WALES

OTHER *WHERE TO WATCH BIRDS* BOOKS PUBLISHED BY CHRISTOPHER HELM

Where to Watch Birds in Devon and Cornwall
David Norman and Vic Tucker

Where to Watch Birds in East Anglia
Peter and Margaret Clarke

Where to Watch Birds in Bedfordshire, Berkshire, Buckinghamshire, Hertfordshire and Oxfordshire
Brian Clews, Andrew Heryet and Paul Trodd

Where to Watch Birds in Kent, Surrey and Sussex
Don Taylor, Jeffery Wheatley and Tony Prater

Where to Watch Birds in the West Midlands
Graham Harrison and Jack Sankey

Where to Watch Birds in

WALES

David Saunders

CHRISTOPHER HELM
London

© 1987 David Saunders
Illustrations and maps by Brian Southern
Christopher Helm (Publishers) Ltd, Imperial House,
21–25 North Street, Bromley, Kent BR1 1SD

British Library Cataloguing in Publication Data

Saunders, David, 1937–
    Where to watch birds in Wales.
    1. Bird watching—Wales
    I. Title
    598'.07'234429   QL690.G7

ISBN 0–7470–3000–6

Typeset by Opus, Oxford
Printed and bound in Great Britain by
Biddles Ltd, Guildford and Kings Lynn

CONTENTS

Contents

ACKNOWLEDGEMENTS

I must straight away extend my thanks to the hundreds of birdwatchers, named and unnamed, who for the past century have watched and enjoyed birds in Wales. Their records and their writings have been the basis of the county avifaunas and bird reports, essential reading for others like myself who wish to follow, and to learn about, the birds of the Principality. To all these pioneers, both present and future birdwatchers owe a considerable debt. Let us repay this by our continued efforts not only to watch birds in Wales, but to ensure that the habitats which our birds use are properly protected, managed and improved.

My special thanks are due to Brian Southern, who so carefully prepared the maps and produced the line drawings for this book; his expertise is greatly appreciated (I trust that it did not take him away too much from his wife and baby daughter). Nick Harris also helped with cartographical matters and for this I am most grateful. Dafydd Davies and Ted Breeze Jones kindly provided the Welsh names for a number of birds recorded in Wales since the latter's list was published in 1973. Thanks are due to Brenda Hibberd, who dragged the author somewhat reluctantly into the computer age and the previously alien world of word-processing; her assistance in these matters was invaluable. My employers, the West Wales Trust for Nature Conservation, kindly placed their computer facilities at my disposal, and to them I am most grateful. The faithful old servant, the Imperial typewriter, now stands on a corner of the desk; it will not be forgotten, indeed it can look forward to a hard-working retirement.

My considerable thanks are recorded for the help, patience and assistance of my wife Shirley, who has shared in birdwatching expeditions throughout Wales since our first to the hills above the Llanthony Valley in 1957.

Thanks are also due in respect of the forbearance of the publishers Christopher Helm Limited, and the assistance of their editorial staff, in particular David Christie, throughout all stages of production.

INTRODUCTION

Wales is a small, mainly upland country of 8,018 square miles (20,766 square km) of which about 60 per cent lies above the 500-foot (150-m) contour. At the same time it is a maritime country, bounded on three sides by the sea: to the south by the Bristol Channel, to the west by St George's Channel and to the north by the Irish Sea. For the geologist, Wales is a land of almost unrivalled opportunities. Here are the oldest rocks, here also some of the youngest. The action of ice is everywhere recorded: glacial lakes, the screes and moraines, overflow channels and other features are a constant reminder of how much of this spectacular landscape was moulded. The rivers are mostly short and fast-flowing, terminating in estuaries of major importance for their birdlife. Three much longer rivers, the Dee, Severn and Wye, murmur into life high on the hills of Wales, and form in parts its eastern march with England. A country, then, of contrasts, for you do not have to drive far in any direction to encounter a great variety and range of habitats. It is for instance but a short drive through the industrial valleys of Glamorgan to the uplands of the Black Mountains, the Brecon Beacons and the Carmarthen Vans. Leave the coast, flatlands and lakes of Anglesey and within half an hour you can be high in Snowdonia. The coastline is equally variable, with sand dunes, saltmarshes, rocky shores, great sea cliffs and then the islands – and what islands they are, Bardsey in the north, and Grassholm, Skokholm and Skomer in the south.

Despite the amount of high ground and spectacular landscape features of great interest, there is not the variety nor the numbers of birds that one encounters in Scotland. The threats to the uplands of Wales are very real, especially those of large-scale afforestation and of agricultural improvements to high-altitude areas. Nevertheless, there are important populations of several key species such as the Hen Harrier, Merlin, Peregrine, Golden Plover and Dunlin. Pride of place among all upland birds, indeed among all the birds of Wales, is without question taken by the Red Kite, for only here and nowhere else in Britain does this species breed. Its survival is assured, as recounted elsewhere in this book, only by much dedicated effort, an effort now spanning no fewer than 80 years, surely the longest-running protection scheme for a single species anywhere in the world. It is still harried by unscrupulous egg-collectors (in 1986 no fewer than six nests suffered from their attentions), while birds such as the Goshawk and Peregrine are targets for equally rapacious falconers. The lakes, marshes and especially the woodlands of Wales are of interest and importance, supporting a rich variety of birds including significant populations of such species as Wood Warbler and Pied Flycatcher. The great bird spectacles of Wales, however, belong to the coast: waders by the thousand – flashing wings and magic calls; clamorous seabird colonies, several being of international importance, where the odour of guano ledges drifts upwards, while Fulmars sweep and glide as only they can along the cliff faces in the summer breeze. Of all the sights, there is probably none more magnificent in the whole of Wales than the massed ranks of Gannets, now approaching 30,000 pairs strong, on lonely Grassholm.

It is often to our remote islands that rare birds come, vagrants from the forests and tundras of Siberia, vagrants from the similar habitats in North America, and even seabirds from the far south. As this book shows, rare birds are by no means restricted to remote islands; they are likely to be seen anywhere, as demonstrated by the record of a Dartford Warbler in Singleton Park, Swansea. Therefore be vigilant whenever you go forth.

The changing patterns of bird distribution make a fascinating study. Turn the pages of the avifaunas and you will see many examples. For instance, the first Fulmars did not nest in Pembrokeshire until 1946, while it is easy to forget that the first Collared Doves arrived in Britain only as recently as 1955, and reached Wales several years later. Such changes in bird distribution are continually taking place, the recent decline and loss of the Nightjar and Woodlark and the spread of the Goosander and Cetti's Warbler being but a few examples. Who ten years ago would have forecast the sudden decline of the Herring Gull, or realised that Dippers would disappear from some rivers as a result of acid waters reducing the number of invertebrates on which they feed? There are man-induced gains as well. The Ruddy Duck is now well established and spreading, following escapes from the collection at the Wildfowl Trust. Do not be surprised if you encounter Ring-necked Parakeets. There has been a population of about 1,000 of these birds breeding on the fringes of London since 1969, the result of escapes or deliberate releases from captivity. The Welsh population is currently a small one close to the large urban centres of Glamorgan. Will it spread elsewhere?

For the birdwatcher, the fact that many classic sites are now nature reserves, managed by one of the at times confusing variety of conservation organisations, is something to be applauded. Much more needs protection, and as I write this Introduction the naturalists' trusts in Wales have launched the Welsh Wildlife Appeal, their goal £3 million, with which to acquire and manage further land. Some areas have been designated Sites of Special Scientific Interest under the provisions of the Wildlife and Countryside Act, 1981, and thus are given a greater degree of protection from damaging activities than in the past. Access to many parts of Wales is now much easier than it was even but a few years ago, not just as the result of road improvements, but also because of the creation of or improvements to footpaths and bridleways. Long-distance footpaths such as that which follows Offa's Dyke along the border with England, or the Pembrokeshire Coast path, enable birdwatchers to reach previously difficult or inaccessible points. Wherever you are, please ensure that you do not disturb the very birds you are watching, otherwise the birds will suffer and other birdwatchers as well as yourself will suffer. Always put the birds' welfare first: you will then have the satisfaction and knowledge of having your own pleasure without detriment or harm.

The aim of this book is to help and encourage birdwatchers, especially beginners, to set forth, to learn more about this most delightful of hobbies, and at the same time to contribute to our knowledge. If we obtain enjoyment, if we obtain knowledge, if we obtain satisfaction from our watching, then we should try to put something back. Please send records of your observations to the county bird recorder, join your local bird club or county trust, please support, please participate. The rewards of so doing can only add to your further enjoyment, and to the further enjoyment of others.

HOW TO USE THIS BOOK

Few birdwatchers have watched birds throughout the length and breadth of Wales, so that from this book hopefully even the most expert will be able to learn of new sites of interest to explore and of the birds which they support. Local knowledge is often all important, and there is a vast amount contained among the 55 site descriptions. Follow this, join your local bird club or naturalists' trust, and your birdwatching opportunities will be much improved. At the same time the experience gained at well-watched points will enable you to search some of the less well-known listed in Appendix A. However, there is a further pleasure, and that is to discover new opportunities, new places to watch, and by so doing add further to our knowledge about birds in Wales.

In 1973, one of the effects of changes in our system of local government was that some county boundaries were amended, while in Wales there was a complete revision of the county names. In most cases this resulted in a linking of counties, save for Glamorgan where the opposite took place. Although administratively this may have been most convenient, birdwatchers, and indeed all naturalists, still follow the old counties system — one might well call it the vice-county system; this is how the bird clubs and societies operate, and long may it remain so! To assist the reader, the new county names are given below together with the vice-counties which they contain.

Clwyd	Denbigh, Flint
Dyfed	Cardigan, Carmarthen, Pembroke (Note that Cardigan is now often referred to as Ceredigion)
Gwent	Monmouth
Gwynedd	Anglesey, Caernarvon, Merioneth
Powys	Brecon, Montgomery, Radnor
Mid Glamorgan	
South Glamorgan	Glamorgan
West Glamorgan	

Measurements

Being a firm believer in the words of Sir Winston Churchill that 'names that have been familiar for generations in England should not be altered to study the whims of foreigners', I have given measurements in traditional units; distances are given in miles, areas in acres and altitude in feet. Since most modern maps use metric units, however, the metric equivalent is given in parentheses after each measurement.

Habitat

Descriptions of each site are given under this heading in an attempt, hopefully successful, to provide a background for the birdwatcher. Brief references to other features of natural history interest which may be encountered or which warrant further inquiry are also included.

Species

The main bird interest is described, together with snippets of background information which may help add to the knowledge of the reader, enabling everyone to get the most out of the visit. No-one can fail to be moved to some excitement by the sight of an unusual bird, a rare visitor, perhaps one with the accolade 'first for Wales' or, for those extremely fortunate, a 'first for Britain'. Indeed, some birdwatchers will travel great distances to witness such an event, so that I have drawn attention to many of the scarce visitors seen in Wales. Hopefully, this will help inspire further careful watching, and many more such sightings.

Timing

If you can be flexible in your arrangements, then follow the broad suggestions given in this section. Generally speaking, on estuaries one is governed by the state of the tide, while for seawatching the hours immediately after dawn are by far the most productive. This latter period is in fact the best whether you are in the depths of woodland or tramping the high sheepwalks.

Access

Maps are provided for each site and these will enable the birdwatcher to locate the area with reference to that essential item of equipment the 1 : 50,000 Ordnance Survey map, the modern equivalent of the old 1-inch-to-1-mile map. The number of each site map, together with the relevant Ordnance Survey map number, is given beside the heading for each locality.

Calendar

This provides a quick reference section. The first part covers birds which are resident throughout the year, though during severe weather many, even all, of some resident species will desert an area, while in the dog days of late July and August, with the breeding season for many species over, small passerines can at times become surprisingly elusive; it also covers birds such as Turnstone, which do not breed but may be seen at any time throughout the year. The rest of the year has been divided into four sections. The period *December–February* is when all winter visitors are present, numbers often reaching a peak early in the year, especially if the rest of Europe experiences severe weather. *March–May* sees the departure of winter visitors, the arrival of summer migrants and the passages of waders and terns; by the end of the period, breeding species will be fully active. *June–July* covers the end of the breeding season for most species, and the commencement of return passage, waders usually being the first to be seen. *August–November* is a period spanning the whole of the autumn migration and the arrival of winter visitors on our shores.

To facilitate quick reference, the sequence of bird names follows Voous's *List of Recent Holarctic Bird Species* (1977), which is that adopted by most recently published field guides. For anyone wishing to see a complete list of the birds of the Western Palearctic in this sequence, I strongly recommend the modestly priced (at present 60p plus postage) 'Check List' produced by the British Trust for Ornithology.

GLOSSARY OF WELSH NAMES

It is appropriate and, I hope, of assistance to include a short glossary of the Welsh names that readers will encounter in the text, or when consulting other works or maps.

aber	mouth	dinas	fort
aderyn	bird	draeth	shore
adwy	gap, pass	drws	pass
afon	river	dyffryn	valley
agen	cleft	eglwys	church
allt	hillside	esgair	ridge
arth	hill	fach	small
bach	small	fawr	large
bala	stream outlet	felin	mill
bannau	peaks	fford	road
berllan	orchard	ffridd	mountain pasture
big	peak	ffrwd	torrent
blaen	head of valley	ffynon	spring, well
bont	bridge	figyn	bog
borth	landing place	foel	bare hill
bren	wood	fynydd	mountain
brig	peak	gaer	fort
bron	rounded hill	gallt	hillside
bryn	hill	garn	mountain
bwlch	pass, gap	garth	hill
bychan	small	glyn	glen
cader	seat	gogof	cave
cae	field	gopa	summit
caer	fort	gors	bog
camlas	canal	graig	rock
capel	chapel	gwastad	level place
carnedd	mountain	gwaun	moor
carreg	rock	gwern	marsh
castell	castle	gweunydd	moors
cefn	ridge	heol	road
cerrig	rocks	isaf	lower
ceunant	ravine, gorge	llan	church
clawdd	embankment	llannerch	glade
clegyr	rock	llechwedd	hillside
clun	meadow, moor	llethr	slope
cnwc	hillock	llwyn	grove
coed	woodland	llyn	lake
comin	common	maen	stone
cors	bog	maes	field
craig	rock	mawnog	peaty
cwm	valley	mawr	large
cymer	confluence	melin	mill
darren	hill	migyn	bog
ddol	meadow	morfa	coastal marsh
ddu	black	mynydd	mountain

nant	stream, valley	rhyd	ford
odyn	kiln	sarn	road
ogof	cave	sgwd	waterfall
pant	valley	tarren	hill
pen	top	ton	meadow
penmaen	rocky promontory	traeth	shore
pennant	head of valley	trwyn	promontory
penrhyn	promontory	twll	chasm
pistyll	waterfall	twyn	hillock
plas	mansion	tywyn	seashore, dune
pont	bridge	uchaf	highest
porth	landing place	waun	moor
pwll	pit, pool	ynys	island
rhaeadr	waterfall	ystrad	valley floor
rhiw	hill	ystwyth	winding
rhos	moor, bog		

1 ANGLESEY LAKES

Map 1
OS Map 114

Habitat

Anglesey abounds in freshwater sites, including the Cefni Reservoir and the various lakes and marshes in the shallow valleys which intersect the island on parallel lines to the Menai Straits. In view of the importance of several of these sites, it is a disappointment that none is managed as a nature reserve by one or other of the conservation organisations, though several are Sites of Special Scientific Interest. Most have a rich aquatic flora, including rare plants such as Frogbit, Flowering-rush, Eight-stamened Waterwort, Lesser Bulrush, Great Fen-sedge, Blunt-flowered Rush, Marsh Fern, Narrow-leaved Marsh-orchid, to mention but a few.

Species

One of Britain's rarest breeding birds first nested in this country in Anglesey when the Black-necked Grebe was discovered there in 1904, though it had probably been undetected for some years before. It remained for just over 20 years before ceasing to nest, and now it is but a rare winter visitor to Wales. Other scarce species which have nested in Anglesey from time to time include the Bittern, Marsh Harrier, Black-tailed Godwit, Ruff and Bearded Tit. There have been new arrivals in recent years: the Reed Warbler in the late 1960s, the Greylag Goose in 1970 and the Ruddy Duck in 1978. The latter is a remarkable story of colonisation, resulting from free-flying young dispersing from the Wildfowl Trust, Slimbridge, Gloucestershire, during the 1950s. Breeding in the wild was first confirmed in 1960 in Somerset, since when the species has grown in numbers by about 25 per cent per annum, mainly in the West Midlands, the Welsh borders and Cheshire. In 1985 no fewer than 113 were counted on Llyn Traffwll, where Ruddy Ducks are present throughout the year. Other breeding wildfowl include Great Crested and Little Grebes, Mute Swan, Canada Goose, Wigeon, Gadwall, Teal, Mallard, Shoveler, Pochard and Tufted Duck. Goldeneyes have summered, and it seems only a matter of time before this handsome duck begins to breed in Wales. Save for an early occurrence in Cheshire, the first British record of breeding by this species was in East Inverness in 1970, since when the number of localities has increased, and in 1984 there were at least 53 pairs in five separate localities which hatched 311 young. The Goldeneye takes readily to nestboxes, and with birds regularly summering away from known breeding sites the opportunity is there for birdwatchers wishing to aid the expansion of this species.

Wildfowl numbers increase in winter. Pochards may rise to 400 at the Cefni Reservoir, while on Llyn Coron the number of Wigeons reaches 1,600. Other visitors include Bewick's and Whooper Swans, Smew and White-fronted Geese, a small flock of which tends to frequent Llyn Bodgylched. Casual visitors in the summer months have included both Black Tern and White-winged Black Tern.

Timing

Early morning visits are best, as there is much less chance of birds having been disturbed. At the same time, however, ensure that you yourself do not cause disturbance.

Access

Cefni Reservoir: SH440774 Park at SH452783 just off the B5111 Llangefni to Amlwch road and follow marked routes.

Llyn Alaw: SH380865 The largest area of open fresh water on Anglesey. The car parks at SH372856, where there is a visitor centre, SH378853 and SH404865 are all approached by unclassified roads.

Llyn Bodgylched: SH585770 May be observed from the B5109 west of Beaumaris or from the footpath which runs north from the road towards the Bulkeley Memorial.

Llyn Coron: SH378700 A footpath from near Bodorgan Station runs close to the northern shore, while two others run to the lake from the A4080 Aberffraw road west of Llangadwaladr.

Llyn Llygerian: SH346898 A footpath leads to the eastern shore from the unclassified road near Llanddygfael Hir.

Llyn Llywenan: SH346815 An unclassified road runs northward close to the west shore from the B5109 ½ mile (0.8 km) west of Bodedern.

Llyn Traffwll: SH325770 A footpath provides nearly a complete circuit of the lake from the village of Llanfihangel yn Nhowyn 3 miles (4.8 km) east of Valley and 1 mile (1.6 km) south of the A5.

Calendar

Resident Little and Great Crested Grebes, Cormorant, Grey Heron, Mute Swan, Greylag Goose, Shelduck, Wigeon, Gadwall, Teal, Mallard, Shoveler, Pochard, Tufted Duck, Ruddy Duck, Moorhen, Coot, Black-headed Gull.

December–February Winter visitors present and numbers usually reach a peak, especially if there is hard weather in England and in western Europe. Additional species at this time are likely to include Long-tailed Duck and Smew.

March–May Winter visitors depart, summer migrants arrive throughout period, breeding species such as Sedge and Reed Warblers arrive in late April.

June–July Summer visitors and residents present. Breeding season draws to a close and wader passage commences, often the first species seen being Green Sandpiper.

August–November Wader passage during August and some southward-moving terns call briefly. Duck numbers begin to increase during September and by the end of period many winter visitors have arrived, including Bittern, Bewick's and Whooper Swans, White-fronted Goose, Pintail and Goldeneye.

Habitat

Cemlyn Lagoon on the north coast of Anglesey has been formed by a shingle-ridge storm beach which has effectively sealed off, save for an overflow channel, the inner reaches of Cemlyn Bay. Behind the beach, an area of brackish water is retained, being flooded by the sea at high spring tides. It has been a nature reserve since the early 1930s, first as part of the Hewitt Estate; then, on the death of Captain V. Hewitt, the lagoon was purchased by the National Trust and subsequently has been managed by the North Wales Naturalists' Trust under a nature reserve agreement. The shingle ridge has an interesting maritime flora, with Sea-kale, Sea Beet, Thrift, Sea Aster, Sea-milkwort, Spring Squill and Sea-purslane.

Species

The highlight of Cemlyn is without question the tern colonies, where, although numbers vary considerably from year to year, there are normally several pairs of Sandwich, Common and Arctic Terns. Roseate Terns are occasionally seen, as are passing Little Terns, probably from the small colonies elsewhere on Anglesey. Other breeding species include Shelduck, Mallard, Red-breasted Merganser, Oystercatcher, Ringed Plover, Redshank and Black-headed Gull. A wide range of waders uses the muddy fringe of the lagoon and the nearby beach, including Grey Plover, Lapwing, Sanderling, Curlew Sandpiper, Dunlin, Curlew, Common Sandpiper and Turnstone. In winter, flocks of Wigeons and Mallards may rise to about 400 and there are always smaller numbers of Teals, Shovelers, Pochards, Tufted Ducks and Goldeneyes present. Bewick's and Whooper Swans regularly visit the lagoon, while the sheltered waters of the bay throughout the winter months often contain Red-throated Diver, Great Crested Grebe, Eider, Common Scoter, Guillemot and Razorbill. More unusual species have lately included Little Shearwater, Lesser Golden Plover and Little Gull.

Sandwich Terns

Timing

Any daylight hours should suffice, but during the summer months the early morning may mean that you have the beach to yourself, at least apart from other readers of this book, plus hopefully a good selection of birds. Winter visits are probably best when the wind is in the southwest or west and Cemlyn Bay provides a sheltered area.

Access

Leave the A5025 at Tregele (SH355927), on the unclassified but signed road. There are two car parks near the lagoon, at Traeth Cemlyn on the east side and near Bryn Aber on the west, and the best views may be had from the shingle ridge, but please keep below the crest to avoid disturbance. Please note that there are access restrictions in the interests of the tern colonies. A summer warden is resident.

Calendar

Resident Cormorant, Shag, Grey Heron, Shelduck, Mallard, Red-breasted Merganser, Kestrel, Coot, Oystercatcher, Ringed Plover, Lapwing, Redshank, Turnstone, Black-headed, Herring and Great Black-backed Gulls.

December–February Red-throated and Great Northern Divers, Great Crested Grebe, Bewick's and Whooper Swans, Wigeon, Teal, Pochard, Tufted Duck, Eider, Common Scoter.

March–May Passage waders include Sanderling, Whimbrel and Common Sandpiper. Terns arrive during April, the Sandwich Tern usually being the first noted. Swallows and martins often feed over the lagoon in large numbers during April and May. Other summer migrants include Cuckoo, Wheatear and Yellow Wagtail.

June–July All breeding species present, first return wader passage commences during July.

August–November Wader passage well under way by late August, when a wide range of species can be expected. Terns usually present in variable numbers until late September. Winter ducks begin to arrive by early October, and by the end of period midwinter species such as divers and swans usually much in evidence.

Habitat

The southwest extremity of Anglesey is dominated by a huge area of sandhills, saltmarshes and dune grasslands, between the mouth of the Menai Straits and the estuary of the Afon Cefni. Prior to the fourteenth century this was a prosperous agricultural area, even with its own harbour at Abermenai. A series of great storms changed all of this as vast quantities of sand were blown inland. The fields and trackways quickly became choked, crops could no longer be grown, there was little grazing, houses and farm buildings began to disappear, and the population, unequal to the struggle, was forced to move inland. Subsequent centuries saw the wind mould the dunes into four main ridges, separated by flat hollows known as slacks — a wild remote area which for long periods was the haunt only of those who grazed their stock and of the rabbiters, for, as the name suggests, Newborough held a vast population of this animal until the arrival of myxomatosis.

In 1948, the Forestry Commission began planting the northern section of the dunes, the area now known as Newborough Forest, which with its serried ranks of Corsican Pines extends for some 2,000 acres (810 ha). Fortunately, the whole of the dunes was not taken over for forestry, and in 1955 1,600 acres (648 ha) was declared a National Nature Reserve, so that one of the finest dune systems in Britain is fully protected. The nature reserve includes three distinct areas: the eastern dunes between Llyn Rhos-ddu, the Braint Estuary and the sea; the rocky promontory of Ynys Llanddwyn; and the saltmarshes fringing the eastern shore of the Cefni Estuary, including Malltraeth Pool. It was to Malltraeth that the noted bird artist Charles Tunnicliffe came in 1945, and here he sketched and painted many of the birds from the surrounding area. His studies of wildfowl and waders on Malltraeth Pool are among his most outstanding work.

Species

Birds of prey were, in years gone by, a speciality among the sandhills, where both the Montagu's Harrier and the Merlin nested. Now, alas, the former is but a rare visitor, though the Merlin is seen each winter. If the fortunes of the Montagu's Harrier in Britain continue to improve, it may not be too much to hope that it returns to Anglesey. Short-eared Owls breed in some years and are regular winter visitors. Ynys Llanddwyn provides on its shores a range of rocky habitats not found elsewhere at Newborough. Cormorants and Shags nest (a few years ago the Shags were found with eggs in November; were these early or late breeders?), Ringed Plovers breed, while Turnstones can be seen throughout the year and may at times number up to 70; the smaller numbers of Purple Sandpipers are restricted to the winter months. The sheltered waters of Llanddwyn Bay attract a number of birds, mainly as winter visitors, including Red-throated and Great Northern Divers, Great Crested and Slavonian Grebes, Eider, Long-tailed Duck, Common Scoter and Goldeneye. Red-breasted Mergansers have nested in Anglesey since 1953, and Newborough is now one of their regular sites, so you may be fortunate to see an attentive female and her brood during midsummer.

Anglesey is the headquarters in Wales for breeding terns: Common, Arctic, Roseate and Little Terns have all nested in the past at Llanddwyn, and further east at Abermenai.

The saltmarshes of the Cefni Estuary extend for over 400 acres (160 ha), dotted with pools of brackish water and tiny creeks. Greylag Geese, which after introductions breed at several sites on Anglesey, regularly flight to the marshes, where they are joined by Canada Geese, several pairs of which breed close by. Shelducks breed in the forest and among the sandhills, and bring their broods rapidly to the estuary for safety. The winter duck population may rise to about 2,000, the flock of 200 or so Pintails being an outstanding sight. Several hundred each of waders such as Oystercatcher, Ringed Plover, Golden Plover, Lapwing, Knot, Dunlin, Curlew and Redshank are present throughout the winter. At the head of the estuary, from which it is separated by a low embankment known as Malltraeth Cob, is Malltraeth Pool. Here, a wide range of wildfowl and waders may be seen, including Bewick's and Whooper Swans, Ruff, Black-tailed and Bar-tailed Godwits, Spotted Redshank and Greenshank. Llyn Rhos-ddu provides a further variation in aquatic habitat, a small freshwater pool which attracts Shoveler, Pochard, Tufted Duck and Goldeneye in winter, while Coots and occasionally Little Grebes breed.

One most unusual species which you may encounter in Newborough is the Golden Pheasant, a native of the uplands of central China. First imported into Britain during the eighteenth century, these pheasants have been released on a number of occasions since and small populations have become established, most successfully in East Anglia. They were introduced to Anglesey in the early 1970s and a small number are now present, though their skulking habits mean that they are rarely encountered.

Timing

If visiting the estuary areas of the Braint and Cefni, it is best to consult the tide tables and to arrive about high water so as to observe waders returning to the mudflats as the tide recedes. For the rest of the area, including both Llyn Rhos-ddu and Llanddwyn, the timing of visits is not critical.

Access

The A4080 passes through the village of Newborough, to the head of the Cefni Estuary and Malltraeth Pool. Good vantage points can be obtained from the road and from the top of the cob. Access to the shore is possible by leaving the A4080 at SH424656, and following the road right through to the shore car park, where during the summer months a small information centre run by the Forestry Commission and Nature Conservancy Council is open. A brisk walk along the shore brings you on to Ynys Llanddwyn, or for the more energetic the long walk may be taken towards Abermenai Point to the southeast. Several footpaths are open through the forest and dunes, one of which passes close to Llyn Rhos-ddu while another skirts the Cefni saltmarshes.

Calendar

Resident Little Grebe, Cormorant, Shag, Grey Heron, Mute Swan, Greylag and Canada Geese, Shelduck, Teal, Mallard, Sparrowhawk, Kestrel,

Red-legged Partridge, Golden Pheasant, Coot, Oystercatcher, Ringed Plover, Lapwing, Turnstone, large gulls, Short-eared Owl and a wide range of passerines of woodland edge and open country.

December–February Red-throated and Great Northern Divers, Great Crested and Slavonian Grebes, Bewick's and Whooper Swans, Wigeon, Pintail, Shoveler, Pochard, Tufted Duck, Common Scoter, Goldeneye, Hen Harrier, Merlin, Water Rail, Snow Bunting.

March–May Departure of winter and arrival of summer visitors, Sandwich Terns being one of the first to be seen.

June–July Breeding season coming to an end, first wader passage noted in the estuaries.

August–November Continual passage of summer visitors until September, when there can be large movements of Swallows and martins. Winter visitors arrive in early October, large numbers of Fieldfares and Redwings from the middle of the month in some years.

4 POINT LYNAS

Map 4
OS Map 114

Habitat

Point Lynas at the northwest tip of Anglesey seems made for seawatching, a narrow promontory extending northwards for ½ mile (0.8 km) from the main coastline. There is a good access road so that one can arrive and commence watching without delay, an advantage for those who have to drive some distance to be ready at dawn. Members of the Cambrian Ornithological Society have diligently carried out watches here for over a decade, their efforts chronicled in successive bird reports.

Species

One of the most numerous species recorded is the Manx Shearwater. While some of these will be on feeding movements from the colonies on Bardsey, many others will be flighting south from the enormous colonies on Rhum and other islands in the Inner Hebrides and from the smaller ones on Rathlin Island and the Copeland Islands off Northern Ireland. Undoubtedly, those from the tiny colony on the Calf of Man will come this way. It was from the Calf that the first Manx Shearwaters were described for science in the mid-seventeenth century, hence the name Manx. Small numbers of Fulmars pass, with peak movements in August and September. Like the Manx Shearwaters, Gannets passing here have come from the north, probably from the great colony of some 16,000 pairs on Ailsa Craig, sentinel of the Clyde, and from the small colony of a few hundred pairs on Scar Rocks, Wigtownshire; others, however, may well be wanderers from the south, from Grassholm, the only gannetry in Wales. Kittiwakes are the most frequent species, perhaps not surprisingly as this attractive gull is one of the most numerous seabirds in Britain. Many thousands pass Point Lynas each autumn, often exceeding in numbers the sum total of all other species seen: in 1985, 16,000 were observed in just over 100 hours' watching. Most exciting of all to observe is the passage of auks, mainly Guillemots and Razorbills, though very occasionally a Puffin or a Black Guillemot may be seen, or, if you are very lucky, even a Little Auk. The Guillemots and Razorbills, often in small flocks, fly low over the sea, a scurrying but determined flight which will take many south through St George's Channel and the Western Approaches to the Bay of Biscay, and in the case of Razorbills to Iberia and the western Mediterranean. Peak numbers are observed from October to December.

Terns can be seen throughout the summer, birds from breeding colonies elsewhere on Anglesey and indeed throughout Liverpool Bay. The main passage south of these birds takes place during late August and September. Although most skuas pass at the same time, there are records of birds as early as mid-July while others may be seen as late as November. Other species seen, though only in small numbers, include divers, grebes, Sooty Shearwater, Leach's Petrel, Scaup, Eider, Goldeneye, Red-breasted Merganser and Black Tern.

Timing

The first essential of seawatching is to ensure that you arrive and are ready to commence at daybreak. Most movement takes place in the hours immediately after dawn, and although, depending on the weather, there will be some movement throughout the day it will generally not compare with that observed in the early hours. The weather is all important, not just on the morning of the watch but also during the preceding days, and at Point Lynas the essential ingredients are a period of stormy and unsettled conditions, with the wind in the northwest or the northern quarter. This is a hint also that very warm clothing is a must, together with suitable quantities of food and drink.

Access

Take any of the several unclassified roads off the A5025 south of Amlwch, or from the town itself, pass through the hamlet of Llaneilian, and continue to Porth Eilian and so to the point itself.

Calendar

Resident Cormorant, Shag, Oystercatcher, large gulls.

December–February Divers and Great Crested Grebe usually offshore, occasional seaducks. Fulmars return to nearby cliffs before end of January. Some passage of auks through whole period.

March–May Terns noted from early April onwards. Passerine passage develops from April onwards, most noticeable being the movements north and east of Swallows, smaller numbers of Sand Martins and a few House Martins.

June–July Terns still present, passage waders seen late in period, regular feeding movements of Manx Shearwaters.

August–November Peak passage time for all seabirds. Large Swallow and martin passage in mid-September, Skylarks, Meadow Pipit, Fieldfare, Redwing, Starling and Chaffinch movement from mid-October.

Habitat

Puffin Island, also known as Priestholm and Ynys Seiriol (the island of Saint Seiriol, who lived there in the sixth century), is some 70 acres (28 ha) in extent and rises to 163 feet (55 m). It is separated from the Penmon Peninsula, the most easterly part of mainland Anglesey, by a sound nearly ½ mile (0.8 km) wide. John Ray visited the island in 1662 and noted the Puffin colony, which, although now much reduced in numbers, exists to this day. Unlike many of our other islands, there is a veritable forest of Elder covering up to a third of the island; other prolific plants include Alexanders up to 10 feet (over 3 m) high, Burdock, Hemlock and Henbane.

The Penmon Peninsula, especially its north coast, is of interest for its seabird colonies. There are extensive quarry workings, the Ordovician limestone having been shipped away in large quantities by sea. When visiting the peninsula, look for the remarkable dovecote close to the church of St Seiriol at Penmon. Although the church dates from the twelfth century, the dovecote was built about 1600; it contains about 1,000 nest holes, which were reached by a ladder from a centre pillar with corbelled steps.

Species

Few Black Guillemots nest in Wales and those which do are confined to Anglesey, with occasional sightings in Caernarvonshire and even south

Black Guillemot

to Pembrokeshire. They returned to Anglesey to nest in 1962, having been recorded there previously by Thomas Pennant in the eighteenth century. The population remains extremely small, and their stronghold, though even here only a handful of pairs, is the north side of the Penmon Peninsula. Why so few in Wales? On the other side of the Irish Sea this species occurs in many localities, extending to the far southwest in Co. Cork and Co. Kerry. It seems strange that it has not become more widely established on the coast of Wales: a question of avian distribution still to be answered. Another species which nests in Wales only at Penmon is the Common Gull. It first bred in 1963, and there are still several pairs breeding in the quarries.

Fewer than 100 pairs of Puffins now nest on Puffin Island, a decline from the former glories of even 70 years ago, but a decline the cause of which is hard to determine. Was it the presence of Brown Rats? The pressure of sharing the colony with increasing numbers of Herring Gulls? Oil pollution? Or even changes in the availability of food? Perhaps we may never know the answers, but we can only hope that Puffin Island will always have its Puffins at this, the second largest colony in North Wales. The other seabirds include Fulmar, Cormorant, Shag, an expanding colony of Kittiwakes, Guillemot, Razorbill and the largest Herring Gull colony in Wales. No doubt the feeding opportunities of the North Wales coast and Liverpool Bay are largely responsible for the improved fortunes of the Puffin Island gull colonies. Very much the same range of seabird species nests along the north side of the Penmon Peninsula.

Do not neglect the area in migration times. It will repay careful observation, as those who discovered the first Yellow-browed Warbler for Anglesey in 1985 bear witness.

Timing
No particular time of day is the best for a visit, though the north side of the peninsula is best visited when the wind is in the southerly quarter.

Access
Take the B5109 eastwards from Beaumaris to Llangoed, beyond which an unclassified road meanders close to the south shore of the peninsula to Penmon and beyond to the most easterly part of Anglesey. The western section of the peninsula is best reached by going north from Llangoed to Glan yr afon and thence to Fedw Fawr. Enquiries should be made in Beaumaris with regard to sailing around Puffin Island.

Calendar

Resident Cormorant, Shag, Buzzard, Kestrel, Peregrine, Oystercatcher, large gulls including Common Gull (though you will need to search hard for this species, especially during the summer months), Rock Pipit, Stonechat, Chough, Jackdaw and Raven.

December–February Divers usually offshore, especially on south side of the peninsula, also various seaducks. The first Fulmars return. Waders on some sections of southern shore, Purple Sandpiper and Turnstone on the rocky areas. First Guillemots and Razorbills return to the cliffs, Kittiwakes gather at their colonies by end of period.

March–May Returning auks more frequent, but not resident until first eggs laid in early May. Terns are seen during early April, Sandwich Tern usually being the first to arrive. Puffins from early April. Wheatears and Ring Ouzels are among the early migrants, the former nesting in the coastal areas.

June–July All breeding species present. Terns regular offshore, although the nearest colonies are some miles away. Other offshore visitors, though these will have travelled greater distances, are Manx Shearwater and Gannet.

August–November Auks have departed by early August, though late in period many moving offshore. Wader passage under way, followed by the arrival of winter ducks and the occasional diver and grebe. Although seawatching at Penmon may not be so productive as elsewhere, scarce species have included Cory's Shearwater, Velvet Scoter and Mediterranean Gull.

6 SOUTH STACK CLIFFS

Map 6
OS Map 114

Habitat

South Stack Cliffs contain some of the most spectacular coastal scenery in North Wales, and extend for nearly 2 miles (3.2 km) on the northwest coast of Holy Island, the most westerly extremity of Anglesey. The main section of cliffs, together with a hinterland of maritime and moorland heath extending onto Holyhead Mountain, is a reserve of the Royal Society for the Protection of Birds. At Gogarth Bay the cliffs rise to about 360 feet (110 m), gradually descending as one moves south. In places they are much eroded, with numerous gullies, sea caves and offshore stacks, while the major folding near South Stack of these ancient Pre-Cambrian rocks is of great geological interest. Cliff-climbers not surprisingly find the whole area a great challenge, though fortunately most observe the voluntary ban on climbing during the seabird breeding season; there are descriptive signs indicating the areas to be avoided from the beginning of February to the end of July. The main stack, South Stack, has a lighthouse (built in 1809) which is reached by a long flight of steps and a narrow footbridge.

In spring and early summer the cliff edges are a blaze of colour, with plants such as Kidney Vetch, Scurvygrass, Spring Squill and Thrift in full flower. The heaths come into their own later in the summer, when the golden carpets of Western Gorse contrast with three species of heather. Other notable plants include Bog Pimpernel, Devil's-bit Scabious, Heath Spotted-orchid and Pale-heath Dog-violet. Two rarities occur here: the endemic Spotted Rock-rose, found only on Anglesey, at one site in Caernarvonshire and at a few localities in the west of Ireland; and a maritime variety of the Field Fleawort, found only at South Stack Cliffs.

Species

Seabirds are one of the main attractions at South Stack, with up to 3,000 Guillemots and smaller numbers of Razorbills and Puffins. Small numbers of Fulmars, Shags, Kittiwakes and the three large gulls also nest on the cliffs. Choughs are another speciality, the close-cropped swards and heaths providing good feeding areas for up to five pairs and a few non-breeding immatures. The occasional accidental clifftop fires do have a benefit so far as the Chough is concerned, by keeping the vegetation in check. During the autumn, the Choughs often gather into loose flocks which may comprise up to 30 individuals. One, sometimes two pairs of Peregrines nest; no doubt the seabird colonies and the Feral Pigeons which share the cliffs provide at least part of this raptor's food supply. Other cliff-nesting birds include several pairs of Kestrels, Stock Doves, Rock Pipits, Ravens, Carrion Crows and Jackdaws. The maritime heath, especially where pockets of scrub have become established, supports birds such as Meadow Pipit, Stonechat, Whitethroat and Linnet. The damp areas of Penrhosfeilw Common usually have several pairs of Lapwings and Redshanks.

Seabird passage can be noteworthy, the west coast of Holy Island being a key vantage point for observing the southward passage of birds which may have been driven into Liverpool Bay by stormy weather. Manx Shearwaters and Gannets are regular offshore, but each autumn such birds as Sooty Shearwater, Arctic and Great Skuas together with large passages of auks are observed. Scarce species offshore have included both Cory's and Little Shearwaters, while notable birds on the cliffs and heaths in recent years have been Red Kite, Red-footed Falcon, Hobby, Quail, Dotterel, Stone-curlew, Nightjar, Bee-eater, Hoopoe, Rock Thrush and Golden Oriole.

Timing

For a general visit no particular time is better than another, but for seabird passage in late summer, or scarce visitors at any time, you must be there in the early morning.

Access

Two unclassified roads lead from Holyhead, the southern one going via Penrhosfeilw, and both continue towards South Stack. There is a car park near the reserve and a network of public footpaths throughout the whole area. The RSPB has a Visitor Centre in Ellin's Tower, open throughout the summer months, which contains a first-floor viewing room overlooking the seabird colonies. In 1987 a remote-controlled video camera complete with windscreen-wiper was installed on the cliffs close to a Guillemot ledge; this enables visitors to watch the birds at really close quarters on a screen in the tower. Choughs and Stonechats can often be seen from the car park. A warden is present from March to September.

Calendar

Resident Cormorant, Shag, Buzzard, Kestrel, Peregrine, Oystercatcher, Turnstone, large gulls, Jackdaw and Raven.

December–February Great Northern and Red-throated Divers, Fulmars return to cliffs and Gannets appear offshore. Hen Harrier, Merlin usually present, while both Guillemot and Razorbill make sporadic visits to the cliffs.

March–May Puffins arrive about the beginning of April, though are not present continuously until about the end of the month. Passage migrants throughout whole period, Wheatear usually the first.

June–July Manx Shearwater passage daily offshore, terns also seen, while by the end of the period the auks have left the cliffs save for a few Puffins which remain into early August.

August–November Seabird passage throughout period, with the greatest range of species in September. Wader passage under way, including Dotterel, Whimbrel and Greenshank. Passerines move through, and late in period large influxes of Skylarks, Meadow Pipits, Fieldfares, Redwings, Starlings and Chaffinches may occur.

7 LLANGORSE LAKE Map 7
OS Map 161

Habitat

Llangorse Lake, some 370 acres (150 ha) and the largest area of natural fresh water in South Wales, has long been recognised as a gem by naturalists. It contains a range of wetland habitats, from the adjacent herb-rich pastures and damp meadows, through marshland, sedge and reed swamp, to the floating-plant communities, and finally the communities of submerged aquatic plants in the shallow waters. Even the muds of the lake bed have their secrets, evidence of the vegetation many thousands of years ago recorded in the pollen grains, and more recently the relics of Iron Age Man, as he lived for safety and convenience on platforms close above the lake surface. The aquatic plants include a number of scarce species, several found nowhere else in Wales, though to the layman the Yellow and White Water-lilies, Fringed Water-lily, Greater Spearwort and Flowering-rush are the most striking. As a coarse fishery Llangorse is among the most productive in Wales, with good populations of Perch, Roach, Bream, Pike and Eel.

Although long recognised as a site of extremely high nature conservation interest, much has been allowed to take place at Llangorse which has diminished its value. At one time, effluent from the local sewage works was discharged into the lake and this, together with general nutrient enrichment from the surrounding farmland, has resulted in significant changes, most notably the loss of some specialised aquatic plants. Easy access has meant the development of aquatic sports, so that no area, even in the depth of winter, remains wholly undisturbed. As a consequence, numbers of both breeding and visiting birds are affected.

Species

There are few more attractive sights on lakes and reservoirs during spring and early summer than that of Great Crested Grebes displaying, or later, when the tiger-striped young have hatched, seeing them closely escorted along the reed face or being carried on the parent's back beneath a tent of arched wings and long scapular feathers. Great Crested Grebes have nested at Llangorse for over 100 years, at what must be one of their most important sites in South Wales, if not in the whole Principality. Numbers have been as high as 20 pairs in the past, though only about a quarter of this number have been present in recent years. This emphasises the need to keep at least part of the lake free of waterborne disturbance, so maintaining a quiet area for these most graceful of waterbirds. The Little Grebe has nested in the past at Llangorse but no longer does so, though it is a regular winter visitor. Red-necked, Slavonian and Black-necked Grebes have all been recorded at infrequent intervals.

Bitterns visit the Llangorse reedbeds in most winters, and there have been occasional sightings in spring and early summer. In the last century this species was even more regular, though the evidence of this is, sadly, the report that 'hardly a winter passes without two or three Bitterns being shot'.

Save for Coots, which have numbered up to 150 pairs, breeding wildfowl are rather few. In winter, however, their numbers rise and Tufted Duck and Pochard are especially numerous, with up to 400 of the latter on occasions. Wigeon, Teal and Mallard each usually number about 100 individuals, and there are smaller numbers of Gadwall, Pintail, Shoveler, Scaup and Goldeneye. Rare visitors have included Long-tailed Duck and Smew. Bewick's and Whooper Swans visit in small numbers throughout the winter.

An idea of the paucity of records of some species in an inland and under-recorded county such as Brecon may be gained from the fact that the first record of Whimbrel for the county was not until 1963, when four were recorded at Llangorse. Even the shooting enthusiasts of Victorian times failed to encounter this wader in the county, or, if they did, failed to obtain specimens. 'What is hit is history, what is missed is mystery' was the adage in those days. Whimbrels are now regularly seen on passage at Llangorse, and it is here that most passage waders are recorded in Breconshire. These have included Oystercatcher, Ringed and Little Ringed Plovers, Black-tailed and Bar-tailed Godwits, Wood Sandpiper, Spotted Redshank, Greenshank and Turnstone. Several species of tern have been recorded at the lake, most especially the Black Tern, which is almost an annual visitor in late summer/early autumn. Lesser Black-backed and Herring Gulls are usually present in small numbers, being joined in winter by Common Gulls. By contrast, Black-headed Gulls occur in huge flocks, especially in late winter and early spring when up to 10,000 roost on the lake, gathering in a tremendous clamour in the late afternoon.

The reedbeds support a large colony of Reed Warblers, and for many years this was their most westerly outpost in central Wales. Sedge Warblers and Reed Buntings also breed in the reedbeds, and a few pairs of Yellow Wagtails nest in nearby fields. The aquatic invertebrates flying low over the water provide a rich feeding source for hirundines, and in late summer enormous numbers of Swallows and Sand Martins gather to roost in the reedbeds, up to 5,000 of each having been estimated. Small numbers of Pied Wagtails also use the reedbeds as a roost, up to 150 being present in late summer, to be followed during the autumn by 5,000 or more Starlings, coming nightly from their feeding grounds farther south in the Usk Valley. Scarce visitors in recent years have included Osprey, Aquatic Warbler, Bearded Tit and Black Kite.

Timing

In view of the numbers of other visitors, and in particular the boating activities, it is advisable to visit early in the day.

Access

There are two main access points to the shore. The first is on the north shore at SO127271, near the village of Llangorse. The other is on the south bank beside the lakeside church of Llangasty-Talyllyn (SO133262), from where a footpath skirts much of the southern and western shore.

Calendar

Resident Great Crested Grebe, Grey Heron, Mute Swan, Mallard, Buzzard, Moorhen, Coot, Lapwing, Lesser Black-backed and Herring Gulls, Reed Bunting.

December–February Winter visitors include Teal, Gadwall, Pochard, Tufted Duck, Goldeneye, visiting parties of Bewick's and Whooper Swans, Kingfisher.

March–May Swallows and martins arrive late March and early April, Reed and Sedge Warblers and Yellow Wagtails later in the month.

June–July All breeding species present. Occasional passage waders. Hirundine numbers build up as July progresses.

August–November Hirundine roost at peak during August and early September before main departure south. Passage waders until late September, when winter visitors start to arrive and include Little Grebe, Wigeon, Teal, Pintail, Shoveler, Pochard, Tufted Duck, Scaup and Goldeneye.

Habitat

In the extreme northwest of Breconshire, hard by the borders with Carmarthenshire and Ceredigion, is the Irfon Valley, the river being a major tributary of the Wye which it joins at Builth Wells. The upper reaches of the valley above Llanwrtyd Wells are most attractive: steep valley sides with stands of conifers, and remnants of once extensive oak woodlands, while above the hamlet of Abergwesyn lines of rock out-crops and cliffs, the result of erosion in glacial times, and then there are quiet upland pastures and beyond glimpses of the open hills. The Nature Conservancy Council has a reserve, the Nant Irfon National Nature Reserve, some 334 acres (135 ha) on the steep western slopes of the valley. It includes some of the highest Sessile Oak woodland in Wales, reaching to 1,300 feet (396 m). Bluebells carpet the ground in late spring, while the other interesting plants include Round-leaved Sundew, Common Butterwort, Bog Asphodel, Ivy-leaved Bellflower and on damp rocks the dainty Wilson's Filmy-fern. Extending north from Abergwesyn is an area of high ground rising to 2,115 feet (644 m) at the rock cairns of Drygarn Fawr, and forming one of the few extensive areas of open ground in the southern half of the mid-Wales plateau. Continue north for a further 3 miles (4.8 km) and you reach the Caerwen and Elan Valley Reservoirs. You will find when you reach the high ground that it is probably yours alone, for this is a lonely part of Wales with few visitors, though alas your solitude is likely to be shattered from time to time, at least on weekdays, by low-flying aircraft on necessary training flights.

Species

During the summer months several pairs of Common Sandpipers breed along the river, and Grey Wagtails and Dippers are present throughout the year except in the hardest weather. The oak woodland supports a range of species including Buzzard, Tawny Owl, Tree Pipit, Redstart, Wood Warbler and Pied Flycatcher. Where there are rocky areas, or in the steep-sided clefts along the escarpment, Ring Ouzels should be located, while Whinchat and Wheatear will be found on the more open ground. Kestrels hunt over the hills, and if you are lucky you may see a Red Kite. Other birds of prey include Short-eared Owl, Peregrine and Merlin, though it is now some years since the latter nested in these parts. Merlins are normally associated during the breeding season with areas of well-developed heather moor, a habitat which has declined in many parts, usually owing to afforestation or conversion to open grass moor-land with a high sheep density. As a result they have declined in Wales, Northumberland and the Orkneys, while the possibility of poisoning by pesticides is another factor which cannot be ruled out. Whatever the reason, there are now probably fewer Merlins in Wales than Red Kites. Some Red Grouse still frequent the hills, and Black Grouse have colo-nised the younger conifer plantations.

The special species of the high ground are without question the Golden Plover and Dunlin; several pairs of each nest here. The latter is extremely easy to overlook unless the trilling purr song of the male is heard. The resident Skylarks can provide a clue, since they often include

Black Grouse

an imitation of the purr in their own song if Dunlins are about, something for the astute observer to bear in mind. Another clue, at least if there are Golden Plovers in the area, is the way that Dunlins follow them, hence the Dunlin's delightful colloquial name of 'Plover's Page'.

Timing
This is not critical so far as the valley birds are concerned, but if you really mean to see some of the upland species such as Golden Plover and Dunlin then be prepared for an early start, or a late return. Both species can be extremely elusive during the main part of the day, and are heard and seen best about dawn, or in the evening towards dusk, when Snipe will also reveal their previously hidden presence.

Access
Leave the A483 in Llanwrtyd Wells by the unclassified road signed Abergwesyn. There are several Forestry Commission picnic areas close to the river, and these provide good vantage points or starting places for your exploration. Beyond Abergwesyn the road is unfenced, and there are several good pull-off points for a car. From these the energetic can climb to high ground. Permits are required for the Nant Irfon NNR, and these may be obtained from the NCC, Dyfed-Powys Regional Office.

Calendar

Resident Sparrowhawk, Buzzard, Kestrel, Merlin, Peregrine, Red and Black Grouse, Tawny Owl, Skylark, Meadow Pipit, Grey Wagtail, Dipper, Goldcrest, Raven, Redpoll.

December–February Resident species present except in hard weather.

March–May Goosander, Golden Plover, Lapwing, Dunlin, Snipe, Curlew, Common Sandpiper, Cuckoo, Tree Pipit, Ring Ouzel, Redstart, Whinchat, Wheatear, Whitethroat, Wood Warbler, Chiffchaff.

June–July All residents and summer visitors present.

August–November Summer visitors depart during August and early September, tits and finches begin to flock, and autumn thrushes and finches move into the valley during October.

Habitat

One of the most beautiful valleys in South Wales, the Taf Fechan extends northwards from the outskirts of Merthyr Tydfil into the very heart of the Brecon Beacons. Follow the road through the valley and past the Pontsticill and Pentwyn Reservoirs, cross the watershed, and after several miles you come to the Talybont Reservoir, built earlier in the century to supply water for Newport. The reservoir is about 2 miles (3.2 km) long and has a maximum width of about 500 yards (457 m). Steep slopes with coniferous woodland surround much of the perimeter, though there are shallow areas along the reservoir margin, especially at the southern end.

Species

Among all the birds using Talybont, pride of place must go to the Goosander. This is probably their main wintering area in Wales, with on occasions up to 100 birds present. The Goosander now breeds on many river systems throughout South Wales, and it continues to extend its range rapidly at the present time, with just over 100 pairs in Wales. Up to 600 Mallards gather here in late autumn and in early winter, a few remaining throughout the whole period. Some 400 each of Pochard and Tufted Duck may be seen throughout the winter. Whooper Swans are regular visitors, though the flock rarely exceeds ten birds; these are probably the same ones which visit Llangorse and other waters in this part of Breconshire. Other winter wildfowl include Goldeneye, Scaup and Red-breasted Merganser. Wader passage in late summer can be good, though much depends on water levels, and several scarce species, at least for inland waters, have been recorded including Sanderling, Pectoral Sandpiper and Little Stint. Small numbers of terns pass through each autumn.

Goosander

Timing

No particular time of day, though in the afternoon the light will be behind the observer.

Access

There is no access to the reservoir area, but this need not be a drawback as the unclassified road from Talybont-on-Usk (SO113228) skirts the western shore and provides excellent views before continuing south, eventually reaching the A4102 at SO067077 on the edge of Merthyr Tydfil.

Calendar

Resident Grey Heron, Mute Swan, Mallard, Goosander, Sparrowhawk, Buzzard, Kestrel, Moorhen, Coot, Kingfisher, Grey Wagtail, Dipper.

December–February Unless the weather is very hard most winter visitors present, including Great Crested and Little Grebes, Cormorant, Whooper Swan, Wigeon, Teal, Pochard, Tufted Duck, Goldeneye and Red-breasted Merganser.

March–May Winter visitors depart, summer migrants arrive in surrounding woodlands. Occasional passage waders in May.

June–July Passage waders return by end of July.

August–November Some tern passage early on, chance of waders until water levels rise. Winter visitors begin to arrive from early October.

10 BARDSEY ISLAND

Map 10
OS Map 123

Habitat

Bardsey, legendary burial place of 20,000 Saints, lies just over 2 miles (3.2 km) south of the tip of the Lleyn Peninsula. The sound which separates the island from the mainland provides its Welsh name, Ynys Enlli, 'the Isle of Eddies'. The tide-rips and overfalls can make the journey, shall we say, interesting, and in stormy weather impossible. Hilaire Belloc, in his classic *The Cruise of the Nona,* describes how he lost his dinghy there, and in a never-forgotten phrase said of the turbulence: 'The sea jumps up and glares at you'.

When viewed from the mainland, Bardsey, which extends for 444 acres (180 ha), looks rather uninviting. The Mountain, as the highest point is called, rises to 548 feet (167 m), having steep rock and scree slopes tumbling to low cliffs and boulder beaches. This ridge of high ground effectively shields most of Bardsey from view. The far gentler western world of the island consists of lesser slopes richly covered in Western Gorse, Bracken and two species of heather, giving way to a network of small fields, 120 in all, divided by low stone and earth walls. Spaced out across the field system and linked by a rough track, the Main Road as it is fittingly called, are no fewer than 11 cottages, built as farmhouses in the 1870s by Lord Newborough. One of Lord Newborough's ancestors, John Wynn app Hughes, the standard-bearer at the Battle of Norwich (1549), was rewarded with the gift of Bardsey by a grateful Edward VI. Associated with the cottages is a school, though this has long ceased to function, and to the north a chapel and the tower of a thirteenth-century abbey. Only one family farms Bardsey at the present time: mainly sheep, ponies and a small area of arable crops. The walled gardens of the cottages, the four withy beds and a small conifer plantation provide excellent shelter for migrating birds. The garden at Cristin, now the Bird Observatory, appropriately harbours the largest tree on Bardsey, a Sycamore.

The south of Bardsey is divided from the north by an isthmus, bounded on one side by the island's only sandy beach and on the other by shingle and pebbles. Here the landing jetty is situated. Most of the southern extremity is an expanse of close-cropped maritime turf with Thrift, Sea Campion and Spring Squill.

On this low southern peninsula stands the lighthouse, constructed in 1821 by Joseph Nelson, one of the great lighthouse-builders. It is one of the few lights to have a square tower, but its chief claim to fame, or rather infamy, is that its light, five flashes every 15 seconds, attracts large numbers of nocturnal migrants, especially on very dark, cloudy nights. Unfortunately, many are killed by flying into the lantern and surrounding structure; the toll on bad nights may be some hundreds of birds, the corpses having to be wheelbarrowed away. Since 1978 a 'false lighthouse', a tall mast with quartz iodide lamps, has been in place close to the lighthouse proper. This draws birds away from the hazards of the tower and buildings, many settling on the ground around the mast and not moving away until daybreak. Not only are small passerines attracted, but Manx Shearwater, Storm Petrel, Water Rail, various waders, Kittiwake, terns, Swift and Cuckoo have been recorded. To be at the Bardsey light when migration is at its height, when the beams are full of flighting birds, is an experience never to be forgotten.

The Grey Seal breeds but infrequently on Bardsey, though it is always to be seen offshore; some no doubt wander from the Pembrokeshire colonies 80 miles (128 km) to the south. Porpoises and dolphins of several species have been recorded, while Basking Sharks are seen in most years. On land, there are Rabbits, Wood Mice, House Mice and Common Shrews. The Palmate Newt is the sole representative of the amphibians and reptiles to have reached the island.

John Ray, considered by many to be the greatest of all our field naturalists, visited Bardsey in the seventeenth century, while 200 years or so later the indefatigable William Eagle Clarke collected bird notes from the lighthouse-keepers. Despite this early interest, and that of a scattering of visitors during the first half of the present century, a writer in 1953 was to comment: 'It is remarkable that an island so well situated as Bardsey should be as little known to ornithologists.' Times were, however, changing. Birdwatchers in increasing numbers were taking up the challenge presented by small islands, and from the time the Observatory opened in 1953 there has been a stream of visitors to help successive wardens assiduously add to our knowledge, not only of the birds, but of all aspects of Bardsey's glorious natural history.

Bardsey is the only bird observatory in Wales, having been founded in 1953 by the West Midland Bird Club, the West Wales Field Society and local residents. The first Honorary Secretary was the noted naturalist and author William Condry, and the first visitors arrived in late July 1953. A succession of wardens has manned the Observatory ever since, save for the period 1971 to July 1973 when transport difficulties meant a temporary closure. Over 100,000 birds have been ringed on Bardsey, and the results of this dedication form a major contribution to our knowledge of bird populations and movements in western Britain.

Species

Bardsey is a stronghold for the Chough, and the six or seven pairs which now breed make this the most important single site for this bird

Choughs

in Britain. The population has been much studied and the results made available in several reports, so that those elsewhere have a fund of valuable information to draw upon when managing other sites for this, the most graceful member of the crow family. It has been discovered on Bardsey that the breeding pairs of Choughs are sedentary and remain together throughout the year; even when in a flock each pair is easily recognisable. They breed from about four years of age, and tend to use the same sites year after year in caves and in the boulder beaches. A male which nested in Seal Cave was at least 17 years of age when it died, a longevity record. Young Choughs are much more mobile, wandering some distance along the Lleyn Peninsula; a few even reach into Snowdonia, while one moved south, 45 miles (72 km) across Cardigan Bay to Llangranog, and settled there to breed. A key factor in maintaining so many breeding Choughs on Bardsey is the large area of close-cropped turf and the liberal quantities of droppings from large grazing animals. Particularly important in late summer are dung beetles, many hundreds of which may emerge from a single horse dropping. Ants are another important food, the mounds on the open sward being torn into by the Choughs searching for the yellow occupants. In winter the seaweed and other debris of the strandline is a source of food, mainly kelp flies and sandhoppers.

The other members of the crow family present include two pairs of Ravens, early nesters on secluded rock outcrops. In most autumns there is an influx from the mainland, usually of up to 25 birds though on several occasions double that number have been counted. With the wind in the east they soar along the face of The Mountain, hanging in the updraught, the air full of wild, joyful 'kronking' calls. Jackdaws nest in Rabbit burrows and crevices, the residents being joined in late summer by large noisy flocks which cross from the mainland. Magpies are gradually increasing, nesting in the withy beds and even in low bramble patches, a habit repeated on the Pembrokeshire islands. Hooded Crows are regular vagrants — the coast of Co. Wicklow, Ireland, is after all only 60 miles (96 km) to the west. Not surprisingly, the Jay, a resident of oak woodland, is a rare visitor to offshore islands, but small flocks were seen in the late autumn of 1983, the year of the huge irruption of this bird into Britain.

After the Chough, the seabirds are the main attraction among breeding species on Bardsey, though numbers do not compare with those at some other sites in North Wales or on the Pembrokeshire islands. Lack of suitable nest sites restricts numbers of cliff-nesting birds. Fulmars first nested in 1957 and there are now about 30 pairs. For about 15 years from the early 1960s the number of breeding Kittiwakes was extremely low, although it has subsequently risen and about 140 pairs now nest, mainly at one site on the east coast. Up to 200 pairs of Guillemots share the same cliff, while similar numbers of Razorbills are more scattered; it seems surprising that not more Razorbills nest, as they take readily to sites among the lower scree slopes. It is in these latter situations that 40 or so pairs of Shags also nest. Although Cormorants are seen daily, their nearest colony, like that of the Puffin, is on the Gwylan Islands off Aberdaron Bay, 4 miles (6.4 km) to the northwest.

The Lesser Black-backed Gull is the most numerous of its family on the island, having slowly increased since 1956, and now numbers about 220 pairs occupying a slope on the north of the island. Herring Gulls have by contrast declined, as they have done at other colonies in Wales. Several pairs of Great Black-backed Gulls nest in most years.

The nocturnal Manx Shearwater is Bardsey's most numerous breeding seabird, with up to 3,000 pairs nesting in burrows on the high ground and others occupying sites in the field walls. It is one of the events of a stay on Bardsey to hear after dark the calls of Manx Shearwaters flighting in from the sea, a signal to gather one's torch and head for the colony to view birds at close quarters — a magic world of calling shearwaters, of dew-soaked Bracken, while away in the distance the Bardsey light stabs the night sky. The status of the other nocturnal seabird, the Storm Petrel, is an enigma. A few pairs probably breed, though proof is difficult to come by. Small numbers visit the island throughout the summer, many probably non-breeders which wander vast distances, calling at islands all along the western seaboard of Britain in movements currently little understood.

Depending on weather conditions and the time of year, there can be spectacular movements of some species offshore, including Manx Shearwaters, Kittiwakes, Guillemots and Razorbills, with smaller numbers of Gannets, Lesser Black-backed Gulls and terns. It is the scarcer species that attract attention, while others may be 'once-in-a-lifetime' birds such as the albatross, most probably a Black-browed Albatross, seen flying south one day in 1976: what fortune for the lucky observer! The Sooty Shearwater is a regular visitor in late summer from southern oceans, while the Great Shearwater from Tristan da Cunha is occasionally seen. Although nesting as close as the Azores and off Portugal, Cory's Shearwater has been recorded only once. One of the great delights for seawatchers is when, on the windiest of days, the diminutive Leach's Petrel, with its distinctive buoyant, at times erratic flight, comes beating past; a few, usually singles, are seen each autumn. Arctic and Great Skuas are annual passage migrants, with over 100 of the former seen in some autumns. Pomarine Skuas are less frequent, while there are only three records of the Long-tailed Skua. Other scarce species seen offshore have been Grey Phalarope, Sabine's, Little and Bonaparte's Gulls and Black Tern.

North American passerines have provided some exquisite gems on Bardsey, such as the first, and so far only, British records of a Summer Tanager (in September 1957) and a Yellow Warbler (in August 1964).

Yellow Warbler

How many others have set out involuntarily to cross the North Atlantic aided by a swiftly moving depression, only to be lost at sea, or even to arrive, and depart, quietly, unnoticed by birdwatchers? Other late-summer and autumn Americans have included Sora Rail, Blackpoll Warbler, White-throated Sparrow, the huge Rose-breasted Grosbeak and three out of 16 Gray-cheeked Thrushes to have been recorded in Britain. Visitors to Bardsey in the spring can also look forward with some anticipation to the chance of American visitors, for a Slate-coloured Junco and a Song Sparrow have both been recorded then, the latter at the same time as a Northern Oriole in Pembrokeshire and a White-throated Sparrow in Caithness.

The list of rare migrants from Europe and Asia to Bardsey is equally impressive and includes the first Cetti's Warbler for Wales, in October 1973; this skulking warbler with, fortunately, a loud and distinctive song has gradually spread northwest in Europe, being first recorded in Britain in 1961. Other species have travelled much greater distances, among them Pallas's, Dusky and Yellow-browed Warblers from central Asia. Two scarce warblers from much nearer home are almost annual in their appearance: these are the Icterine and Melodious Warblers, both of which usually arrive during August and September. A River Warbler found dead at the lighthouse in September 1969 was only the third recorded in Britain. The Great Reed Warbler has been seen on two occasions in early summer, though few would have expected to hear its strident frog-like song on a remote Welsh island. As if there were not already enough to whet the appetite, other rare visitors include Night Heron, Honey Buzzard, Black-winged Stilt, Alpine Swift, Bee-eater, Wryneck, Tawny Pipit, Thrush Nightingale, Black-eared Wheatear, Collared Flycatcher, Penduline Tit, and Little, Yellow-breasted, Black-headed, Ortolan and Rock Buntings.

Timing

So much depends on your interests. If it is migrants, then the early autumn — September/October — is best; there is a good seabird passage and small migrants can be prolific at times, though much depends on the weather situation over the whole of northern Europe. May must be the most attractive month, for the island flowers are then coming to their peak, spring migration is well under way, and the breeding seabirds have all returned to their colonies. The weather is often as good during May as at any other time of year.

Access

Bardsey is owned by the Bardsey Island Trust, details of which are available from Dafydd Thomas, Stable Hen, Tywyddyn Du, Criccieth, Gwynedd, LL52 0LY. The Trust has a number of holiday properties for letting on the island.

The Observatory is open from late March to November and anyone over the age of 14 is welcome, beginners and experts alike. Enquiries to Mrs H. Bond, 21A, Gestridge Road, Kingsteignton, Newton Abbot, Devon. There is room for up to 12 people; in addition to the bedrooms, there is a common room, dining room and a well-equipped kitchen. Visitors need to take their own food and cater for themselves: be careful to allow extra — islands engender huge appetites, and even in midsummer the boat can be delayed by rough weather. In certain weeks the warden runs courses, and during these there is a resident cook. The

Observatory boat leaves Pwllheli each Saturday at 08.30 hours, heading south past St Tudwal's Islands and then westwards, a journey of about 20 miles (32 km) taking two hours.

Calendar

Resident Cormorant, Shag, Mallard, Kestrel, Peregrine, Moorhen, Oystercatcher, Lapwing, Curlew, Herring and Great Black-backed Gulls, Little Owl, Rock Pipit, Chough, Raven.

December–February Red-throated Diver. Fulmar, Guillemot and Razorbill return to the cliffs, the latter two making only sporadic visits, usually at dawn. Depending on weather conditions further east, there may be major influxes of thrushes, finches and Starlings. Merlin and Snipe usually resident.

March–May Manx Shearwater, Lesser Black-backed Gull and Kittiwake return early in the period, winter visitors depart though there may be stragglers well into April. First summer visitors usually Ring Ouzel, Wheatear and Black Redstart, followed shortly after by Swallow, Sand Martin and Chiffchaff. Other warblers and more hirundines are a feature of April, together with smaller numbers of Whimbrel, Common Sandpiper, Redstart and Pied Flycatcher. Late summer migrants include Turtle Dove, Swift and Spotted Flycatcher. Although not landing, Puffins should be looked for offshore from early April (about 400 pairs nest on Ynys Gwylan off Aberdaron); Guillemots and Razorbills do not remain ashore permanently until the first eggs are laid, usually about the end of April/early May. Vagrants likely to occur throughout whole period, Hoopoe and Woodchat Shrike being the two most regularly seen.

June–July All breeding species present, though by end of period Guillemots and Razorbills have left the cliffs. A few late migrants possible, though before July is out southward passage will have commenced. Purple Sandpipers from early July, while a few Turnstones usually summer on the island.

August–November Kittiwakes complete their breeding season in late August and quickly forsake the cliffs, though many are seen offshore daily throughout the autumn. Fulmar, Manx Shearwater and Storm Petrel complete their breeding season during September. Seabird movement at its peak in September, with shearwaters, Gannets, skuas, gulls and terns the main species involved, joined in October by large passages of auks and occasional scarce species such as Sabine's Gull and Leach's Petrel. Given good conditions passerine passage can be spectacular, with added attraction of scarce visitors. In late October and November usually large movements of larks, pipits, thrushes, finches and buntings, with occasional sightings of geese and swans.

11 COED ABER

Map 11
OS Map 115

Habitat

From a *Sphagnum* moss flush high on a shoulder of the Carnedd range, the Afon Goch commences its short, tumbling dramatic journey to the sea at Conwy Bay. Two miles (3.2 km) into its course it reaches one of Snowdonia's many geological highlights, a band of igneous granophyre forming a cliff some 120 feet (37 m) high. Over this the river plunges in a series of steps and terraces, to rush, swollen by several equally boisterous tributaries, a further 2 miles to the sea. Much oak woodland remains on the steep sides of the valley, but even in this secluded area some has been lost, replaced by ranks of introduced conifers of several species. Elsewhere there are wet areas where the Alder dominates, while as you climb out of the valley the woodland becomes more open and there are Hawthorn thickets, scattered Crab Apple and Rowan. The valley is renowned for its mosses and lichens, an indication of minimal aerial pollution. A number of scarce plants have been recorded, while among the butterflies the elusive White-letter Hairstreak has been seen in the past. Does it still survive? Certainly its food plant, the Wych Elm, is found here. The Pine Marten is even more difficult to locate, but it still occurs in Snowdonia, most especially in dense woodland, or on open moorland where scree slopes and rocky tors provide shelter.

Species

Dippers and Grey Wagtails nest along the river and Kingfishers are occasionally seen, usually at least one pair breeding in the valley. Another resident of the waterways is the Red-breasted Merganser, a fine bird to see especially when the small ducklings are about. The deciduous woodland provides the main bird interest, the summer visitors being Redstart, Garden Warbler, Blackcap, Wood Warbler, Chiffchaff, Willow Warbler and Pied Flycatcher.

Do not neglect the conifers, for they support several attractive species. Goldcrests and Coal Tits seem to be everywhere, but the bird to look for is the Siskin. A hundred years ago it was virtually confined to the Scottish Highlands, yet now it breeds, at least locally, throughout Britain. Much of this expansion has occurred within the last 30 years, something aided at least partly by a liking for peanuts at bird tables. In North Wales Siskins probably first nested in the early 1960s, but such is their secretive nature at the nest that breeding was not proved until 1972. Now they frequent many of the larger conifer areas, their musical flight call, a short 'tsyzing', and their twittering song quickly attracting attention so that the bird is hardly likely to be overlooked. Look out also for the Common Crossbill, which often frequents conifers; when its population in eastern Europe reaches a high level, large numbers move westwards and colonise new areas for several years.

Resident woodland species in the valley include Sparrowhawk, Buzzard, Tawny Owl, Green and Great Spotted Woodpeckers, Mistle Thrush, Willow Tit, Nuthatch, Treecreeper, Jay, Raven, Chaffinch and Bullfinch. As you climb southward out of the valley, you should encounter species such as the summer-visiting Tree Pipit and

Whinchat, and on the open moor Wheatear and possibly Ring Ouzel, and if you are very lucky even a fleeting glimpse of a Merlin.

Timing
No particular time of day, though a visit in early morning during mid- to late May is probably the best.

Access
Turn south off the A55 Bangor to Llandudno road at SH656727 in Aber village; a minor road leads through the valley, and there is a car park at SH663719. From here, a nature trail takes one on a circuitous route to Aber Falls and back over a hill and through some coniferous plantations. A booklet describing the trail is available from the Nature Conservancy Council North Wales Regional Office.

Calendar

Resident Sparrowhawk, Buzzard, Kestrel, Merlin, Pheasant, Woodpigeon, Tawny Owl, Little Owl, Kingfisher, Green and Great Spotted Woodpeckers, Skylark, Grey Wagtail, Dipper, Goldcrest, tit family, Nuthatch, Treecreeper, Jay, Raven, Siskin, Redpoll.

December–February Winter visitors, including Fieldfare, Redwing and Brambling.

March–May Arrival of summer visitors, including Cuckoo, Tree Pipit, Redstart, Whinchat, Wheatear, Ring Ouzel, Garden Warbler, Blackcap, Wood Warbler, Chiffchaff, Willow Warbler, Spotted and Pied Flycatchers.

June–July All breeding species present, most now feeding young.

August–November Summer visitors depart by end of August/early September, but the occasional late Blackcap and Chiffchaff may be located well into October. Winter thrushes appear during October, while resident tits, Treecreeper and Goldcrest form loose flocks which wander through the woodlands.

12 GREAT ORME

Map 12
OS Map 115

Habitat

Some 2 square miles (5.2 square km) in extent and rising to 675 feet (206 m), the massive limestone headland of the Great Orme extends northwest, forming the eastern arm of Conwy Bay. The holiday resort of Llandudno sprawls at its landward base, a continuation of human occupation extending back to Paleolithic times, when some of Wales' earliest inhabitants huddled in the headland caves, and hunted across plains and marshes long submerged beneath the Irish Sea. Neolithic Man buried his dead here — there is a cromlech near the half-way tram station; what would he have thought of such a development, and the visitors who use it today? Almost an island, it is not surprising that early religious Man sought solitude here, as for instance did St Tudno in the sixth century. More recently but still nearly 700 summers away, Bishop Anian, who had christened the first Prince of Wales, the future Edward II, built a palace here; perhaps not unexpectedly, it was burnt by Owain Glyndwr.

The cliff and plateau vegetation is a rich mixture of limestone and heath with an area of limestone pavement, the fissures and knolls – grykes and clints – supporting a number of plants rarely found elsewhere on the head. Despite its proximity to a large population and busy holiday resorts, the Great Orme is as much a botanist's paradise now as when the first naturalists passed this way in the late eighteenth century. There are rich rewards for those with time to search: plants such as the Goldilocks Aster, Dark-red Helleborine, Spotted Cat's-ear, Nottingham Catchfly and Spiked Speedwell. Cotoneasters have spread onto the head from nearby gardens, but one member of the family, first discovered on the Great Orme in 1783 and not known from anywhere else in Britain, still clings here, some five bushes strong, despite past ravages by collectors and the herd of wild goats descended from the Royal herd at Windsor. Butterflies abound on sunny days, the dwarf forms of the Silver-studded Blue and Grayling being of note.

Species

Seabirds are a speciality at the Great Orme, though alas two species no longer breed there. The Black Guillemot is said to have nested in the eighteenth century, but is now rarely seen. Puffins remained until much more recently, probably last nesting in the 1950s, and individuals are seen offshore in most years and might well eventually return to occupy some secluded cliff crevice; it will need a sharp observer during June and July to spot birds carrying fish back to the nesting site. The first record of the Fulmar for Caernarvonshire was of two at the Great Orme in April 1937; breeding was confirmed in 1945, and there are now about 100 pairs occupying ledges above the road as well as on the sea cliffs. Cormorants and Shags nest, as do Herring and a few pairs of Lesser Black-backed and Great Black-backed Gulls. Pride of place must go to a noisy colony of over 1,200 pairs of Kittiwakes, this being their largest colony in North Wales. Sharing the same ledges are some 700 pairs of Guillemots and nearly 100 pairs of Razorbills. Look out for House Martins nesting on the cliffs: an ancestral habitat, for where else did they nest before we provided homes with eaves?

Peregrine and Kestrel breed on the cliffs and Choughs have done so in the past, their nearest regular site being 4 miles (6.4 km) to the west beyond the Conwy. During the hard winter of 1962/3, several Choughs even fed in the streets of Llandudno. Choughs still visit the head, 11 on 25 October 1985 being a notable flock for this area. The varied habitats, especially on the more sheltered slopes, support a wide range of passerines, including Stonechat and Wheatear, the latter at probably its only coastal site in Caernarvonshire. Several pairs of Little Owls are usually present, and are not infrequently seen during daytime. The Great Orme would probably repay more comprehensive observation at migration times in respect of both seabird passage offshore and small birds on the head itself, where species recently recorded have included Black Redstart, several warblers, Goldcrest, Firecrest, Pied Flycatcher, Coal and Blue Tits, Great Grey Shrike, Siskin, Redpoll and Snow Bunting.

Timing

Not critical here, but beware: the marine drive and footpaths become very busy during the summer months, so it is well worth making an early start if you desire some degree of solitude. Certainly an early start will be essential for seawatching and for autumn migrants.

Access

The marine drive from Llandudno provides a complete circuit of the head, in addition to which a road crosses the centre. A tramway is another route to the high interior, from where a nature trail leads west to the seabird colonies and the southwest coast. Excellent views are also obtained from the pleasure boats which sail out of Llandudno.

Calendar

Resident Cormorant, Shag, Kestrel, Peregrine, Oystercatcher, Herring and Great Black-backed Gulls, Feral Pigeon, Little Owl, Skylark, Rock Pipit, Stonechat, Jackdaw, Carrion Crow, Raven.

December–February Winter visitors such as divers and grebes offshore, occasional seaducks including Common Scoter. First Fulmars return during January, with Kittiwakes in February, while Guillemots and Razorbills make infrequent visits to the cliffs, always during the early morning and usually when weather conditions are settled.

March–May Gannets offshore, Lesser Black-backed Gulls, Guillemots and Razorbills return to the colonies permanently about the end of April, by which time Kittiwakes are commencing nest-building. Summer visitors arrive, with Wheatear and Black Redstart in mid-March usually the first, quickly followed by Swallow, Sand Martin and Chiffchaff by end of month. Sandwich Terns possible offshore. Other migrants move through in April, with continuing Swallow passage, and small numbers of Redstarts, Sedge Warblers, Whitethroats and Willow Warblers.

June–July Gannets now regular offshore, all breeding species present with Guillemots and Razorbills completing their short stay ashore by end of July

August–November Seabird passage under way during first part of period, Manx Shearwater, Gannet, Kittiwake and terns being predominant species. Kittiwakes leave colonies by about third week of August but are usually seen offshore, Fulmars depart during mid-September. Soon afterwards winter species such as Red-throated and Great Northern Divers appear offshore, while Common Scoters pass in small parties. Some passage waders seen but usually only Turnstone present on the head itself. This is the most likely time of year to see Choughs on the Great Orme. Passerine migration from late August onwards, with departing Swallows conspicuous in September, Skylark, Meadow Pipit, Fieldfare, Redwing, Starling and Chaffinch during late October, when possibility of Black Redstart.

Habitat

Snowdonia — does its Welsh name Eryi mean that Golden Eagles once soared above its narrow valleys, above its ridges and summits, nesting on remote crags, hoping no doubt to escape the attentions of shepherds? Alas, there are only tantalising hints. Edward Lhuyd himself, greatest of Welsh naturalists, probably failed to see the bird, though the evidence which he collected, and the reports of others, seem to confirm that Golden Eagles had indeed been present here, possibly nesting until about 1700 but disappearing forever within a few years. The absence of the Golden Eagle, and of other northern species, means that the mountains of Wales are somewhat impoverished ornithologically when compared with those of Scotland. Do not let this dissuade you from walking the hills, or going high into the mountains of Snowdonia, provided of course that you are properly equipped.

The Nature Conservancy Council manages several National Nature Reserves in Snowdonia, including one of the most renowned, Cwm Idwal, 984 acres (398 ha), the first NNR in Wales and aptly described as 'holy ground for the history of early botany and geology'. Some of the scarce and special plants of Snowdonia can be found there, including the Snowdon Lily, Purple Saxifrage, Alpine Meadow-rue and Moss Campion. The glacial lake of Llyn Idwal, like a number of other unspoiled upland waters, has some interesting plants: Awlwort, Floating Bur-reed, Pillwort, Quillwort, Shoreweed and Water Lobelia, and latter fringing the shallows during July and early August with its pale lilac flowers. Another NNR, the largest in Wales, Y Wydda (Snowdon), extends over 4,145 acres (1,677 ha) and includes the very summit of Snowdon itself.

Species

The Ring Ouzel is a bird of mountain and moorland, its breeding range extending directly down the central spine of Wales, rarely descending below 1,000 feet (305 m) and often reaching onto the very summits. Ring Ouzels require within their nesting territory a crag or gully, perhaps a stunted Rowan, even a disused mineshaft or quarryman's building. If searching for this bird, concentrate on areas where such features are evident, though usually the penetrating whistle and harsh 'tac-tac-tac-tac-tac' notes will reveal the bird's presence even at long range. Ring Ouzels arrive in late March and early April and stay until late summer, before returning to winter quarters in northwest Africa. Another summer visitor to the high ground is the Wheatear, arriving even before the Ring Ouzel, and just as much at home in rocky areas as on the open grasslands, provided there are nest holes. Wrens are encountered to the very tops of the mountains, and are often the only small bird present there during hard weather in midwinter. On the open mountain grasslands Skylarks and Meadow Pipits are numerous, the latter a frequent host to the Cuckoo on slopes up to about 1,500 feet (457 m) in altitude.

Two members of the crow family are striking, at times noisy residents of the high ground. The Chough feeds on the sheep-grazed turf of the mountains, having been recorded up to at least 2,900 feet (884 m); altitude, however, is no problem for this bird, which has been found nesting at 19,000 feet (5,790 m) in the Himalayas. A survey of the Chough in Wales, carried out in 1982 as part of the International Chough Survey, and faithfully reported in the journal *Nature in Wales,* revealed that there were some 51 breeding pairs in Caernarvonshire, of which no fewer than 27 nested in Snowdonia. Despite what seems to be an abundance of suitable natural sites in cliffs and crags, the inland-breeding Choughs prefer to use quarries and mineshafts. While large numbers of sheep continue to graze our uplands, there seems little likelihood of significant changes taking place in the Snowdonia Chough population. The main threats are from disturbance, probably unavoidable in the active quarries, and egg-collectors. Ravens frequent the high ground throughout the year, hard weather resulting in the death of sheep being to the birds' advantage. Numbers have probably regained the level of the early nineteenth century, before persecution by gamekeepers and shepherds reduced the bird for many years to the status of a scarce resident restricted to remote coastal and upland areas. Three falcons, the Kestrel, Merlin and Peregrine, may be encountered in Snowdonia; the Merlin is by far the rarest, for it needs large heather moors on which to breed.

The Snowdonia lakes attract small numbers of winter wildfowl, the groups of Whooper Swans being the most prominent. Goosanders usually winter here: will they come to nest? This seems quite likely in view of their rapid extension of range along several of the river systems in central and in South Wales and on the Dee in the northeast. Pochard, Tufted Duck and Goldeneye are diving ducks which, together with the Coot, may be seen on all the larger waters throughout the winter. A summer visitor to the shores of these lakes is the Common Sandpiper, its shrill 'willy-wicket' song, certainly the sound of the lakes and rivers in early summer, soon attracting the watcher's attention; its flight is unlike that of any other wader, very low over the water with flickering wingbeats and short glides, and as soon as it lands the characteristic bobbing action will be observed and the call heard. Other birds of the lakes and rivers are the Dipper and Grey Wagtail, while Pied Wagtails seem to be everywhere, even up to the high ground.

Timing

Not material. It is more a question of the weather, which can change extremely rapidly on the mountain tops so that care must be taken, even in high summer, to acquaint oneself with the forecast for the day before setting out. Make sure that you are properly equipped, and do not proceed unless you are certain of both the conditions and your own capabilities.

Access

While several of the Snowdonia lakes such as Llyn Gwynant, Llyn Dinas and Llyn Cwellyn are visible from the road, probably the best way of seeing Snowdonia and its upland birds is to follow one of the three nature trails. Each has its own leaflet, available from the NCC North Wales Regional Office.

Cwm Idwal Leave the A5 at the Ogwen Cottage Mountain School (SH648603) and take the footpath south up the slope to the NNR, where a path leads right around Llyn Idwal.

The Miners' Track Built during the nineteenth century for the copper mines near Glaslyn, you head south from the A4086 at Pen y Pass (SH647557). The track takes one close to Llyn Teyrn and eventually to Llyn Llydaw, one of the largest of the Snowdonia lakes. For those properly equipped, it continues, linking with the Pyg track above Glaslyn, to the summit of Snowdon.

Cwm y Llan Leave the A498 at Pont Bethania (SH627500) and follow the Watkin Path, the first part taking the watcher to the Snowdon Slate Works below Craig Ddu. For those properly equipped, it is possible to continue beyond to Bwlch Ciliau and Bwlch y Saethau and so on to the summit of Snowdon.

Calendar

Resident Cormorant, a regular visitor to the lakes throughout the year, Grey Heron, Buzzard, Kestrel, Merlin, Peregrine, Herring and Great Black-backed Gulls are regular visitors in all months, Little Owl, Skylark, Meadow Pipit, Grey and Pied Wagtails, Dipper, Wren, Chough, Jackdaw, Carrion Crow, Raven.

December–February Depending on conditions, Whooper Swan, Teal, Pochard, Tufted Duck, Goldeneye, Goosander and Coot on the lakes.

March–May Winter visitors depart. Wheatear and Ring Ouzel the first summer visitors to arrive, though by early April small numbers of Swallows over the lakes, soon to be joined by Common Sandpipers. Other visitors include Cuckoo, Tree Pipit and Redstart.

June–July Summer visitors still present, occasional passage waders at lakes in late July. Chough family parties merge together into small flocks.

August–November Summer visitors leave the high ground by early September. Winter ducks from early October, other visitors shortly afterwards include Fieldfare and Redwing.

14 TRAETH LAVAN

Map 14
OS Map 115

Habitat

At low tide, the eastern end of the Menai Straits is almost blocked by the vast expanse of Traeth Lavan — the Lavan Sands; only a narrow deep-water channel remains, close under Beaumaris on the Anglesey shore. Traeth Lavan, one of the richest haunts for wildfowl and waders in the whole of Wales, extends for some 26 square miles (73 square km) from Llanfairfechan westwards to the estuary of the Ogwen close to Bangor. At their maximum, the sands stretch some 3 miles (4.8 km) seawards, a seemingly inhospitable seascape of sand, mudflats and mussel beds, with a low shingle ridge flanking the west side of the tiny Ogwen Estuary.

Species

Pride of place must go to the late-summer concentrations of Great Crested Grebes and Red-breasted Mergansers which use Traeth Lavan as a moult area, the numbers being of national importance. Up to 500 Great Crested Grebes are present from late July to October, though some may be seen throughout the year, a few even in spring and early summer. The number of Red-breasted Mergansers gathering has risen over the past quarter of a century, probably as the bird has extended its range, from about 70 in 1962 to over 400 in recent years. Small numbers of Slavonian and Black-necked Grebes occur annually, and Red-necked Grebes are occasionally seen. Several species of diving duck regularly winter, including Scaup, Goldeneye, Long-tailed Duck and Velvet and Common Scoters.

Great Crested Grebes

Traeth Lavan is important for several species of dabbling duck, total numbers of which may rise to 2,000 birds, mainly Shelduck, Wigeon, Teal and Mallard, with fewer (usually less than 100) Pintails. Vast flocks of waders feed on Traeth Lavan, with up to 15,000 birds of ten species

43

during midwinter. Oystercatcher and Dunlin predominate and together total about 12,000 birds, with smaller numbers of Lapwing, Knot, Bar-tailed Godwit, Curlew and Redshank, and occasional Black-tailed Godwit, Greenshank and Turnstone.

Closely related to the Mallard is the Black Duck, one of the most abundant dabbling ducks in eastern North America. The first record of a Black Duck in Britain and Ireland was in February 1954, when a female was noted by an astute observer among other fowl in a poulterer's shop in Waterford, it having been shot on a marsh to the west of Mullinvat, Co. Kilkenny. Since then 12 or so have been recorded, including a remarkable male which first took up residence on Traeth Lavan off Aber in February 1979. Finding one of the local female Mallards to his liking, he mated, and has remained in residence ever since, together with a number of hybrid offspring which lead to much confusion among birdwatchers.

Timing

It is essential to check on the tide times and to arrange a visit for a couple of hours either side of high water. At these times, ducks and grebes will move close inshore and the wader flocks will be concentrated on the restriced areas of mudflat.

Access

With a coastline and footpath some 6 miles (9.6 km) in length there is much to choose from and there are a number of access points to the shore, most notably at Ogwen (SH614724), Aber (SH647731) and Llanfairfechan (SH677754).

Calendar

Resident Great Crested Grebe, Cormorant, Grey Heron, Shelduck, Mallard, Black Duck, Red-breasted Merganser, Oystercatcher, large gulls.

December–February Divers and small grebes, Wigeon, Teal, Pintail, Scaup, Long-tailed Duck, Common Scoter, Goldeneye, Ringed, Golden and Grey Plovers, Lapwing, Knot, Dunlin, Bar-tailed Godwit, Curlew, Redshank, Turnstone.

March–May Departure of winter visitors, passage waders throughout much of period including Sanderling and Whimbrel, occasional terns, especially Sandwich Tern.

June–July Numbers of Great Crested Grebes and Red-breasted Mergansers begin to increase during July and peak in August. Tern passage commences and wader numbers begin to increase.

August–November Return passage of waders well under way throughout August, including small numbers of Little Stint, Curlew Sandpiper, Black-tailed Godwit, Spotted Redshank and Greenshank. Winter visitors begin to arrive during September and tern passage continues until October.

Habitat

The best introduction to the Rheidol Valley is to take one of the 'Great Little Trains of Wales' and travel from Aberystwyth to Devil's Bridge. The line has a gauge of 1 ft 11 in and was built in 1901–02 to carry lead and zinc ore from the mines in the valley to the harbour at Aberystwyth. Extending for 10 miles (16 km), it takes one from almost sea level to some 650 feet (198 m), from the valley floor a contour-hugging climb along the southern slopes affording spectacular views to the north.

At the seaward end of the valley the river meanders across a floodplain, exposing shingle beds and leaving oxbows where it has frequently changed its course. At one point there are several small gravel pits, one of the few lowland freshwater sites in north Cardiganshire. Further inland is a reservoir, part of the Central Electricity Generating Board hydroelectric scheme. Water is brought from the Nantymoch and Dinas reservoirs in the hills to the north, and travels by pressure tunnel to drive the generators of the Cwm Rheidol power station, before being released into the river.

The main feature of nature conservation interest in the valley is the large area of Sessile Oak woodlands. These still cover many of the steep hillsides, despite clearances for agriculture, overgrazing, and the planting of conifers. At Devil's Bridge is the Coed Rheidol National Nature Reserve, some 106 acres (43 ha) managed by the Nature Conservancy Council, while a little further down the valley is Coed Simdde Lwyd, 71 acres (28 ha) owned by the West Wales Trust for Nature Conservation.

Species

Before exploring the valley, it is always worth looking at the gull flock where the Rheidol meets the sea in Aberystwyth Harbour, and also on the nearby beach. Mediterranean and Little Gulls are now regularly seen, mainly during the late winter and early spring, usually as single birds but in the case of Little Gull up to 24 have been recorded. Sabine's, Ring-billed and Glaucous Gulls have also been seen, an indication of the success that birdwatchers throughout Britain now have in identifying scarce gulls which, as they appear in a great range of plumages depending on age, were probably overlooked in earlier years. Late autumn is the time to search for Black Redstarts around the harbour buildings or nearby where the few remains of Aberystwyth Castle stand. Throughout the winter Red-throated Divers are present offshore, and on the rocky shore at College Rocks, and even within the harbour, there are Purple Sandpipers and Turnstones. Small numbers of diving ducks use the Rheidol gravel pits in winter, while Common Sandpiper, Kingfisher, Sand Martin, Grey Wagtail and Dipper can be seen along the river in summer. Look out also for Red-breasted Mergansers, which have recently come to breed on the neighbouring Ystwyth. A female Goosander with a solitary chick seen on the Rheidol in July 1985 was the first absolute proof of breeding by this handsome duck in Cardiganshire, and is surely the forerunner to its rapidly becoming established on other rivers in the county.

The woodlands contain all the expected species, including summer visitors such as Tree Pipit, Redstart, Wood Warbler and Pied Flycatcher.

Turnstones

Ravens are usually to be seen, while Sparrowhawks and Buzzards are the most likely birds of prey. If you are lucky, there may be a glimpse of a Red Kite as it soars along the escarpments before returning to higher ground to feed.

Timing
Winter visits to the harbour and beach should be made as the tide begins to recede, though as there is no great intertidal area the distance even at low water is not too great for easy observation. For the valley itself, any time of day will be in order.

Access
The harbour is easily accessible on foot, while the promenade provides easy viewing points from the shore and enables one to watch from the comfort of a car if required; at least in winter there will be no parking problems, but in summer it is a different story. The narrow-gauge train runs from Aberystwyth to Devil's Bridge between Easter and mid-September: enquire at the station or in tourist information centres as to the times of departure. An unclassified road leaves the A44 at Capel Bangor (SN657803) and traverses the whole valley. Beyond the CEGB information centre, which is well worth a visit, the road becomes extremely narrow and finally ends at the disused lead mines below Allt Gigfran. There is a tiny parking space at the Coed Simdde Lwyd reserve (SN703787) from which a footpath takes one up the slope. The western boundary is the hanging valley, a glacial feature in which the Nant Bwa Drain plunges 500 feet (150 m) from the plateau above, well worth seeing in times of spate. The A4120, which runs east from Aberystwyth on the high ground to the south of the valley, has several good vantage points, though one has to park on the roadside as there are currently no viewing places provided.

Cale. dar

Resident Grey Heron, Red Kite, Sparrowhawk, Buzzard, Kestrel, Coot, Oystercatcher, Herring and Great Black-backed Gulls, Green and Great

Spotted Woodpeckers, Rock Pipit, Grey and Pied Wagtails, Dipper, Goldcrest, tit family, Nuthatch, Treecreeper, Jay, Raven.

December–February Red-throated Diver, Pochard, Tufted Duck, Purple Sandpiper, Turnstone, Little Gull, Fieldfare, Redwing, Brambling.

March–May Common Sandpiper, Cuckoo, Sand Martin, Tree Pipit, Redstart, Whitethroat, Garden Warbler, Blackcap, Wood Warbler, Chiffchaff, Willow Warbler, Spotted and Pied Flycatchers.

June–July Manx Shearwaters and first tern passage offshore by late July. Kingfisher likely on river. All summer migrants and residents still present, but become more difficult to locate as breeding season draws to a close.

August–November Turnstones return, a chance of other passage waders, Mediterranean and Sabine's Gulls possible, tern passage continues until late September. Black Redstart, Fieldfare and Redwing during late October, while other winter visitors such as diving ducks and divers begin to arrive.

16 CORS CARON

Map 16
OS Maps 135/146

Habitat

Travel back in time to the end of the last Ice Age and look north from the outskirts of present-day Tregaron. A huge but shallow lake, the result of a glacial moraine damming the valley, would be seen: perhaps it teemed with waterfowl, the envy of the hunter people who huddled on the shore. Gradually the lake infilled, first with the plants of open water, then tall reeds and other emergent vegetation, and finally trees such as Willow, Alder and Birch. Later, during a wet period, the trees died and *Sphagnum* mosses — the bog mosses, master builders of peat bogs — began to dominate. Several thousand years elapsed, and now, like a huge upturned saucer, the bog centre rises about 30 feet (9 m) above the original lake bed.

Cors Caron is now largely protected as a National Nature Reserve managed by the Nature Conservancy Council. It is a classic site for studies into the development sequence of raised mires; fortunately, much west of the Teifi has not been exploited for peat. Cross-leaved Heath, Bog Asphodel, Bog Rosemary, Cranberry and Round-leaved Sundew are just a few of the special plants which occur. The Large Heath butterfly is at the southern extremity of its range, while the reserve supports a range of animals including Polecats and Otters.

Species

Cors Caron has been a NNR since 1955, with a resident warden so that much information has now been accumulated on its birdlife. Some 170 species have been seen, of which 40 breed including Teal, Mallard, Water Rail, Red Grouse, Snipe, Curlew, Redshank, Black-headed Gull, Tree Pipit, Redstart, Grasshopper Warbler and Redpoll. Regular visitors include Grey Heron, Whooper Swan, Wigeon, Red Kite, Hen Harrier, Buzzard and Merlin. Rare species in recent years have been Purple Heron, Marsh and Montagu's Harriers, Quail and Great Grey Shrike. The Red Kite is particularly noteworthy, either as it glides along the eastern hills or when it descends to hunt over the bog; the latter it does especially in winter, when that other fine raptor the Hen Harrier is present, up to five individuals having been seen on a single occasion. At one time Cors Caron was a noted wintering ground for small numbers of Greenland White-fronted Geese, but now they rarely visit, remaining instead on the Dyfi to the north.

Timing

Visit in the mornings, especially when using the tower hide at the northern end, for then the light is behind you as you look across the bog.

Access

General views are obtainable from the A485 which runs northwest from Tregaron, or better still from the B4343 which runs northeast from the town following the eastern boundary of the bog. Just beyond Maesllyn Lake (SN700634) is a limited parking area; from here one can walk about a mile (1.6 km) north along the disused railway line to a public observation hide overlooking a large section of the reserve, including shallow pools much used in winter by wildfowl, among them the Whooper Swans which move between here and several small lakes in the surrounding hills. Access to the reserve proper is by permits, available from The Warden, Minawel, Ffair Rhos, Pontrhydfendigaid, Ystrad Meurig, Dyfed, SY25 6BN, or from the Dyfed-Powys Regional Office of the NCC.

Calendar

Resident Grey Heron, Teal, Mallard, Buzzard, Kestrel, Coot, Moorhen, Water Rail, Snipe, Skylark, Meadow Pipit, Carrion Crow, Raven, Reed Bunting.

December–February Whooper Swan, Wigeon, Shoveler, Red Kite, Hen Harrier, Merlin, Fieldfare, Redwing, Siskin, Redpoll.

March–May Winter visitors depart, but sometimes Hen Harriers and even Whooper Swans remain until late April, while there is always a chance of seeing a Red Kite over nearby hills. Breeding Curlew and Redshank return, while summer migrants include Tree Pipit, Redstart, Whinchat, and Grasshopper, Sedge and Willow Warblers.

June–July All breeding species present. Passage waders from mid-July, usually Whimbrel and Green Sandpiper but Greenshank and Wood Sandpiper have been recorded.

August–November Summer visitors depart, wildfowl numbers increase during late September and early October, and raptors begin to feed more frequently over the bog. First Whooper Swans usually appear in early November.

Habitat

The Dyfi is one of the most enchanting estuaries in the whole of Britain, being bounded to the north by Cader Idris and its foothills, and to the south by the lesser slopes of north Cardiganshire, the outliers of Plynlimon, which are intersected by almost secret valleys such as the Clettwr, Einion and Leri. The Dyfi, which has flowed from its source below Aran Fawddwy, forms the boundary between North and South Wales at this point.

At the estuary mouth lie Ynyslas Dunes, one of the most popular holiday beaches in Wales, but please do not let this deter you from making a visit even in the height of summer, for even then there are always likely to be birds offshore. The main part of the dunes forms part of the Dyfi National Nature Reserve, and there is an excellent information centre here run by the Nature Conservancy Council, particular emphasis being given to the large number of visiting school parties that make use of the teaching opportunities provided by the dunes and nearby shores. The dunes are protected by boardwalks at sensitive points so as to prevent erosion and their ultimate destruction. On the landward side are several dune slacks, shallow pools in winter, and even in midsummer with water not far beneath the surface. Here are such plants as Common Bird's-foot-trefoil, Restharrow, Biting Stonecrop, Common Centaury, Early and Northern Marsh-orchids, and Bee and Pyramidal Orchids. In one recent summer no fewer than 170,000 Marsh Helleborine plants were counted: what a sight the slacks looked, a seemingly endless carpet of white flowers.

Stand on the highest point of the boardwalk and look inland: the main part of the estuary extends some 5 miles (8 km) away to the east, while to the southeast lies Cors Fochno. Despite many inroads by reclamation for agriculture and peripheral peat-cutting, this still remains the largest area of unmodified raised mire in the country, much of it now owned by the NCC. A wide range of peat-loving plants flourishes here, including Bog Myrtle, Bog Rosemary, Cranberry and Royal Fern. Of special interest is the colony of the Rosy Marsh Moth discovered here in 1965, over 100 years after it became extinct in the fens of East Anglia.

The estuary itself is a mixture of saltmarsh, mud and sandflats, though Common Cord-grass introduced as part of an agricultural reclamation scheme has reduced by about a third the amount of feeding areas for many waders. Where the estuary begins to narrow and makes its first major bend is the Royal Society for the Protection of Birds reserve at Ynyshir, opened in 1970. The name provides a hint as to the early nature of the land here, for Ynyshir means 'long island', and the wooded ridge was probably once an island set among extensive marshes which have long since vanished. Now the reserve covers some 630 acres (155 ha), a superb mixture of habitats from the open estuary through to woodlands and then the Bracken-covered hills above the villages of Furnace and Eglwysfach.

Species

It is well worth searching the sea off the mouth of the estuary and southwards towards Borth. The depth is shallow and the resultant warm waters make the area attractive to a range of marine species. Manx Shearwaters are regular here, sometimes moving close inshore, while occasionally Sooty Shearwaters have been seen. Both Storm and Leach's Petrels occur, especially when stormy weather brings autumn passage birds close inshore. There are two intriguing records of rare petrels in north Cardiganshire, both during the last century. A Cape Pigeon, an Antarctic species, was shot here in 1879, though it was not accepted on to the British List as this species was regularly caught by sailors and kept on board ship. One might ask that, if this were the case, why were not more reported, and after all its arrival unaided in British waters seems at least as likely as that of some other vagrants which have long been accepted. Also considered highly improbable (though one never knows with birds!), a Collared Petrel shot just south of Aberystwyth in 1899 was likewise not accepted; this species breeds on islands in the tropical and subtropical Pacific Ocean.

The sea between Ynyslas and Borth is perhaps the most important wintering area in Wales for Red-throated Divers, and peak counts have exceeded 100 birds. Family parties are present from mid-September, and with luck you should be able to observe them fishing close inshore. Great Northern Divers occur, usually as single birds, but Black-throated Divers are, as in many other areas, extremely rare. Even more striking than the peak numbers of Red-throated Divers is the midwinter peak of Great Crested Grebes, up to 550 birds being recorded. Local ornithologists, having recognised its importance, hope to carry out co-ordinated counts across much of this section of Cardigan Bay, which is clearly a key wintering ground in Britain for divers and grebes.

Gannets, Cormorants and Shags are normally to be seen offshore, as are small numbers of seaducks, the latter mainly in winter though parties of Eiders and Common Scoters may be seen in any month. Skuas occur on autumn passage and less frequently in spring, no doubt attracted by the flocks of terns which gather to fish at the estuary mouth. Sandwich Terns usually predominate and on occasions several hundred may be present, with smaller numbers of Common, Arctic and Little Terns and occasionally Roseate and Black Terns. The gull flocks are well worth investigating, careful observers having located Mediterranean and Little Gulls annually in recent years, with occasional records of Ring-billed, Iceland and Glaucous Gulls. Mixed flocks of Guillemots and Razorbills raft offshore, especially in October and again in April; their nearest colonies are on New Quay Head, some 25 miles (40 km) to the south, and on the south side of the Lleyn, a similar distance to the northwest.

Turn away from the sea and look inland, where Cors Fochno supports a small flock of Black Grouse; there can be few other places in Britain where this species exists at almost sea level. Most ornithologists, however, concentrate on the estuary, where the upper third is a wildfowl refuge and for the remainder local wildfowlers provide wardens and submit records of all birds taken. Shooting of the small flock of Greenland White-fronted Geese is subject to a voluntary ban throughout the whole estuary. This, the largest and most distinctive subspecies of the White-fronted Goose, breeds on or close to plateau lakes on the west coast of Greenland between Upernavik and Godthab. It winters entirely in Britain and Ireland, most using sites in the west of Scotland and in Ireland (particularly the Wexford Slobs), so that the small number which visit Wales represent a fraction, though a precious fraction, of the

Greenland White-fronts

population. The decline in the numbers of the Greenland White-fronted Goose, one of the rarest geese in the world, from about 20,000 in the 1950s to about 12,000 in the late 1970s, is part of a long-term decline mirrored in Wales. Here, numbers have fallen from about 1,100 at the beginning of the century to fewer than 100 at the present time, all of which winter on Cors Fochno or the nearby estuary of the Dyfi. Although their winter habitat is protected and none is shot, the presence of low-flying military aircraft is a constant problem, for even at a distance of 10 miles (16 km) they put the geese to flight and on a bad day the birds may be on the wing for up to three hours as the result of continuous disturbance. What effect is the loss of feeding time and the stress of such disturbances having on this relict flock?

Shelducks breed on the Dyfi, but peak numbers usually occur in midwinter, when up to 300 may be present. Several thousand Wigeons frequent the estuary throughout the winter, together with about 1,000 Mallards and a slightly smaller number of Teals. Although some Goldeneyes arrive as early as September, most are not seen until midwinter, when numbers may rise to 40: a spectacular sight, especially when there is a good proportion of males among the flocks. Long-tailed Duck and Smew are scarce visitors, the latter usually only when the lakes and reservoirs of eastern England are frozen. Red-breasted Mergansers breed close to the upper reaches of the estuary, where the first ducklings were seen in 1969; once they have left the nest the broods link up, so that sizeable gatherings may result such as that of 60 ducklings at Ynyshir in July 1983. In winter the Red-breasted Merganser is still much in evidence on the estuary, where up to 100 have been seen at one time. Look for signs that Goosanders have successfully nested: since they are now seen more frequently in spring, it can surely be only a matter of time before this duck establishes itself on the upper reaches, part of a long-term improvement in its fortunes.

A few pairs of Oystercatchers, Lapwings, Snipe and Redshanks breed on the estuary-side marshes, while, surprisingly, up to six pairs of Ringed Plovers manage to survive at Ynyslas despite the tramp of many feet. More are seen on passage, mainly during the autumn, while a few overwinter on the estuary together with large numbers of Lapwings, Dunlins and Curlews. Most other waders are seen here, including up to 30 Grey Plovers, about 100 Knots, ten Black-tailed and 100 Bar-tailed Godwits, while a handful of Spotted Redshanks and Greenshanks are also recorded. Unusual waders in recent years have included Kentish Plover, Dotterel, Little Stint, Curlew and Buff-breasted Sandpipers, Ruff, Lesser Yellowlegs and Spotted Sandpiper.

The RSPB has carried out a range of management tasks at Ynyshir and some 67 species of bird now breed on the reserve. Redstarts, Pied Flycatchers, Blue and Great Tits take readily to nestboxes provided by the warden. All three species of woodpecker are present, as well as Nuthatch and Treecreeper. Eight species of warbler breed, while if you leave the woods close to the estuary shore and climb Foel Fawr you should encounter another range of birds, among them Tree Pipit, Whinchat, Stonechat, Wheatear and Yellowhammer. Fifty years or more ago Nightjars nested in many localities in Cardiganshire, including the dunes at Ynyslas and on Cors Fochno. A steady decline has since occured throughout Britain, the reasons for which are not clearly understood, though loss of suitable habitat will have played its part. Over recent years Ynyshir was one of the last places in Ceredigion where Nightjars were known to nest, though even here there were no more than two pairs. Now there are none.

Whinchat

Ynyshir has had its share of scarce species, a tribute to the vigilance of wardens and visitors alike. These have recently included White Pelican, Little Egret, Spoonbill, Ruddy Shelduck, Montagu's Harrier, Quail, Lesser Yellowlegs, Hoopoe, Golden Oriole, Great Grey Shrike and Lapland Bunting.

Timing

Visits to Ynyslas for seawatching should preferably be in the early morning, as soon after dawn as the light permits; for resident species choose high water, at which time birds will often be close inshore, sometimes just off the beach. The tide is also the important factor on the estuary itself, when the best watching is usually from about an hour after high water and before the tide recedes sufficiently for birds to disperse to feeding grounds at greater distances. Spring tides push birds further up the estuary, and this is when the pools, and the river at Ynyshir, attract most species. For the woodland and the hill, timing is immaterial, though an evening walk as the shadows lengthen over the distant estuary is very pleasant. You can still daydream of the Nightjars which used to nest here, even if they have been lost for our lifetime.

Access

For Borth and Ynyslas, take the B4353 where it leaves the A487 Machynlleth to Aberystwyth road at Tre'r-ddol if coming from the north, or near Bow Street if coming from the south. The south road eventually runs close behind the sea-wall at Borth, which provides a good vantage point for watching out to sea. At Ynyslas, leave the B4353 and continue straight on to the beach car park: this gives access to the dune system and the lower estuary. A permit is required to visit Cors Fochno, and this may be obtained from the Dyfed-Powys Regional Office of the NCC. Good views of the bog can, however, be obtained from the roadsides, and also from the Leri embankment where a footpath follows the west bank from the railway bridge south. Visitors for Ynyshir should turn off the A487 at SN685952, close to Furnace bridge, and follow the signs to the reception centre. The reserve is open daily from 09.00 hours with a £2.00 entrance fee in 1987: enquiries to The Warden at Cae'r Berllan, Eglwysfach, Machynlleth, SY20 8TA. There are four hides at Ynyshir: three on the estuary, at Marion Mawr, the saltings and the heronry, and one in the woodland at Penrhyn Mawr.

Calendar

Resident Little Grebe, Cormorant, Shag, Grey Heron, Shelduck, Mallard, Eider, Common Scoter, Red-breasted Merganser, Buzzard, Kestrel, Pheasant, Moorhen, Coot, Oystercatcher, Ringed Plover, Redshank, large gulls, Stock Dove, Barn and Tawny Owls, Kingfisher, woodpeckers, Skylark, Meadow Pipit, tit family but not Marsh Tit, Raven, Chaffinch, Greenfinch, Goldfinch, Linnet, Bullfinch, Yellowhammer, Reed Bunting.

December–February Red-throated Diver, Great Crested Grebe, Bewick's and Whooper Swans, Greenland White-fronted Goose, Wigeon, Teal, Tufted Duck, Goldeneye, Water Rail, Lapwing, Grey and Golden Plovers, Dunlin, Curlew, Black-tailed and Bar-tailed Godwits, Turnstone, Fieldfare, Redwing, Brambling, Siskin.

March–May Winter visitors depart, the last divers and grebes may be in summer plumage when they leave. First summer migrants arrive in late March, Sandwich Tern offshore, Wheatear on the dunes and Chiffchaff in the woods being quickly followed by Sand Martin and Swallow. Passage continues throughout period, with Whimbrel and Common Sandpiper among the waders and Turtle Dove, Swift and Spotted Flycatcher being the last migrants to appear.

June-July All residents and summer visitors present. Manx Shearwater and Gannet begin to appear offshore and wader numbers begin to increase during mid-July.

August–November Wader and tern passage well under way during August and September, summer visitors largely slip away unnoticed from the woods though a late Chiffchaff may draw attention with a few final bursts of song. Winter ducks begin to appear. Large movements of Skylarks, Meadow Pipits, thrushes and finches from mid-October, when first Greenland White-fronts appear together with occasional Hen Harrier and Merlin.

18 SOUTH CARDIGANSHIRE COAST

Habitat

The 20 miles (32 km) or so of coastline between Aberaeron and the mouth of the Teifi Estuary contain a number of sites of interest to birdwatchers. In the south, there is the narrow estuary of the Teifi and the broad bay where it crosses the bar to meet the sea. The only island in the county, Cardigan Island, stands guardian close to the northern shore, some 40 acres (16 ha) and separated by only a narrow channel from the mainland. A flock of Soay Sheep has grazed here since being introduced from Woburn in 1944, when there were few of these animals outside the ancestral home on St Kilda. The flock usually numbers about 100 and is normally easily visible from the mainland. From Cardigan Island the coast turns east and then northeast into the bay of the same name, a mixture of low cliffs, often backed by steep slopes covered with Bracken, Common Gorse and in places Heather. There are bays and coves, some hidden from view and rarely visited, others the haunt of holidaymakers. The peninsula of Ynys Lochtyn, just north of Llangranog, and the aptly named Bird Rock west of New Quay are the most interesting places on the seaward coast for birdwatchers. Resident birdwatchers are few in this part of the world, so that wherever you go, especially in the autumn and winter, you are likely to add to our knowledge. Please do not keep the information to yourself; make sure that you send it to the county bird recorder.

Species

Guillemots and Razorbills breed at a scattering of sites, mostly in small, generally inaccessible colonies, with larger ones at Bird Rock and near Lochtyn, several hundred pairs nesting at each site, though even here the best views are obtained only from a boat, with more distant ones from the land. For many years from 1962, Bird Rock was the site of the only Kittiwake colony in Cardiganshire; more recently another has been established at Lochtyn, where about 100 pairs now nest. All three species, but especially Guillemots and Razorbills, can be seen offshore throughout the year.

Cardigan Island, a reserve of the West Wales Trust for Nature Conservation, is rather disappointing for seabirds, though a small colony of Razorbills has been established since 1983. There is a mixed colony of Lesser Black-backed, Herring and Great Black-backed Gulls and a small number of Fulmars and Shags. In 1969 the WWTNC managed to eradicate Brown Rats, which had been present since a shipwreck in 1934. Burrows were excavated by a Trust working party in the late 1970s, and over subsequent years small numbers of Manx Shearwaters about to fledge were transported from Skomer. It is hoped that some will return to their adoptive island and so establish a colony. There is some cause for optimism: an egg was found in one burrow in 1984, and other burrows showed signs of use in the following summer. Sail past the west side of Cardigan Island and you will see a group of Puffins standing strangely still; a closer inspection reveals that they are plywood Puffins, first set up in 1985 in an effort to attract passing birds to land and breed. Who will be the first to report feathered Puffins from Cardigan Island? They have now been absent for 50 years.

The various bays along the coast usually have a few Red-throated Divers in winter, and Common Scoters can often be seen. The Teifi Estuary is the haunt of Shelduck, Wigeon, Teal and Mallard, together with common waders such as Oystercatcher, Ringed Plover, Dunlin, Curlew and Redshank. A shortage of observers probably means that the full potential of this site has still to be realised. At the head of the estuary above Cardigan, the expanse of Pentood Marshes provides a particularly attractive area for wintering wildfowl, while Water Rail and Reed Warbler are among the more unusual species nesting. If the planned nature reserve is established there and management work put in hand, there is no reason why the marshes should not become one of the best wildfowl sites in west Wales.

The cliff coast between Cardigan Island and New Quay supports about ten pairs of Choughs, two-thirds of the Cardiganshire population. The Lochtyn area is probably as good as anywhere else in southwest Wales to see this species, and there is often a flock of up to 25 birds present in the late summer. A Chough ringed as a nestling on Bardsey Island in 1980 was discovered here in 1982 and remained at least until late 1984, one of the longest movements recorded for this largely sedentary species.

Timing

For visits to the Teifi Estuary, watch from immediately after high water for the best results, and preferably in the early part of the day if using the Ceredigion shore, otherwise you will be looking into the sun. Waterborne activities, especially in August and early September, can cause some disturbance. Do large movements of seabirds coast offshore during the autumn? There is an urgent need for concentrated dawn watches from such places as New Quay Head.

Access

Although there are some coastal paths, Cardiganshire is not so well served in this respect as neighbouring Pembrokeshire, though access is fairly easy at key spots. A footpath leads from the western side of New Quay to Bird Rock, where the seabird colonies are visible from just north of the Coastguard Lookout, but do take great care. The Lochtyn Peninsula is easily reached by the coastal path which heads north from Llangranog, a popular holiday cove so that parking in the summer can be a problem. Despite this, you often have the headland to yourself or nearly so. Roads lead to other beaches, for example those at Cwmtudu, Penbryn, Tresaith and at Aberporth, where the sheltered bay is a good spot to look for wintering divers and grebes. Cardigan Island is easily viewed from the coastal path which starts at the Cliff Hotel at Gwbert and skirts the golf course. Roads follow both the east and the west sides of the lower Teifi Estuary, so that access and viewing is straightforward, and indeed on the east bank can be accomplished from the car itself. The former railway line running south from Cardigan Station, beside the cattle market, is the best place to observe the upper estuary and Pentood Meadows, though at the time of writing a by-pass proposal is being discussed for Cardigan which could alter one section of the low embankment.

Calendar

Resident Cormorant, Shag, Grey Heron, Mute Swan, Shelduck, Mallard, Buzzard, Kestrel, Peregrine, Oystercatcher, Herring and Great Black-backed Gulls, Feral Pigeon, Rock Pipit, Stonechat, Chough, Jackdaw, Raven.

December–February Red-throated Diver, Fulmars return to cliffs in early January, Wigeon, Teal, Goldeneye, Common Scoter, Ringed Plover, Lapwing, Dunlin, Curlew, Redshank, Black-headed and Lesser Black-backed Gulls, Kittiwakes return in February, Guillemots and Razorbills offshore throughout whole period with occasional brief visits to the cliffs.

March–May Guillemot and Razorbill commence egg-laying about the end of April. Passage migrants from late March, Wheatear and Ring Ouzel being among the first to arrive, later arrivals include Grasshopper Warbler and Whitethroat.

June–July Manx Shearwaters and Gannets frequent offshore, first terns may be seen on return passage, wader numbers increase in the estuary from late July.

August–November Fulmars leave in September, and although Kittiwakes will have left in late August some remain offshore throughout period. Red-throated Divers may arrive as early as September, though usually not until well into October. Manx Shearwater passage dies away as September proceeds. On the estuary, birds such as Wigeon, Teal, Ringed Plover, Lapwing, Dunlin, Curlew and Redshank begin to appear, while during August and September there is always a chance of passage Whimbrel. Arctic and Great Skuas may be seen offshore, also terns during August and September, when birds such as Kingfisher and Grey Wagtail move down to the coast.

19 BURRY INLET NORTH SHORE AND LOUGHOR ESTUARY

Map 19
OS Map 159

Habitat

The Burry Inlet with its vast mudflats is of international importance for winter waders and wildfowl. From Pembrey Burrows to Llanelli and thence into the Loughor narrows there are a number of excellent birdwatching spots. A journey by train, for the railway closely follows the shore, provides an excellent general impression of the low coastline, and of the estuarine expanse of up to 4 miles (6.4 km) reaching to the north shore of Gower (see also pages 88–89, Burry Inlet south shore and Whiteford Burrows). The only truly wild area of hinterland is in the extreme west beyond the Country Park, though even here large conifer plantations now almost completely shroud the dunes where Merlins once nested among the Marram Grass. Even the Country Park posed a threat at one time, when ambitious plans were proposed to take over the remaining unspoilt dunes and estuary, an idea successfully opposed both by local naturalists and by residents. Elsewhere there has been much urban development, though in many instances only the crumbling remains of factories remind us of the great industrial days; few ships now come to Llanelli, and the harbour at Burry Port is used only by pleasure craft, where both sail and steam vessels formerly loaded cargoes of coal for the factories of Britain and the rest of Europe.

Species

Merlins may have ceased to breed, but the coastal strip is still a likely place to see this bird of prey in winter. No doubt the flocks of Skylarks, Meadow Pipits and finches are an ample food source. It is well worth the birdwatcher paying some attention to these flocks, as they sometimes contain less frequent species such as Shore Lark, Water Pipit, Twite and Snow Bunting. Hen Harriers also winter on the coastlands, mostly to the west of Burry Port. Do not neglect the vicinity of the power station, for Black Redstarts occur there on both spring and autumn passages in most years.

Until recently, the only regular breeding place for Yellow Wagtails was on the levels near Machynys, the furthest west this bird extends in Wales, but alas this now seems deserted. It was here that Lesser Whitethroats first really became established as a breeding bird in Carmarthenshire, since when they have extended westwards. A species lost and a species gained, part of the intrigue and excitement of changing bird distributions. The scattered reedbeds close to the coast always contain Sedge Warbler and Reed Bunting, while Reed Warblers have nested here since the late 1960s. The first Carmarthenshire record of Cetti's Warbler was in a reedbed at the West Wales Trust for Nature Conservation reserve at Ffrwd Farm Mire, Pembrey, in 1960. It is well worth examining all the coastal reedbeds for this noisy warbler, which has been expanding its range in Britain since it first nested in southern England in 1972. A Cirl Bunting at Pembrey Harbour in 1969 was a brief reminder of a bird which once nested at a few sites in South Wales, but is now restricted in Britain to a last stronghold in Devon with a few pairs in Cornwall, Somerset and occasionally elsewhere.

59

Seaducks of a variety of species are seen, with Scaup, Eider, Goldeneye and Red-breasted Merganser being the most frequent. Red-throated Divers and Great Crested Grebes are the most regular representatives of their families to winter here, occasionally joined by rarer relatives. Difficulties of observation owing to the vastness of the area prevent a proper assessment being made of the true status of all these species. Co-ordinated counts from both shores, possibly aerial surveys, could reveal that the Burry Inlet is an even more important wintering area for wildfowl than previously realised. Among dabbling ducks the Wigeon is the most numerous, normally several thousand being present, while there may be up to 650 Pintails. Brent Geese are occasionally seen, as are White-fronted Geese, probably from the flock in the Tywi Valley.

The Burry Inlet has always been noted for its wader flocks, which in midwinter total up to 45,000 birds. The main species, accounting for almost half the number, is the Oystercatcher, many of Icelandic origin. These birds were once considered a threat to the commercially important stocks of Cockles and Mussels, and the question became rather controversial during the 1960s when, for several years, the Oystercatchers were culled, against a background of justifiable protest.

Oystercatchers

Golden Plover and Lapwing flocks are a conspicuous feature of the Burry Inlet and of the coastal fields in winter, with a small number of the latter nesting at suitable localities. Grey Plovers, which have come here from breeding grounds in the high Arctic, can generally be seen, perhaps up to 250 in the whole estuary so you will have to work hard to find them. Knots and Dunlins occur in almost equal numbers, with a combined midwinter total of about 13,000 birds. Up to 2,000 Bar-tailed Godwits have been seen on Llanelli beach — what a superb spectacle that must have presented — but such numbers are rarely repeated and most observers see much smaller flocks. The peak total for Black-tailed Godwit is usually about 250 birds, while Curlew and Redshank may reach 1,000 each.

The dedicated band of watchers on the north shore have been rewarded by the arrival of a number of scarce species in recent years. These have included Leach's Petrel, Killdeer (on the low-lying fields near Pwll), Wilson's Phalarope, Little Gull, Sabine's Gull and Black Guillemot, the last-named species a county first as recently as October 1973, when one was seen at Burry Port.

Timing

It is essential that you check your tide table. If you do not and you arrive at low tide or thereabouts, then the birds will have dispersed over a wide area of the estuary, for the tidal range is up to 26 feet (7.9 m). Watch during the hour or two after high water, or when the tide is coming in and the waders are forced off the lower sandbanks. If by any chance waders are not easily seen, do not forget to search such places as the Machynys area with its pools and reedbeds, the fields at Pwll — of Killdeer fame — and the harbour areas at Burry Port.

Access

Commencing in the west, there is a route to the shore at SS410995 from Pembrey, while a track eastwards affords viewing across the saltings towards Burry Port. Access to the north shore is by way of Pembrey Golf Course or a little further east to the old harbour. The breakwater here provides a good vantage point for viewing the creek, and some watching is possible from a car. To the east, similar opportunities exist for birdwatching from the car at the Burry Port power station, a conspicuous feature and well signed from the town. From here one can walk along the shore to overlook Cefn Padrig. Turn off the A484 at the Red Lion in Pwll (SN486007): this is the best access to the shore, and more importantly to the wet fields to the west. Llanelli beach and the North Dock area are easily reached from the town centre, while within a short distance to the south is a long section of coast at the head of the Burry Inlet which is worth giving attention to. Access is by way of Machynys (SS510982), Tir Morfa (SS533984) and Bryn Carnarfon (SS545983). The Loughor Estuary is well worth exploration, and indeed is probably missed even by local birdwatchers on occasions. Try the Ffosfach and Pencoed areas (SS563995) and further north at Llangennech (SN567009). There are plans currently afoot to construct a barrage at the mouth of the Loughor and so create a large freshwater lake; this could prove an interesting feature so far as local bird populations are concerned.

Calendar

Resident Cormorant, Grey Heron, Shelduck, Eider, large gulls though none breed (Herring Gulls formerly nested on the roof of the now demolished Royal Ordnance factory at Pembrey).

December–February Red-throated and Great Northern Divers, Great Crested Grebe, Wigeon, Teal, Pintail, Hen Harrier, Merlin, Oyster-catcher, Ringed and Golden Plovers, Lapwing, Knot, Sanderling, Dunlin, Black-tailed and Bar-tailed Godwits, Curlew, Redshank.

March–May Winter visitors depart, but always at least a few individuals of most species remain throughout the period. Spring wader passage includes Whimbrel during April and May.

June–July A chance of terns moving into the estuary late in July, wader numbers begin to increase at about the same time, Whimbrel, Spotted Redshank and Greenshank being among the first to appear, and in quiet creeks possibly Green Sandpiper.

August–November Wader passage at peak during August and September as wintering species begin to arrive, winter ducks, divers and grebes usually appear from October onwards.

20 LOWER TYWI VALLEY AND TALLEY LAKES

Habitat

The lower Tywi from Llandeilo to the tidal waters of Carmarthen some 13 miles (20.8 km) to the west meanders through a wide, flat valley. Picture the scene a thousand years ago or more: there would have been vast marshes and fens, thick carrs of Willow and Alder, and the river would have frequently flooded. What marvellous wetland birds might have thrived here? Nowadays the valley contains some of the richest grazing land in the whole of Wales, though even now in winter the floods appear. A climb to Paxton's Tower on the south side on a crisp January day will give a splendid, almost aerial view of the scene, glistening water on green farmland and a touch of snow on the distant Carmarthen Vans.

There are three main birdwatching sites in the valley. At Llandeilo, the West Wales Trust for Nature Conservation Castle Woods nature reserve occupies much of the woodland extending westwards past the summit on which the ruined Dinefwr (Dynevor) Castle stands. North lies the Deer Park, 110 acres (45 ha) of pasture woodland complete with Fallow Deer. One hopes that the National Trust, which now owns the site, will bring back the ancient white cattle of Dinefwr, which wandered here from the time the castle was in occupation and before. At the foot of the wooded escarpment is a wide expanse of water meadows and remnant oxbows cradled by a great bend of the Tywi. Some areas of open water remain throughout the summer, but these are much enlarged in winter.

Fly like the Cormorants which regularly pass up and down the valley, 4 miles (6.4 km) downstream to where remnants of another castle stand on the great mound of Dryslwyn. Again there are water meadows and floodpools. Another 6 miles (9.6 km) brings you to the hamlet of Abergwilli, close by Carmarthen. We are told that on the night of Llanybyther Fair, 17 July 1802, in the episcopate of Bishop Murray, there was a great flood which caused the Tywi to switch its course to run at the foot of the southern slope, leaving in its turbulent wake a superb oxbow lake, the best example of its kind in South Wales and now known as the Bishop's Pond. The pond is a reserve of the WWTNC, part held under lease from a private owner and the rest under lease from the Dyfed County Council. In summer, the water levels drop and the surface is carpeted with Yellow Water-lilies, while the margins are fringed with Reed Sweet-grass, in Wales largely confined to the Tywi Valley and the coastal flats bordering the Bristol Channel.

Tallychau — 'the head of the lakes' — or Talley takes its name from its situation close by the two lakes which drain northwards to the Afon Cothi, a tributary of the Tywi. In the solitude, the great Rhys ap Gruffwd, Prince of Deheubarth, founded a house of the White Cannons in the late twelfth century, the only one in the whole of Wales. Now all that remains is part of the tower and the remnants of some outer walls. A short distance away is the shore of the upper lake, which together with its neighbour extends for some 44 acres (18 ha), one of the most important open freshwater sites in this part of Wales. The lakes are owned by the Royal Society for the Protection of Birds, but are managed by the WWTNC.

Species

It is wildfowl and waders that are the main attraction in the Tywi Valley, though the number of species remaining to breed is small. By late July, Mallard numbers begin to increase on the oxbows below Dinefwr as moulting birds take up temporary residence on these secluded waters, where up to 500 may be recorded well into the autumn. Passage waders are not infrequent, usually Green Sandpiper with occasional Dunlin, Whimbrel and Greenshank. Common Sandpipers breed on shingle banks along the river. Little Ringed Plovers have been seen in recent summers at one site in the valley, evidence of this bird's continued expansion in range as a breeding species in Britain; there seems no reason why it should not become firmly established on some of our larger rivers where suitable open shingle banks and ridges have been formed. Mallards breed, and there are usually several pairs of Mute Swans in the valley. A quite remarkable colonisation of the Tywi by Goosanders has taken place since breeding was first suspected in 1979; several pairs now nest between Llandeilo and Carmarthen, and birds are to be seen throughout the year, though the males disappear for several months from May onwards.

Although diving ducks occur in good numbers at Dinefwr, and to some extent at Dryslwyn, the best place to see them is at Talley. Pochard and Tufted Duck are the most frequent and both have bred here, and other visitors include Scaup, Goldeneye, Smew and Goosander. Both Great Crested and Little Grebes breed, while the Red-necked Grebe seen in October 1966 was the first recorded in Carmarthenshire. Strange as it may seem, there is no record of Mute Swans at Talley, perhaps an indication of how poorly covered even notable, but remote, sites such as this are in a thinly populated part of the county. Bewick's and Whooper Swans have occasionally been seen, probably wanderers from the small flocks that winter along the Tywi Valley. In the early 1970s, up to 2,500 White-fronted Geese wintered in the meadows about Dryslwyn. This was one of three main wintering grounds in Britain for the Siberian race of this goose. Numbers have subsequently dropped, though the reason is not clear, and have recently not exceeded 400. Wandering individuals or small parties of several other species are regularly seen, including Bean, Greylag and Barnacle Geese, and in March 1971 a Lesser White-fronted Goose, the first and so far only record for Wales. Another rare visitor was a Ring-necked Duck at Dryslwyn in late December 1981 and near Dinefwr the following month.

Castle Woods are one of the most striking woods in southwest Wales, despite the decimation of their Wych Elms by Dutch Elm disease. Whatever the season, the woods always seem alive with birds. All three species of woodpecker are present, the Lesser Spotted Woodpecker being noteworthy, with no fewer than five pairs in 1984. The ringing calls of the Nuthatch are a characteristic sound of the woods, while the shy Treecreeper is also a numerous resident. Among the summer visitors, the Redstart and Pied Flycatcher are two that most birdwatchers hope to see; with care, few need be disappointed. Birds of prey include Sparrowhawk, Buzzard and Tawny Owl, while Kestrels used to nest in the castle keep before the necessary work of renovation was commenced by Cadw. From vantage points in the woods it is usually

Lesser Spotted Woodpecker

possible to see Grey Herons feeding along the riverbank or around the oxbows; the largest colony in the county is at Alltygaer, Dryslwyn, and usually contains up to 55 pairs.

Timing

When visiting Castle Woods, especially if it is in spring or early summer, try to make the early morning: you will then find bird song at its peak, and the scent of Bluebells in the dew will be something else to remember the visit by. The timing of visits to Dryslwyn and the Bishop's Pond are not critical so far as the wildfowl are concerned.

Access

Castle Woods A system of footpaths leads from Penlan Park, the town park of Llandeilo, through South Lodge Woods, past Llandyfeisant Church visitor centre, and so to the main Castle Woods. The reserve is open at all times, and from late March to September a warden is present, living in a snug hut close to the church. There are regular guided walks on certain dates throughout the summer, and enquiries concerning these should be made at the Llandeilo Tourist Centre or Llandyfeisant Church.

Dryslwyn The water meadows are best viewed from several points on the B4300, a quiet enough road for such activities. Excellent general views can be obtained of the whole area from Dryslwyn Castle, to which there is unrestricted access. If you are lucky, the White-fronted Geese may well fly past at eye level as you sit on this lofty perch.

Bishop's Pond Not easily viewed other than from the bridge which crosses at one point, and which is reached from the A40 at SN445210. There is no general access along the banks of the pond.

Talley Lakes No access to the lakeshore, but the B4302 does overlook the lakes at one point. Better still, follow the unclassified road which runs above the western shore, from where there are several viewing places, especially over the upper pool.

Calendar

Resident Cormorant, Grey Heron, Mallard, Goosander, Sparrowhawk, Buzzard, Coot, Tawny Owl, Lesser Spotted Woodpecker, all common woodland species, Raven.

December–February Little Grebe, Bewick's and Whooper Swans, White-fronted Goose, Wigeon, Teal, Shoveler, Pochard, Tufted Duck, Goldeneye, Peregrine, Snipe, Lapwing, Golden Plover, Curlew.

March–May Great Crested Grebe, Little Ringed Plover, Common Sandpiper, Sand Martin and all other summer migrants, Spotted Flycatcher and Swift being among the last to arrive.

June–July All breeding species present, first passage waders, usually Green Sandpiper begin to appear, Mallard numbers begin to increase.

August–November Summer visitors depart usually by early September, winter wildfowl start arriving, with large numbers of Lapwings and Golden Plovers and smaller numbers of Curlews by end of period. Winter thrushes move into the valley during early November, White-fronted Geese by the end of the month.

Habitat

It is just over 2 miles (3.2 km) from Tywyn Point to Ginst Point. To the
north and east of this line are the estuaries of the Taf, tidal for 6 miles
(9.6 km) to St Clears; the Tywi, tidal for 10 miles (16 km) to Carmarthen;
and the Gwendraeth, a mere 3 miles (4.8 km) to Cydweli (Kidwelly).
Here at this ancient town, Roger, Bishop of Salisbury and a minister for
Henry I, built his castle in 1115. All three estuaries encompass
thousands of acres of sand and mudbank, exposed at low tide so that
the sea seems to disappear beyond the horizon. This was a hazardous
spot to navigate in the days of coastal trading, as the numerous wrecks,
some still visible, on Cefn Sidan Sands bear witness. One of these is the
remains of the 834-ton iron barque *Craigwhinnie,* bound from Calcutta
to Hull and stranded in December 1899, fortunately without loss of life.
A vain effort was made to refloat her, even to the extent of jettisoning her
cargo of linseed, which washed ashore on the nearby beaches and
provided a welcome food supply for thousands of geese, ducks and
finches.

A range of estuarine habitats occurs. There are flats dominated by
Cord-grass, while there can be few finer open sandy beaches than those
which run west from Ginst Point or southeast from Tywyn Point. There
are deep narrow creeks on the south side of the Gwendraeth, rocky
shores at Salmon Point Scar, and scrub-crowned cliffs at Wharley Point,
junction of the Taf and Tywi. There is an impressive plant list from these
coastal lands, which includes the Welsh Gentian in a few dune slacks
where once the Fen Orchid, a nationally rare species, was recorded.
Does it still survive to the east of the estuaries?

Species

Cormorants frequent the shallow waters, which undoubtedly provide a
rich feeding area for the birds, many coming from the colony on St
Margaret's Island 15 miles (24 km) to the west. At times the resting birds
congregate in large flocks on the cliffs on the east side of the Taf or on
favoured sandbanks, no fewer than 285 having been seen off Tywyn
Point on one occasion. Grey Herons are equally frequent, and a colony
was discovered in the cliffside scrub at Craig Ddu in 1945; numbers
reached a peak of 34 pairs in 1953 and currently there are about 20 pairs
present. There is another, smaller, colony close to the Tywi about 4
miles (6.4 km) downstream from Carmarthen. All the divers and grebes
have been recorded in or close to the estuaries, and one can be fairly
certain that the shallow waters of Carmarthen Bay support good
numbers throughout the winter months, though systematic observations
are difficult owing to the area and distances involved.

Common Scoters are present in Carmarthen Bay, in a broad arc from
Saundersfoot to Gower, throughout the year. Maximum numbers are
reached in late winter, when up to 25,000 birds may be present, the
shallow waters and rich shellfish beds being the attraction for this
handsome duck. At times the flocks move close inshore, but the large
area and difficulties of observation at sea make proper assessment hard

to come by. One of the challenges for local birdwatchers must be further and more detailed studies of the seaducks of Carmarthen Bay. There will be rewards for the dedicated observer, mention having already been made of the divers and grebes. Velvet Scoters have occasionally been recorded, but systematic observation will surely reveal this species as a regular visitor in small numbers. A male Surf Scoter was found dead at Ginst Point in January 1971; it seems strange that this was the first Welsh record of an American duck previously recorded in a number of counties from Orkney to the Isle of Wight. Other diving ducks seen offshore, or just inside the estuaries, include Eider, Long-tailed Duck, Goldeneye and Red-breasted Merganser. In winter the upper reaches of the estuaries support modest numbers of Wigeons, up to 700 in the Taf, and smaller numbers of Teals and Mallards. A few Pintails are seen each winter, while Shelducks breed. It is a pity that the pioneer venture of creating a wildfowl habitat at Coed, on the upper reaches of the Tywi Estuary, has not been continued. The range of common species, and the occasional rarity seen there, serve only to underline what may be achieved with foresight and imagination.

Ringed Plovers breed at a number of isolated spots around the three estuaries and westwards within the Pendine Range, these being their only breeding sites remaining in southwest Wales. A wide variety of waders has been recorded in all three estuaries. One of the highlights must be the midwinter gathering of Sanderlings on Cefn Sidan, where up to 1,600 have been seen on a single count. Golden Plovers are plentiful, flocks of up to 400 being present on the Gwendraeth and Taf where, mingling with Lapwings, they resort to the low-lying grasslands and flight out to the estuaries. Small numbers of Grey Plovers are seen throughout the winter; they reach a maximum of about 30 during the early autumn, with Tywyn and Ginst Points being the places to search. Single Ruffs and occasionally small groups are seen on the Gwendraeth Estuary each autumn, so three on Cefn Sidan in December 1985 was an unusual record. As Black-tailed Godwits usually number fewer than 100 birds, the 400 at Cydweli Quay in December 1972 was exceptional. Bar-tailed Godwits are normally more numerous and flocks of several hundred can be located in midwinter. Greenshanks regularly overwinter, as probably does the occasional Spotted Redshank, while if you are looking for Turnstones then Salmon Point Scar is the most likely spot in the whole estuary complex to see this well-camouflaged wader.

The many rare visitors of recent years have included Little Egret, Spoonbill, Avocet, Cream-coloured Courser, Little Ringed Plover, Long-billed Dowitcher, Baird's, Buff-breasted and White-rumped Sandpipers, Grey Phalarope, Sabine's Gull, White-winged Black and Gull-billed Terns and Little Auk. An adult and an immature Crane in early 1984, the first to be recorded in Carmarthenshire, were a superb highlight; alas, Welsh hospitality was lacking — the adult was shot and now resides in the Carmarthen Museum.

Do not neglect the hinterland of the estuaries. Black Redstarts are sometimes observed about the castles at Laugharne and Llanstephan. Peregrines and Buzzards are the most regular predators, while both Hen and Montagu's Harriers hunt over the land to the south of the Gwendraeth; indeed, the latter may well have nested there in the early 1960s. Great Grey Shrike, Twite and Snow Bunting should also be looked for.

Timing

For estuary-watchers, a tide table is an essential part of one's equipment. A visit can then be planned which ensures that the birds are close inshore as the tide rises, or as the first mudbanks are exposed after high water.

Access

Taf Estuary Ginst Point is reached on foot from Laugharne by way of a path which skirts the estuary side of Sir John's Hill, and then south along the sea-wall or, better still, below it so as not to disturb birds in the fields or on the estuary itself. An alternative route is by car, leaving the A4066 Laugharne to Pendine road at SN287097. This drops quickly to the coastal flat fields of Laugharne township, excellent for Lapwing and Golden Plover and for winter thrushes and finches. Follow the MOD boundary fence eastwards for nearly 2 miles (3.2 km) until the road reaches Ginst Point, though this last section may be closed on weekdays when the Proof and Experimental Station is testing weapons.

Tywi Estuary Good general views may be obtained from Llanstephan, and also from Ferryside from where an unclassified road runs south through St Ishmael's to the rocky shore of Salmon Point Scar. Access to the upper reaches of the estuary is not so easy, though it is possible to walk a little way north along the shore from Ferryside.

Gwendraeth Estuary One can walk eastwards from Salmon Point Scar into the Gwendraeth Estuary. Alternatively, you can go by car through Cydweli to Cydweli Quay; you do not have to move far from the car, if at all, to obtain good views of the head of the estuary from here. By contrast, the south shore is much more difficult of access, something accentuated by the presence of a RAF bombing range towards Tywyn Point. Access to the point itself is by way of the disused Pembrey Airfield and then through Pembrey Forest to Cefn Sidan Sands.

Calendar

Resident Cormorant, Grey Heron, Shelduck, Mallard, Eider, Common Scoter, Buzzard, Oystercatcher, Ringed Plover.

December–February Divers, grebes, Wigeon, Teal, Pintail, Goldeneye, Red-breasted Merganser, Knot, Sanderling, Dunlin, Black-tailed and Bar-tailed Godwits, Curlew, Redshank, Greenshank, Snow Bunting.

March–May Main departure of wildfowl and waders during first part of period, but some passage until May, when summer visitors such as Whimbrel and Common Sandpiper can be expected, the latter usually on the upper reaches of the estuaries rather than on the open flats. Occasional parties of terns seen.

June-July Ringed Plover broods fledging, Shelduck broods in evidence on the estuaries, start of return wader passage, Common Scoter numbers build up offshore.

August–November Peak wader passage, with greatest variety of species during first part of period. During October numbers of ducks increase both in the estuaries and offshore, divers and grebes may be seen, especially from November onwards.

Habitat

In 1967, the Royal Society for the Protection of Birds acquired some land above the Gwenffrwd, a tributary of the Tywi, and a little further east at the Dinas where the Doethie, emerging from its gorge, joins the Tywi at Junction Pool. This is the site of Twm Shon Catti's cave, Twm being a somewhat legendary Robin-Hood-type figure based largely on the early exploits in the life of Thomas Jones (1530–1609) of Tregaron, pardoned by Elizabeth in the first year of her reign for unknown offences. Over the years since 1967 the reserve has steadily been added to, so that the RSPB now manages some 6,828 acres (2,763 ha), a key holding containing a mosaic of mid-Wales habitats. Elsewhere in the valley, the Nature Conservancy Council and the West Wales Trust for Nature Conservation own small areas of woodland.

Both the Tywi and its tributaries vary considerably within quite short distances. There are torrents cascading over boulders from pool to pool, then tranquil slower-moving waters, the summer haunt of that most jewel-like of damselflies, the aptly named Beautiful Demoiselle. Small fields and patches of woodland line the riverbank, hemmed in by ground which rises steeply, broken in places by rock outcrops, even small cliffs. There are extensive areas of hanging oakwoods, above which lie vast tracts of heavily grazed uplands where, in the wet hollows, the botanist can find Round-leaved Sundew and Common Butterwort. For those prepared to search, there are other gems such as the Alpine, Fir and Stag's-horn Clubmosses to be discovered on these at times bleak moors.

Much of the woodland has remained unmanaged for the past century; sheep have grazed unchecked, so that the ground flora is impoverished and regeneration of the Oak almost unknown. In the nature reserves, fences have been erected to exclude or control sheep grazing and some tree-planting has been carried out. Certain birds, however, most notably the Wood Warbler, prefer the open woodland floor, so that a careful balance of management has to be maintained. High above the Gwenffrwd the RSPB has established a new woodland, Coed Vaughan, a fitting memorial to Captain H. R. H. Vaughan, who lived for many years just down the valley and did so much to ensure that the Red Kite received protection.

Species

Most birdwatchers come to the Upper Tywi Valley in the hope of seeing Red Kites, for this part of Wales and over the high hills and sheepwalks into Ceredigion has long been their last remaining stronghold in Britain. Towards the end of the nineteenth century, the British population had been so reduced by nest-robbing and the killing of adults that only a handful of birds remained, all in this part of Wales. The first Kite Protection Committee was formed in 1903, and as a result it was just possible to ensure the birds' continued survival, though for many years there were no more than ten pairs and at times only half that number, so close to extinction had the kite become. Recently, the population has increased and now numbers about 48 pairs, which in 1986 reared a record total of 29 young. The pressures remain, however: habitat loss as open hill land is taken up by forestry plantations; hard winters; and above all the continuing unscrupulous activities of egg-collectors, pariahs among naturalists, who secretly but skilfully pursue their self-interests with 'a ruthlessness more characteristic of the worst excesses of the Victorian era'. Birdwatchers also beware — Red Kites in the breeding season are extremely susceptible to disturbance, so please do your watching from public roads and footpaths; some lucky visitors to the Gwenffrwd in August 1985 saw five Red Kites circling over the car park, while kites are often seen over the outskirts of towns such as Lampeter and Tregaron.

On the high ground there is a remnant population of Red Grouse, though you will have to search hard for these. Ravens are much more obvious; their 'kronking' calls on days in May as a family party flies along the escarpment provide one of the joys of the early summer in these hills. A few pairs of Wheatears can be found on the high ground, and as you begin to descend from the open moorland to where scattered bushes and small trees have become established you should find two other summer visitors, the Whinchat and Tree Pipit, the latter extending into the open woodlands. Merlins are occasional on the high ground, Sparrowhawks, Buzzards and Kestrels are more frequently seen, and with any luck a Peregrine may speed across the valley.

The woodlands of the upper Tywi in spring and early summer are alive with birds. Nestboxes in all the nature reserves attract large numbers of Pied Flycatchers: in the Dinas alone, some two-thirds of the 215 nestboxes are usually occupied by this species. This boost for the population, which ensures one of the highest densities of Pied Flycatchers in Britain, may well be the reason for the species' westward extension down the valley in recent years and its colonisation of woodlands in southeast Carmarthenshire and Pembrokeshire. Redstarts and Wood Warblers are common, and there is a whole range of woodland species including Mistle Thrush, Garden Warbler, Blackcap, Marsh and Willow Tits, Nuthatch and Redpoll. Siskins are recent colonists of the conifers. Lesser Spotted Woodpeckers can sometimes be located, while there was an exceptional sighting of two Hawfinches at the Gwenffrwd reserve in May 1985. This shy finch, one of the most elusive of our breeding birds, can often be located only by those familiar with its characteristic 'tick' call note. A few pairs of Woodcock nest in the damp woodlands of the Upper Tywi Valley, and visitors at dawn or dusk may well be fortunate enough to observe the roding display flight of a bird otherwise rarely seen.

The rivers have Grey Wagtails, Dippers, and in late summer occasionally Kingfishers as they disperse from breeding sites further down the valley. There are several colonies of Sand Martins in the riverbanks and Common Sandpipers also nest here, their cheery song quickly drawing the observer's attention. Goosanders are a highlight on the rivers; they first nested here in 1980 and now there is a scattering of pairs.

Timing

Early morning is best, though for late risers there can be few more pleasant ways to spend a summer evening than by a visit to the Dinas, followed by a pint at the Towy Bridge Inn as you look for river birds.

Access

Leave Llandovery on the unclassified road for Rhandirmwyn, beyond which you have a choice. Bear right up the valley to the Dinas reserve, which is open all the year and has an excellent woodland walk; there is a car park and information centre at SN788472. Beyond here the road continues to the massive Llyn Brianne dam and reservoir, spectacular but ornithologically not very interesting. Alternatively you can cross Rhandirmwyn bridge and turn right for Cwrt-a-Cadno, this taking you past the Gwenffrwd reserve and the warden's house at SN749460; the reserve is open from Easter to August on all days except Fridays, and intending visitors should report to the Dinas information centre between 10.00 and 17.00 hours. Further up the same road is the Nant Melin reserve of the WWTNC; a footpath leads up through the woods from the bridge at SN730465 to the reserve itself. For those unable to leave the car, the roads do provide excellent vantage points for viewing large parts of this scenic area.

Calendar

Resident Goosander, Red Kite, Sparrowhawk, Buzzard, Kestrel, Peregrine, Grey Wagtail, Dipper, Dunnock, Robin, Blackbird, Song and Mistle Thrushes, Goldcrest, tit family, Nuthatch, Treecreeper, Jay, Raven, Chaffinch, Greenfinch, Siskin, Linnet, Redpoll.

December–February Winter thrushes and finches unless weather is hard, in which case the valley at times seems almost birdless.

March–May Woodcock. Summer visitors from about the beginning of April include Cuckoo, Sand Martin, Tree Pipit, Redstart, Whinchat, Wheatear, Ring Ouzel, Garden Warbler, Blackcap, Wood Warbler, Chiffchaff, Willow Warbler, Pied Flycatcher.

June–July Breeding season in full swing, but by end of period most woodland species have finished, and virtual cessation of song means that location of remaining birds is difficult. River birds such as Goosander, Common Sandpiper, Sand Martin, Grey Wagtail and Dipper still obvious.

August–November Kingfisher likely on rivers. Summer visitors largely make an early departure, while from mid-October onwards winter thrushes and finches arrive. Resident species such as Goldcrest, tits, Treecreeper and Nuthatch form wandering bands which often leave woods and work along hedgerows.

23 BERWYN RANGE

Map 23
OS Map 125

Habitat

The Berwyn Range in the south of the county runs southwest as a more or less rectangular block of high ground, bounded to the north and west by the valleys of the Afon Dyfrdwy, which includes Llyn Tegid (Bala Lake), to the south by Lake Vyrnwy, while to the east the ground falls more gently away, intersected by river valleys such as those of the Ceiriog and Tanat. Nearly half of the range is in Montgomeryshire. Forestry in the Denbighshire section has fortunately taken over only comparatively small areas, and save for a few oases of conifers the centre remains largely untouched. The ground is higher than at Mynydd Hiraethog to the north, on the summit ridge reaching peaks of 2,590 feet (798 m) at Cadair Bronwen and 2,730 feet (832 m) at Moel Sych, where there is a line of west-facing cliffs. It is on these summits, and nowhere else in Wales, that the Cloudberry is located; this is its most southerly outpost in Britain, its nearest site being in the Pennines. Other upland plants include the graceful white-plumed, wind-blown Cottongrass, Bog Asphodel, Marsh St John's-wort, Round-leaved Sundew and, if you are prepared to search, the Marsh Clubmoss. With luck you may also discover the tiny Bog Orchid, though it will be purely by chance, for this orchid rarely exceeds 2 inches (5 cm) in height and has rather insignificant yellow-green flowers to suit its retiring nature.

Golden Plover

Species

The birds found on the uplands here are largely the same as those on Mynydd Hiraethog (see pages 76–78). Red Grouse are still found where the heather moorland remains intact, for without *Calluna* heather, their chief food source, Red Grouse quickly move on. Undoubtedly, the reduction in heather moorland throughout much of central Wales has reduced the grouse population. Other scarce breeding birds of the uplands include Hen Harrier, Merlin, Peregrine, Golden Plover, Dunlin and the occasional pair of Short-eared Owls, while Dotterel and Whimbrel may occur on spring passage.

Timing

Early morning or late evening is by far the best time.

Access

Not easy, and for the most part definitely an area only for those able and well prepared for much walking. Just a single track crosses the range, from Pentre at SJ136348 in the east to SJ052404 on the B4401 just south of Cynwyd. Two unclassified roads run towards Moel Sych from the village of Llanrhaeadr-yn Mochnant; the southern one offers the best opportunity even for those who do not wish to leave the car, for there is a car park and public toilets at Pistyll Rhaeadr (SJ074295).

Calendar

Resident Hen Harrier, Buzzard, Kestrel, Merlin, Peregrine, Red and Black Grouse, Black-headed Gull, Short-eared Owl, Skylark, Meadow Pipit, Grey and Pied Wagtails, Dipper, Ring Ouzel, Mistle Thrush, Carrion Crow, Raven, Linnet.

December–February Jack Snipe, Fieldfare, Redwing, Brambling in the valleys, chance of Snow Bunting on the tops, though probably few birdwatchers go to look.

March–May Lapwing, Golden Plover, Dunlin, Snipe, Common Sandpiper, Curlew, Cuckoo, Tree Pipit, Wheatear, Redstart, Whinchat, Ring Ouzel all arrive to breed, Dotterel and Whimbrel occasionally on passage.

June–July All breeding species present.

August–November Summer visitors depart, the uplands seem rapidly to become deserted; even the resident birds are hard to find, especially at the onset of colder weather.

Habitat

Travel southwest from the town of Denbigh by way of the A543 and after about 5 miles (8 km) the road climbs on to Mynydd Hiraethog, a large moorland area with several pools — Llyn Aled, Llyn Alwen and Llyn Bran — and numerous boggy areas and *Sphagnum* moss flushes. Much of the land is a rolling upland of about 1,400 feet (427 m) altitude, with the highest point south of the road where Mwdwl-eithin ridge rises from 1,570 (479 m) to 1,760 feet (536 m). To the southeast, in the headwaters of the Afon Alwen, a tributary of the Dee, are the massive Alwen and Llyn Brenig Reservoirs. Both are largely surrounded by coniferous plantations, the western extremity of the Clocaenog Forest, one of the largest areas of coniferous woodland in Wales.

Species

The moorland pools and reservoirs attract small numbers of wildfowl. Great Crested Grebes remained a scarce breeder until the early 1970s, when up to five pairs nested in the county, Llyn Brenig being one of their regular sites. The Grey Heron population in Denbighshire is small, probably fewer than 30 pairs, but some come regularly to the reservoirs, and to the hilltop bogs during the summer months. There are usually several colonies of Black-headed Gulls on the moors, with numbers fluctuating from year to year. Teals have nested in the past, but this is a notoriously difficult species to prove breeding and without a doubt some are overlooked; the broods hide away rather than coming to open water, so that injury-feigning and distraction displays by the adults are usually the first and only sign that Teals have nested. Mallards breed widely, and both this and the previous species, together with Wigeon, Pochard, Tufted Duck, Goldeneye and Goosander, frequent Llyn Brenig during the winter. Small numbers of Whooper Swans also come here and to some of the larger upland pools, but Bewick's Swans are rare, most remaining on valley waters in the east of the county.

The moorlands have their other residents, and in 1981 up to 35 pairs of Golden Plovers may have nested. Dunlins are much less frequent; probably fewer than ten pairs breed in the whole of the county. A few pairs of Lapwings, Snipe and Curlews breed. There is the occasional pair of Short-eared Owls, while other raptors to look for are the Hen Harrier, Merlin and in winter the Peregrine. Meadow Pipits are plentiful, and where there is upland grassland Skylarks and Wheatears put in an appearance. A few pairs of Ring Ouzels are usually present, while other species of the moorland edge include Tree Pipit, Whinchat, Mistle Thrush and Reed Bunting.

There are Red Grouse in the heather. Black Grouse, however, seem to prefer areas where conifers front on to the moorland, the population on Mynydd Hiraethog being small. Their communal displays known as 'leks' take place largely in the early morning in spring, and again in October, when generally only males are present. The males joust with much calling, the loud 'to wha' notes carrying considerable distances on quiet days; females gather nearby, and mate with the more successful males. Sometimes, when the Black Grouse population is small and widely scattered, single males call and display far from the communal grounds.

The developing plantations support a changing bird population. When the trees are small, look for Short-eared Owl, Whinchat and Grasshopper Warbler. Later, the main species in the mature plantations will be Woodpigeon, Goldcrest, Coal Tit and Chaffinch, with the occasional Buzzard and Tawny Owl, even possibly Long-eared Owls though these will take much searching for. Look out also for Siskins and Common Crossbills; the former now nests in the forest, and the latter may well do so from time to time, though their presence in high summer may not necessarily mean that breeding has taken place.

Common Crossbills

Timing
Visit in early morning, indeed dawn if you wish to watch and listen to Golden Plover and Dunlin on the hill. The time of one's visit is otherwise not critical.

Access
The A453 traverses the area, with an unclassified road going north from this at SH929567 near Pont y Clogwyn to the high point of Foel Lwyd, passing as it does so Llyn Aled and the Aled Isaf Reservoir, from which the Afon Aled flows north eventually to reach the sea at Rhyl.

For the forests, the Alwen Reservoir and Llyn Brenig, turn south at SH959593 on the B4501 for Cerrigydrudion. You are immediately in the forest, and there are numerous picnic sites and parking places. There is a nature trail at SH962572, a visitor centre at SH967547 on the shore of Llyn Brenig, and another at SH952537 on the shore of the Alwen Reservoir. Do not neglect to visit the Archaeological Trail at SH984573.

Calendar

Resident Great Crested Grebe, Cormorant a regular visitor to the larger waters even in winter, Mute Swan, Teal, Mallard, Hen Harrier,

Sparrowhawk, Buzzard, Kestrel, Merlin, Red and Black Grouse, Pheasant, Moorhen, Coot, Black-headed Gull, Woodpigeon, Tawny and Short-eared Owls, Great Spotted Woodpecker, Skylark, Meadow Pipit, Grey and Pied Wagtails, Dipper, Dunnock, Robin, Blackbird, Song and Mistle Thrushes, Goldcrest, Coal Tit, Carrion Crow, Raven, Chaffinch, Goldfinch, Siskin, Linnet, Redpoll, Reed Bunting.

December–February Whooper Swan, Wigeon, Pochard, Tufted Duck, Goldeneye, Peregrine, Jack Snipe, Woodcock, Common Gull, Fieldfare, Redwing, Snow Bunting.

March–May Winter visitors depart, Golden Plover, Lapwing, Dunlin, Snipe and Curlew return to the moorland, soon followed by Wheatear and Ring Ouzel, while on the lower ground Cuckoo, Tree Pipit, Whinchat and Redstart take up their territories.

June–July All breeding species present, sometimes large feeding movements of Swifts over the hills in hot weather. Raven and Mistle Thrush, having completed breeding, in family parties or even small flocks.

August–November Summer visitors largely slip away unnoticed, occasional passage waders such as Green and Common Sandpipers. Winter visitors from early October, though by then the hills seem almost deserted by birds.

25 RHOS-ON-SEA

Map 25
OS Map 116

Habitat

Virtually the whole 11-mile (17.6-km) coastline of Denbighshire is one long sandy shore backed by holiday resorts, as at Kimnel Bay, Towyn, Abergele and Colwyn Bay. Coastal birds such as Oystercatcher and Little Tern have long ceased to breed, and only a couple of pairs of Ringed Plovers miraculously hold on. The only cliff-nesting seabirds have colonised the limestone quarries nearly ½ mile (0.8 km) inland at Llanddulas, where Fulmars and Herring Gulls nest. Herring Gulls, incidentally, nest on rooftops at a number of localities along the coast. In the extreme west, the shore at Rhos-on-Sea provides the first sheltered area from west and southwest winds after the Dee Estuary 20 miles (32 km) eastwards. The shore habitat here is hotels and houses, so quickly turn your back on these and search out to sea or along the rocky beaches of Penrhyn Bay.

Species

There are few birds in summer, but from early August through to March it is well worth spending time at Rhos-on-Sea. All the divers have been seen, though only the Red-throated Diver is so regular that you can be sure of seeing one. Great Crested Grebes winter offshore in small numbers, while there are occasional records of Red-necked, Slavonian and Black-necked Grebes. Manx Shearwaters and Gannets appear in late summer, and Fulmars are seen almost throughout the year. Common Scoters are resident offshore here, where even in June the flock may total several hundred, or to the west at Pensarn. Their numbers rise in winter to as high as 10,000, and they are occasionally joined by Velvet Scoter and other winter visitors, including Scaup, Eider, Long-tailed Duck and up to 100 Red-breasted Mergansers. Both Arctic and Great Skuas pass in small numbers. There have been several records of Black Guillemots, and occasionally Little Auks have been found dead on the beach.

Despite the limited shoreline and feeding areas, a range of waders can usually be seen at Rhos-on-Sea. Up to 1,000 Oystercatchers winter here, together with about 500 Knots, 500 Curlews, and — most dramatic of all in terms of numbers — over 700 Turnstones, which find the rocky shores to the west of Rhos-on-Sea much to their liking. Search in the same area for Purple Sandpipers, the numbers of which can rise to about 100 in midwinter. Other waders occurring in smaller numbers include Grey Plover, Bar-tailed Godwit, Redshank and Greenshank. A few Sanderlings pass, and Spotted Redshanks have been recorded. Very surprising is the absence so far of Curlew Sandpiper, the only county record being of a bird shot inland in 1931. None of the scarcer species has yet been recorded; surely it is only a matter of time and careful observation before this is rectified.

Timing

Early morning is best, whatever the state of the tide, in order to ensure the least disturbance from other beach-users.

Access

A road follows the whole of the seafront, and during the winter months observations from this using the car are usually possible.

Calendar

Resident Cormorant, Shelduck, Common Scoter, Oystercatcher, Ringed Plover, Redshank, Turnstone, Black-headed, Lesser Black-backed, Herring and Great Black-backed Gulls, Rock Pipit.

December–February Red-throated Diver, Great Crested Grebe, Fulmar, Wigeon, Scaup, Eider, Long-tailed Duck, Velvet Scoter, Red-breasted Merganser, Grey Plover, Knot, Purple Sandpiper, Dunlin, Bar-tailed Godwit, Common Gull, Guillemot, Razorbill.

March–May Winter visitors depart, spring passage brings new arrivals including Sanderling, Whimbrel, Common Sandpiper, Kittiwake, Sandwich and Common Terns.

June–July Manx Shearwater, Gannet and Shag appear offshore, while terns become more evident late in period.

August–November Seabird passage, with last terns usually in late September, when winter visitors such as divers, grebes and seaducks reappear.

Habitat

In the Middle Ages the Dee was navigable right up to Chester, 22 miles (35.2 km) from the open sea, a major port until at least the fourteenth century. The good citizens of the city were, however, fighting a losing battle: vast quantities of silt were accumulating in the estuary, making the journey hazardous and eventually impossible. A new harbour was then built at Parkgate, but even here the tides held sway, continuing to deposit silt, and by the middle of the eighteenth century this could not be used. Now Parkgate is fronted by nearly 1 mile (1.6 km) of saltmarsh and a further 2 miles (3.2 km) of mudbanks. Most of the saltmarshes on the Dee are situated on the Cheshire bank, but there are fragments on the Flintshire shore. Everywhere there is Common Cord-grass, first introduced in 1928 and now covering vast areas, colonising the open flats in a thick sward, reducing feeding areas, and excluding some of the less vigorous estuarine plants such as Glasswort, Sea Meadow-grass, Sea Aster, Scurvygrass and Sea-purslane. Move to the upper marshes about high-water mark and Sea-milkwort, Sea Arrowgrass and Common Reed will be encountered. Although some 150 miles (240 km) from their nearest large breeding colonies on the coast of Pembrokeshire, the almost unique haul-out of Grey Seals on the West Hoyle Bank at the mouth of the Dee can rise to as high as 200 animals in summer.

Species

The attention of many birdwatchers was first drawn to the Dee, and to its immense wader flocks, by the superb photographs of densely packed Oystercatchers, Knots, Dunlins, Curlews, Redshanks and others, taken by Eric Hosking on the Hilbre Islands — Hilbre, Little Hilbre and Hilbre Eye off West Kirby on the northwest corner of the Wirral. The rocky islands, in total 15 acres (6 ha) in extent and now a nature reserve, are approached on foot at low tide by the watchers who wish to see the

Dunlins

wader flocks as the tide rises or to wait for migrating landbirds. We digress, however, for this is not Wales but England — though the birds do not observe Man's boundaries; suffice to say they roam at will across the sands of the Dee.

Since the 1960s, detailed counts have been made of waders on estuaries throughout Britain as part of the Birds of Estuaries Enquiry organised by the British Trust for Ornithology. It is now possible to assess the importance of the Dee in a national, indeed international, context. The information collected clearly shows this to be one of the most important estuaries for wintering birds in northwest Europe. Over 140,000 waders, some 10 per cent of the British population, may feed here in midwinter. All of the common and most of the uncommon waders gather, with the numbers of Knot and Dunlin both reaching 40,000. Oystercatcher numbers can rise to 20,000, though many disperse over nearby low-lying fields to feed on earthworms, as well as seeking Cockles on the estuary. Numbers of Ringed Plover, Sanderling and Bar-tailed Godwit can be large, while small numbers of Grey Plovers and Black-tailed Godwits frequent the upper estuary. Jack Snipe, Snipe, Curlew and Redshank prefer the saltmarshes, the latter being very much at home in the creeks among the Cord-grass saltings. Small numbers of several other species occur, particularly at migration time; these include Little Stint, Curlew Sandpiper, Ruff, Whimbrel, Spotted Redshank and Greenshank, while scarce species noted have been Kentish Plover and Baird's and Buff-breasted Sandpipers.

Shelducks breed at quite a few points in the vicinity of the estuary. Their broods of downy young are such an engaging feature of the mudflats during June as they are guarded by both parents, who at times have to adopt an aggressive defence against the attentions of marauding gulls and Carrion Crows. As the young develop they gather into crèches, sometimes up to 100 strong, guarded by just a few adults, until they fledge when about seven weeks old. Most of the Shelducks from northwest Europe migrate during June and July to converge on the Waddenzee, chiefly the Grosser Knechtsand, where at a peak up to 100,000 by-then-flightless birds will have gathered on the sandbanks: a quite remarkable facet of the Shelduck life cycle. The actual migration is nocturnal, the Shelducks from the west coast not hesitating to fly direct across mainland Britain, over areas where they are otherwise rarely seen. A small number, probably of Irish origin, moult in Bridgwater Bay, Somerset, where the flock may rise to some 3,500 strong. As the autumn proceeds so birds filter back, a major concentration taking place on the Dee with up to 4,000 in the middle reaches, one of the largest winter flocks in Britain and some 4 per cent of the North European population.

Most of the dabbling ducks, Wigeon, Teal, Mallard and Pintail, concentrate on Burton Marsh at the head of the estuary, with smaller numbers and wandering parties elsewhere. The flock of 5,000 Pintails is among the largest anywhere in Europe; fewer than 30 pairs nest in Britain, and most of those which winter here come from Iceland, Scandinavia and western Russia. The open estuary attracts small numbers of Scaups, Common Scoters (now much reduced in numbers), Goldeneyes and Red-breasted Mergansers, these being joined in hard weather, when the Cheshire Meres and other inland waters are frozen, by Pochards, Tufted Ducks and Coots. Small numbers of Great Crested Grebes are present throughout the winter, and occasional Red-throated Divers move into the estuary though most prefer to remain at sea.

Breeding birds on the saltings and marshes, in addition to the Shelduck, include Mallard and occasional Shoveler, Oystercatcher, Lapwing, Redshank, Skylark, Meadow Pipit, Yellow Wagtail, Stonechat, Grasshopper, Sedge and Reed Warblers, Linnet and Reed Bunting. Black-headed Gulls and Common Terns formerly nested, but owing to disturbance few try to do so these days, most seeking the sanctuary of the reserve at Shotton Pools.

Timing
With such a vast area for birds to disperse over at low tide, it is imperative that a visit is planned so as to take advantage of the high-tide concentrations of the flocks. Do not, however, neglect to see the estuary when the Dee is confined to its lowest channel, for only then can the full beauty be appreciated, the vastness and the solitude of an area hardly used by Man, yet, like many such sites, under threat from reclamation schemes and impoundment.

Access
There are several access points along the Welsh side. At Flint (SJ245735) the shore is accessible, while just north at SJ236738 a footpath follows the sea-wall and provides a good vantage point for North Flint Marsh and the Bagillt Bank. Beyond Greenfield the sea-wall continues as far as Mostyn, and along much of this section there is a low-water channel close under the Welsh shore, beyond which lies an extensive sandbank. Finally, the railway footbridge at Ffynnongroyw (SJ142810) gives excellent views overlooking Mostyn Bank and the bay north towards Point of Air.

Calendar

Resident Cormorant, Grey Heron, Shelduck, Mallard, Shoveler, Oystercatcher, Ringed Plover, Lapwing, Snipe, Redshank, large gulls, Skylark, Meadow Pipit, Reed Bunting.

December–February Great Crested Grebe, Mute Swan, Brent Goose, Wigeon, Gadwall, Teal, Mallard, Pintail, Scaup, Common Scoter, Goldeneye, Red-breasted Merganser, Golden and Grey Plovers, Knot, Sanderling, Dunlin, Jack Snipe, Black-tailed and Bar-tailed Godwits, Curlew, Greenshank, Turnstone, Black-headed Gull.

March–May Winter visitors depart, summer visitors and passage migrants include Whimbrel, Common Sandpiper, Yellow Wagtail.

June–July Shelduck broods in crèches, but most have fledged and departed by end of period. Some terns move into the estuary.

August–November Wildfowl and wader numbers begin to increase, some passage species such as Little Stint and Curlew and Green Sandpipers seen, terns remain in estuary until well into September. By October most wintering species have arrived.

Habitat

The shingle spit with its guardian lighthouse at Point of Air marks the northwest side of the mouth of the Dee Estuary. The habitats here range from the sand dunes facing north into Liverpool Bay to the shingle spit, inside which extend the vast saltmarshes and mudflats of the estuary. Some 450 acres (182 ha) are now a reserve of the Royal Society for the Protection of Birds, by agreement with Welsh Water and the Dee Wildfowlers' Club.

Species

Little Terns, a threatened species at many colonies in Britain, once nested at Point of Air. Perhaps they can be encouraged to return to the shingle areas; after all, they do not require much room, but it must be room away from treading feet. They face many natural hazards, too — Hedgehogs and Stoats, gulls and Carrion Crows — and, if they avoid all of these, just one extra high tide can wash the nests away. Large numbers still gather here in the late summer, when up to 500 have been noted, while at the same time the flock of Common and Arctic Terns may be 3,000 strong, in addition to which Sandwich Tern numbers may rise to 300. A careful search among the clamorous gathering should reveal a few Roseate Terns, not an easy task when so many birds, adults and immatures in a variety of plumages, are present. A few Black Terns also pass at this time.

Up to 1,000 wildfowl winter in the vicinity of Point of Air, Shelduck and Mallard being the main species with small numbers of Teal, Wigeon, Pintail, Shoveler, Common Scoter, Goldeneye and Red-breasted Merganser. Red-throated Divers, Great Crested Grebes, Guillemots and Razorbills occur throughout the winter in the estuary mouth, or just out to sea where the water remains shallow. The flocks of winter waders, part of the massive concentrations which make the Dee so important, can number up to 20,000 in midwinter. Oystercatcher, Knot, Dunlin and Redshank are most numerous, while others to be seen include Sanderling, Black-tailed and Bar-tailed Godwits, Curlew and Turnstone. The point is a major high-water gathering place for all these birds, and provides a spectacle for the birdwatcher seen nowhere else to this degree in Wales.

Seawatching from the Point of Air can at times be quite good, with Fulmar, Manx Shearwater and even Gannets in late summer, while Leach's Petrel, Grey Phalarope, Pomarine Skua and Sabine's Gull are among scarce visitors seen recently. The marshes and shoreline support a range of winter birds, including Hen Harrier, Merlin, Peregrine, Water Rail, Short-eared Owl, Shore Lark, Water Pipit, Twite and Lapland and Snow Buntings.

Timing

For seawatching, a visit, suitably equipped, at dawn is a necessity. A visit to the estuary means careful checking of tide tables to ensure that one's arrival is around the vital high-water hours. For searching along the strandline for small passerines or the nearby dunes and marshes for birds of prey, the time of day is less critical.

Access

Leave the A548 Prestatyn to Flint road at SJ114834 by the unclassified road for the coast. From here, one can walk west along the shore, backed by dunes, or east towards the point, or south for a short distance into the estuary. Great care must be exercised so that the wader and tern roosts at high tide are not disturbed.

Calendar

Resident Few breeding species but some wildfowl and waders seem to be present throughout the year, including Cormorant, Shelduck, Mallard, Oystercatcher, Ringed Plover, Curlew, Redshank, Black-headed, Lesser Black-backed and Herring Gulls.

December–February Red-throated Diver, Great Crested Grebe, Brent Goose, Wigeon, Teal, Pintail, Shoveler, Common Scoter, Goldeneye, Red-breasted Merganser, Hen Harrier, Merlin, Peregrine, Golden and Grey Plovers, Lapwing, Knot, Sanderling, Dunlin, Snipe, Black-tailed and Bar-tailed Godwits, Turnstone, Short-eared Owl, Shore Lark, Water Pipit, Twite and Lapland and Snow Buntings.

March–May Winter visitors departing but wader passage continues well into May, with Whimbrel coming through from mid-April. First Sandwich Terns seen about the beginning of April, when passerine passage noted with birds such as Wheatear and Ring Ouzel among the dunes and Sand Martins and Swallows overhead.

June–July Resident species present, parties of terns throughout period with numbers building up from mid-July.

August–November Wader numbers rapidly increase during August, main influx of winter visitors from mid-October. Seabird passage offshore from mid-August until late September.

Habitat

Birdwatching in the heart of a huge industrial complex, in this case the British Steel Corporation works at Shotton on Deeside, may not seem very inviting. Within the perimeter of this seemingly inhospitable landscape, however, is an area of lagoons, cooling pools and associated reedbeds. As a contribution to European Conservation Year 1970, the Corporation declared the area a nature reserve and wisely placed its management in the hands of a dedicated group of local volunteers who have subsequently carried out much research and management.

Species

One of the most exciting developments at Shotton was the provision of nesting rafts on the pools, which were rapidly colonised by Common Terns. Previously the birds had struggled to breed on the Dee marshes in the face of increasing human disturbance, predation by Foxes and flooding by high tides. In the safety of the rafts, the colony has grown rapidly from 13 pairs in 1970. Other breeding species within the reserve include Little Grebe, Shoveler, Kestrel, Redshank, Black-headed Gull, Yellow Wagtail, Whinchat, Reed Warbler and Corn Bunting. The latter is now an extremely scarce species in Wales, though until about 50 years ago it was well distributed in coastal districts westwards to Lleyn and Pembrokeshire.

Corn Bunting

There is a good winter duck population. Scarce visitors have included Black-necked Grebe, Bittern, Garganey, Long-tailed Duck, Hen Harrier, Spotted Crake, Temminck's Stint, Pectoral and Broad-billed Sandpipers, Greater Yellowlegs, Wilson's Phalarope, White-winged Black Tern, Red-spotted Bluethroat and Great Grey and Woodchat Shrikes.

Timing

A visit at any time of year is worthwhile, though no particular time of day is better than any other.

Access

By permit only, normally valid for three years, and available from Personnel Services, British Steel Corporation, Coated Products, Shotton Works, Deeside, Clwyd, CH5 2NH.

Calendar

Resident Little Grebe, Grey Heron, Mallard, Shoveler, Sparrowhawk, Kestrel, Moorhen, Coot, Redshank, Black-headed Gull, Skylark, Pied Wagtail, Wren, Robin, Goldfinch, Linnet, Yellowhammer, Reed Bunting, Corn Bunting.

December–February Wigeon, Gadwall, Pochard, Tufted Duck, Goldeneye, Peregrine, Fieldfare, Redwing, Brambling, Siskin, Redpoll.

March–May Winter visitors depart, first summer visitors arrive, Swallows and Sand Martins usually over the pools by end of March, when Garganey occasionally call. Common Terns and Black-headed Gulls take up residence for breeding. From mid-April, summer visitors such as Yellow Wagtail, Grasshopper, Sedge and Reed Warblers, Whitethroat and Spotted Flycatcher seen.

June–July All summer residents present, Black-headed Gulls and Common Terns fledge from early July, Green and Wood Sandpipers possible by end of month.

August–November Summer visitors depart, with Swallows and Sand Martins around well into September, passage waders throughout period, winter ducks from late September, while Fieldfare and Redwing arrive in October.

29 BURRY INLET SOUTH SHORE AND WHITEFORD POINT

Map 29
OS Map 159

Habitat

The southern coast of the Burry Inlet, in contrast to the northern shore (see pages 59–62), is a lonely region of extensive saltmarshes, in places over 1 mile (1.6 km) wide, one of the largest areas of moderately grazed saltmarshes in Britain. Except between the cockle villages of Penclawdd and Crofty, the road is well back from the shore, following the northern escarpment of Gower. Cockles have been dug on the Burry Inlet since Iron Age Man descended from his hill camps, of which there is plenty of evidence in Gower, through the woodlands and so to the flats. The Cockle fishery based at Penclawdd was one of the most important in Wales. In 1884 it was said to be worth £15,000 per annum and it provided employment for a large number of women, who each day, with their donkeys, followed the receding tides on Llanrhidian Sands as they raked for Cockles to be sent to markets all over South Wales. Few now make their living here from the industry. To the west of the sands, beyond Great Pill, lies the massive dune system of Whiteford Burrows, extending 2 miles (3.2 km) northwards from the hamlet of Cwm Ivy and Landimore Marsh, so that its furthest point is almost half way across the Burry Inlet. The whole area of the burrows is owned by the National Trust, the first of their Enterprise Neptune purchases, the campaign to protect key sections of the British coastline. A large part is now a National Nature Reserve managed by the Nature Conservancy Council. There are so many good things at Whiteford — its remoteness, the birds, plants and insects, rare and common — to enthrall the visitor. Plants include Moonwort, Yellow Bird's-nest, Fen Orchid, Bird's-foot-trefoil, Yellow Bedstraw and Sea Pansies.

Species

The birds which gather on the saltings and further out on the great flats are part of the same flocks observed on the Carmarthenshire side of the estuary. Careful counts by members of the Gower Ornithological Society, regularly chronicled in their annual reports, indicate some of the riches: some 400 Brent Geese, 1,200 Shelducks, 6,000 Wigeons, 1,300 Teals, 2,300 Pintails, 17,000 Oystercatchers, 3,000 Knots, 2,800 Dunlins, 300 Bar-tailed Godwits, 1,500 Curlews, 600 Redshanks and 400 Turnstones. The Eider is of special interest, despite the fact that it breeds no further south than Walney Island. Ornithologists first noted these birds at Whiteford in 1919, but old fishermen said they had been here for as long as they could remember, and old fishermen have long memories. Eiders occur throughout the year, and are so much a feature that the Glamorgan Wildlife Trust adopted the bird for its emblem. Numbers vary, and in recent years have been about 170 in late winter. Red-breasted Mergansers have nested on the Burry Inlet, and small numbers are seen in almost all months. In winter, there is a good chance of seeing raptors such as Hen Harrier, Merlin, Short-eared Owl and even the occasional Peregrine over the saltings. Divers, grebes and seaducks, especially Common Scoter, are present in winter just west of Whiteford Point, the latter being part of the huge flock which spreads right across Carmarthen Bay.

Timing

Best just after high water, as the tide recedes to reveal the first feeding areas for waders and before divers, grebes and seaducks move too far offshore.

Access

The B4295 at Penclawdd runs close to the shore and provides a good viewing point for this section of the upper estuary, as does Salthouse Point (SS523958), an old causeway on the shore near Crofty. A minor road leads to the point from the crossroads in Pen-caer-fenny. Beyond Crofty, a minor road bears off the B4295 and follows the edge of the saltings for about 2½ miles (4 km) until it rejoins the main road in Llanrhidian. West of here is some 4 miles (6.4 km) of saltmarshes intersected by many tidal channels, and with no prime vantage points and no good access other than by the track leading north from Weobley Castle (SS477926). Better to pass quickly on to Whiteford, parking in Cwm Ivy where there is an information kiosk at SS437940. From here, a footpath leads north for over 2 miles (3.2 km), giving fine views of the reserve and the Burry Inlet. There is a bird hide on Berges Island, details of which are available at the kiosk.

Calendar

Resident Cormorant, Grey Heron, Shelduck, Mallard, Eider, Red-breasted Merganser, Common Scoter, Buzzard, Oystercatcher, Ringed Plover, Lapwing, Snipe, Curlew, Redshank, Turnstone, large gulls, Skylark, Meadow Pipit.

December–February Red-throated and Great Northern Divers, Great Crested, Slavonian and Black-necked Grebes, Brent Goose, Wigeon, Teal, Pintail, Shoveler, Scaup, Long-tailed Duck, Goldeneye, Hen Harrier, Merlin, Peregrine, Golden and Grey Plovers, Knot, Sanderling, Jack Snipe, Black-tailed and Bar-tailed Godwits, Spotted Redshank, Common Gull.

March–May Winter visitors depart, while passage waders are seen well into May when the last Whimbrels fly north. Wheatears usually from mid-March, and from the end of the month Swallows and Sand Martins passing on most days.

June–July Seabirds begin moving into Carmarthen Bay and at times are seen close offshore, especially Manx Shearwaters and Gannets. Waders start to return, Green Sandpiper often one of the first, though you will need to look for this species in the creeks rather than on the open shore.

August–November Wader passage at its peak early in period, with overwintering species also arriving. A large increase in the gull population, with many Common Gulls beginning to roost on the estuary. Winter finches, including Brambling and Snow Bunting, possible from November.

30 CWM CLYDACH

Map 30
OS Map 159

Habitat

Some 7 miles (11.2 km) north from the centre of Swansea is the Royal Society for the Protection of Birds Cwm Clydach reserve, situated in the narrow valley of the same name. The RSPB in Wales has concentrated in recent years on two threatened habitats, heather moorland and broadleaved woodland. The latter once covered 90 per cent of the Principality, but now accounts for no more than 3 per cent. Many of the fragments remaining are threatened, not just from felling or conversion to conifers, but often through a lack of management, and especially by overgrazing. In an effort to provide protection for the top-grade woodlands, and advice and assistance to all woodland owners and managers, 'Coed Cymru' — Save Welsh Woodlands — was launched in 1984. In Cwm Clydach, following an initial acquisition of 120 acres (49 ha), further sections of woodland have been acquired, so that a major reserve is now in being close to a large urban centre, having many educational possibilities for local schools.

Species

Most woodland species to be expected in mid- and South Wales will be seen in Cwm Clydach. Birds of prey include Sparrowhawk, Buzzard, Kestrel and Tawny Owl, and once an Osprey passed by. Woodpigeons are numerous, but on the other side of the balance sheet the Nightjars which formerly occupied woods like this have gone. All three woodpeckers are present. The Lesser Spotted Woodpecker is rather local in Wales so that it is a bonus to have at least one pair on the reserve. Its small size — it is no larger than a House Sparrow — and retiring nature mean that this is a bird easily overlooked: its drumming is much quieter than that of its larger cousin, and where numbers are low, and the pairs widely separated, it may be heard only for a short time in early spring. Certainly you will have to search hard for a glimpse of the Lesser Spotted Woodpecker. Tree Pipits and Whinchats occupy the fringes of the valley above or at the edge of the woodlands, with Wheatears on the hills. Hole-nesting species such as Redstart, Pied Flycatcher and several of the tit family are frequent in the woods. Summer visitors include Whitethroat, Garden Warbler, Blackcap, Wood Warbler, Chiffchaff and Willow Warbler. In winter, Woodcock are recorded in small numbers and there are usually Fieldfares and Redwings about.

Timing

No particular time of day, though early morning is recommended.

Access

Leave M4 at junction 45 and take the A4067 Brecon road, at the crossroads at SN695014 in the centre of Clydach, and follow the unclassified road through the valley until the reserve car park is reached at SN682053. The reserve is open at all times. Beyond the reserve the road, now unfenced, climbs on to higher ground with a picnic site at SN668068 overlooking the Lliw Reservoirs.

Calendar

Resident Sparrowhawk, Buzzard, Kestrel, Pheasant, Stock Dove, Woodpigeon, Collared Dove, Tawny Owl, Green, Great Spotted and Lesser Spotted Woodpeckers, Skylark, Meadow Pipit, Wren, Dunnock, Robin, Blackbird, Song and Mistle Thrushes, Goldcrest, Long-tailed, Marsh, Willow, Blue and Great Tits, Nuthatch, Treecreeper, Jay, Magpie, Raven, Chaffinch, Greenfinch, Goldfinch, Bullfinch, Yellowhammer.

December–February Snipe, Woodcock, Fieldfare, Redwing, Brambling, Siskin, Redpoll.

March–May Chiffchaff usually the first summer visitor to the woodlands and Wheatear to the uplands, both before the end of March, later arrivals include Swallow, Tree Pipit, Redstart, Whinchat, Garden Warbler, Blackcap, Wood and Willow Warblers, Spotted and Pied Flycatchers.

June–July All breeding species present, though by end of period the woods seem strangely quiet after all the song and bustle of earlier in the season.

August–November Departure of summer visitors. Some residents, especially tits, form small post-breeding flocks which can be joined by Goldcrest, Treecreeper, even by finches on occasions. Autumn sees the arrival of such visitors as Woodcock, Fieldfare and Redwing.

Map 31
OS Map 171

31 FLAT HOLM

Habitat

Flat Holm, the only true island in the whole of Glamorgan, lies 3 miles (4.8 km) out to sea from Lavernock Point between Penarth and Barry. To the south, some 2½ miles (4 km) distant, is Steep Holm, which belongs to Somerset. Barely 52 acres (21 ha) in extent, and less than ½ mile (0.8 km) in length, it is, as its name suggests, a low-lying island; the only cliffs rise to little more than 50 feet (15 m) on its eastern side, on the top of which stands a lighthouse. The early Welsh Saints had a predilection for remote, and indeed the not so remote, islands and Flat Holm did not escape their attention. St Cadoc made frequent visits, and one of his disciples, Gwalches, is buried here. Farming activity is recorded as far back as the sixteenth century, and continued until the island was evacuated in the 1940s. Other activities, including the establishment of an isolation hospital, and a great deal of military activity, first during the reign of Queen Victoria and then during the early years of World War II as part of the defences for the Bristol Channel ports, have all shaped the island habitats. The last people to farm here were the Harris family, Fred Harris living on Flat Holm for over 40 years — and he had been on Steep Holm before that. More recently, the island has been leased by Trinity House to the South Glamorgan County Council, who have designated it a Local Nature Reserve and set up the imaginative Flat Holm Project, which involves renovation of the buildings and the establishment of facilities for visiting naturalists.

The vegetation of Flat Holm has been much modified by human activity, by countless generations of Rabbits present since the fourteenth century, and in more recent years by the gull population. There are large areas of low, windswept scrub, rough pasture and maritime swards. The chief item of botanical interest is the Wild Leek, a plant of the Mediterranean region, found in Wales only on Flat Holm and at a single site in Pembrokeshire. Elsewhere in Britain it is virtually restricted to a few sites in Cornwall.

Species

The most striking feature is the large gull colony, which was first established in the late 1940s, probably as an overspill from the by then enormous colonies on Steep Holm. In 1954 there were five pairs of Lesser Black-backed Gulls and a similar number of Herring Gulls; ten years later there were 616 pairs and 380 pairs respectively, and by 1974 there was a teeming colony of just over 8,000 pairs, divided equally between the two species. Subsequently there was a decline, by 1980 the population numbering 2,380 pairs of Lesser Black-backed Gulls and 1,300 pairs of Herring Gulls, and this decline has continued ever since, the latest counts, in 1983, being of 2,033 and 624 pairs respectively. The dramatic drop in numbers seems clearly linked with botulism, probably the result of intensive feeding on rubbish dumps, a habit shared by both species in the upper reaches of the Bristol Channel (unlike at the Pembrokeshire colonies, where most Lesser Black-backed Gulls feed on fish caught well out to sea). Great Black-backed Gulls were first found nesting here in 1962, though there have never been more than five pairs.

A number of Shelducks nest in old Rabbit burrows, and there are several pairs of Oystercatchers. The rest of the breeding birds comprise a variety of small landbirds and include Meadow Pipit, Wren, Robin, Blackbird and Song Thrush. In autumn, large numbers of migrating Skylarks, Meadow Pipits, thrushes and finches pass over as they move southwest along the coast of Wales. Consistent observations will without question reveal Flat Holm as an excellent place for finding some of our scarce migrants in due season.

Timing
A visit will depend entirely on the boat service, while eventually the accommodation will provide a superb opportunity for those wishing to spend a few days, or longer, ashore.

Access
Enquire of the Flat Holm Project, Old Police Station, Harbour Road, Barry, South Glamorgan.

Calendar

Resident Cormorant, although not nesting, always present offshore. Shelduck, Oystercatcher, Herring and Great Black-backed Gulls, Woodpigeon, Skylark, Meadow Pipit, Wren, Robin, Blackbird, Song Thrush.

December–February Occasional divers and grebes offshore, Common Scoter.

March–May Lesser Black-backed Gulls return to the colonies early in period. Summer passage migrants from late March, with Wheatear and Ring Ouzel the earliest, quickly followed by Swallow and Sand Martin and the occasional Chiffchaff. Small numbers of most other migrants throughout April and early May, with Turtle Dove and Swift the last to arrive.

June–July All resident breeding birds present, small numbers of Manx Shearwaters and occasional Gannets offshore.

August–November Seabird movement offshore, particularly when stormy weather drives birds such as skuas and terns well up the Bristol Channel, while some undoubtedly cross England and move down the Severn Estuary. Large passages of Swallows and Sand Martins in early September and winter visitors in October, with Fieldfares and Redwings passing through.

Habitat

Most of the east side of Swansea Bay has been lost to industrial development, but one sizeable remnant remains to the south of where the Kenfig River enters the sea. Here about 1,200 acres (486 ha) of calcareous sand dunes have accumulated, swallowing up many centuries ago the prosperous town of Kenfig which nestled hard by what was a navigable river in pre-Conquest times. Now all that remains above ground is the top of the keep of the Norman Castle, but what a treasure-house for future archaeologists lies hidden away beneath the sand. Several more recent dwellings are of interest, such as Mawdlam Church, Kenfig Farm and Sker House, the latter the grange of the Cistercian monks of Neath Abbey and the source of many romantic legends. The novel *The Maid of Sker*, by R. D. Blackmore of Lorna Doone fame, is based on the house and the surrounding area.

Kenfig has been a Local Nature Reserve administered by the Mid Glamorgan County Council since 1978, but its importance for birds and plants had been recognised since at least the beginning of the century. It was here that the father of Welsh ornithology, Colonel H. Morrey Salmon, came in the years before the Kaiser's War, to photograph the Merlin and other dune birds. In *The Birds of Glamorgan*, published in 1967, he lamented the changes which had taken place on the coast of South Wales:

'Immediately after the first world war the coast was still relatively inaccessible to the majority of people except at the terminal points of the railways; but it soon changed, and wherever a roadway led down to the coast beach or cliff it was open to the motor car. The quiet solitudes of the great sand-dune areas and their adjacent beaches, with their abundant bird-life were the first to suffer; their colonies of Little Terns, their breeding pairs of Merlins, their Nightjars, their few nesting pairs of Black-headed Gulls (then unique in the county) had vanished before the second world war.'

At Kenfig you can see a superb succession, from the embryonic and mobile dunes fronting the shoreline through to the older dunes and slacks. Here some of the botanical treasures can be found, as well as a wealth of common species such as Bird's-foot-trefoil, Evening-primrose, Carline Thistle, Viper's-bugloss and, in the slacks, Marsh-orchids, Yellow Rattle and Round-leaved Wintergreen. Further inland, there are areas of dune grassland with patches of scrub here and there, and close to the river an Alder carr. Of special importance is the 70 acres (28 ha) of Kenfig Pool, one of the largest natural freshwater sites in South Wales. It is not just birds at the pool, for 20 species of dragonfly and damselfly have been recorded, and that is nearly half those on the British List.

Species

Breeding species at the pool are small in number, but include Great Crested Grebe, Mute Swan, Teal, Mallard, Shoveler, Tufted Duck, Moorhen and Coot. Ruddy Ducks have not been so quick to colonise

South Wales as in Anglesey, but have now nested here for a couple of years. Garganeys have probably nested occasionally at this, their furthest site west; this is a scarce species in Wales, more frequently seen as an early spring passage migrant, and probably fewer than 100 pairs nest in the whole of Britain. An interesting breeding record in 1985 was that of a Mandarin Duck which reared six young at Kenfig Hill, about 4 miles (6.4 km) inland, the first record for the county of a duck which did not gain admission to the British List until 1971 and whose presence is wholly dependent on several feral populations. Other breeding species include Oystercatcher, Ringed Plover, Lapwing, Snipe and Redshank. Cetti's Warblers have been recorded for several years and it can only be a short time before they nest, though proving this will be extremely difficult.

The pool comes into its own in winter, when several hundred Pochards and Tufted Ducks take up residence, while the Coot population swells with immigrants from eastern Europe. Wigeon, Teal and Mallard also number several hundred as they dabble in the shallows or graze on nearby fields. The flock of Gadwalls, which on occasions may rise to 80, is the largest in Wales. Visitors in smaller numbers include Scaup, Long-tailed Duck, Goldeneye and Smew, and there is always the chance of the splendid spectacle of a family group of Whooper Swans and occasional Bewick's Swans.

It is worth seawatching in late summer from Sker Point. Small numbers of Manx Shearwaters are usually to be seen, increasing from late July onwards. Other species recorded in recent years have included Storm and Leach's Petrels, Pomarine Skua, Sabine's Gull and Roseate Tern.

Rare visitors to Kenfig, the result of much diligent watching, are such that it must be among the best sites in mainland Wales for those wishing to add exotic species to their list. Several North American species have recently been seen, including Pied-billed Grebe, American Wigeon, Surf Scoter, Pectoral and Buff-breasted Sandpipers, Bonaparte's and Ring-billed Gulls and Royal Tern. Rarities from closer home have included Little Bittern, Purple Heron, Spoonbill, Ferruginous Duck, Spotted Crake, Kentish Plover, Alpine Swift, Aquatic, Barred and Yellow-browed Warblers, Red-breasted Flycatcher, Bearded Tit, Woodchat Shrike and Lapland Bunting.

One other rare visitor deserves special mention. Imagine the excitement on the afternoon of 30 August 1982 when a Little Whimbrel was located near Sker Farm, the first record of this species in Britain and only the second for Europe. This bird breeds in a restricted area of eastern Siberia and normally winters from the Moluccas eastwards to New Guinea and Australia. Small wonder that well over 1,000 birdwatchers came from all over Britain and beyond to see this once-in-a-lifetime vagrant, a close relative of the legendary Eskimo Curlew which was first discovered by pioneers working for Hudson's Bay Company in the high Canadian Arctic. Vast flocks of the latter species were seen on migration in the United States, where they were shot in thousands, so that by the end of the nineteenth century it was so infrequently seen that its survival was in jeopardy; a small population survives to this day, though its future remains in the balance. But we digress from this most excellent of birdwatching localities.

Timing

Visit at any time of day, but early mornings are strongly recommended. If in winter you wish to see the largest number of waterfowl, choose a time when boating is taking place on nearby Eglwys Nunydd, the reservoir a little to the north; when disturbed, the birds rapidly move to take temporary refuge at Kenfig, much to the delight of the assembled watchers.

Access

Leave the M4 at junction 37 and head for North or South Cornelly, from where unclassified roads are signed to Kenfig. A car park is at SS801809, and adjacent to this is the reserve centre; a warden and assistant wardens are employed. There are numerous footpaths which head towards Sker Point and other places on the shore, and to Kenfig Pool, where there is an observation hide at the southwest corner; when the hide is locked, the key is available from the reserve centre.

Calendar

Resident Great Crested Grebe, Cormorant, Grey Heron, Mute Swan, Canada Goose, Teal, Mallard, Shoveler, Tufted Duck, Ruddy Duck, Sparrowhawk, Kestrel, Moorhen, Coot, Oystercatcher, Ringed Plover, Lapwing, Snipe, Redshank, large gulls, Meadow Pipit, Skylark.

December–February Bittern, Bewick's and Whooper Swans, Shelduck, Wigeon, Gadwall, Pintail, Pochard, Long-tailed Duck, Goldeneye, Hen Harrier, Merlin, Peregrine, Water Rail, Dunlin, Jack Snipe, Curlew, Common Gull, Short-eared Owl.

March–May Winter visitors depart. Summer migrants arrive, passage Sandwich Terns, Swallows and Sand Martins among the first, a chance of Wheatears among the dunes, while Garganeys are seen in late March and early April in some years. Whimbrel, Cuckoo and Swift in late April.

June–July All resident species present, some seabird movement offshore, chiefly Manx Shearwaters and occasional Gannets. First returning waders, even a chance of Sanderling on the beach by late July.

August–November Passage movements well under way until mid-September, when winter visitors begin to arrive at the pool, chance of the occasional diver and grebe offshore.

33 LAVERNOCK POINT

Map 33
OS Map 171

Habitat

Just over 1 mile (1.6 km) beyond the southern outskirts of Penarth, the coast, which has been following a northeast to southwest line, takes a right angle towards the west at Lavernock Point. Here the Liassic limestone cliffs are about 50 feet (15 m) high, and some 14 acres (5.6 ha) of clifftop grassland and dense Hawthorn scrub are a reserve of the Glamorgan Wildlife Trust. There is a rich flora which includes Adder's-tongue, a diminutive member of the fern family found in old pastures and similar long undisturbed habitats. Lesser Butterfly-orchid and Green-winged and Bee Orchids are prominent in spring and early summer.

Species

Breeding birds include most of the common passerines such as Wren, Dunnock, Blackbird, Whitethroat and Linnet. It is, however, as an observation point for watching migrants and for seawatching that Lavernock Point is most renowned. Being in the extreme east of the Bristol Channel means that for seabirds one is much dependent on strong southwest winds bringing birds into the mouth of the Severn Estuary, then, as the wind drops or swings to the northwest, so they push back out to sea, many coming close inshore to delight the watchers. One of the most regular species is the Manx Shearwater, most of which in late summer will be on feeding movements from the colonies on the Pembrokeshire islands, while in September these same birds will be ready to move to their winter quarters off South America. Small numbers of Gannets and Kittiwakes together with occasional Guillemots and Razorbills are seen, the latter two species mostly in midwinter. Terns pass in small numbers from late July to late September, some undoubtedly having crossed over central England by way of the river valleys. Other seabirds occasionally recorded here include Black-throated and Great Northern Divers, Fulmar, Balearic and Sooty Shearwaters, Storm and Leach's Petrels, Common and Velvet Scoters, Pomarine, Arctic and Great Skuas, and Mediterranean and Sabine's Gulls: all an indication of the ornithological riches that even a spot such as this, far from the open sea, can provide the dedicated observer.

Lavernock Point is also an excellent place for observing visible migration throughout the autumn, when large movements of Skylarks, Meadow Pipits, Fieldfares, Redwings, Starlings and Chaffinches can be seen, following the coastline. Sometimes unexpected species are seen, as for example the Jays during the autumn of 1983, when there was a huge invasion of this species from Continental Europe with the result that they were seen far from their natural woodland habitat. Scarce species at the point have included Honey Buzzard, Red Kite, Richard's Pipit, Black Redstart, Bonelli's Warbler, Firecrest, Pied Flycatcher, Red-backed Shrike and Common Crossbill. A Nightingale sang briefly in April 1985, but soon moved on to more congenial territory; there are few breeding records of this species in Wales.

Timing

Being close to the towns of Penarth and Barry, and with Cardiff only a few miles away, the point with its camping site is a popular spot. Birdwatchers are well advised to make their visit in the early morning, and this will be essential at migration time.

Access

Leave the B4267 Penarth to Barry road at ST178687 and take the unclassified road which leads directly to the point. There are clifftop footpaths.

Calendar

Resident Woodpigeon, Skylark, Meadow Pipit, Wren, Dunnock, Robin, Blackbird, Song Thrush, Jackdaw, House Sparrow, Greenfinch, Linnet, Yellowhammer.

December–February A chance of wandering geese, usually White-fronted, passing by, possible seaducks and Guillemots and Razorbills offshore.

March–May Summer passage migrants much in evidence from late March onwards, Swallow, Sand Martin and Chiffchaff among the first to arrive, Turtle Dove and Swift the last.

June–July Small numbers of Manx Shearwaters offshore, especially from July onwards, when a few Gannets may also be seen.

August–December August and September the best months for observing seabird passage but much depends on weather conditions, those willing to be patient being rewarded by a good range of species. Autumn passage of passerines dominated during September by large numbers of Swallows and Sand Martins, while birds such as Chiffchaff and Willow Warbler may be located, main movements from late October with Skylark, Meadow Pipit, Starling and Chaffinch by far the most numerous. Wandering bands of tits, even Goldcrest, may appear at this time.

Habitat

From Pennard Pill westwards for 2½ miles (4 km) is the broad sweep of Oxwich Bay, a shallow bay backed by dunes which in turn trap an extensive area of saltmarsh, freshwater marsh and lagoons, all of which drain to the sea by way of Nicholaston Pill. The dunes show all stages of succession, from the embryonic dunes of the shoreline, the erosion systems and blowouts of the seaward faces, through to the oldest dunes where trees such as Birch and Oak have become established. There are numerous fine plants to be found here, including such rarities as the Welsh Gentian and a maritime variety of the Round-leaved Wintergreen. For the birdwatcher, the fens and marshes are of great interest. They were originally reclaimed in the sixteenth century, and for over 300 years provided rich summer grazing. Fish ponds dug in the early nineteenth century still remain, the largest, of some 18 acres (7.2 ha), aptly named Serpentine Broad. The reedswamp extends for some 100 acres (40 ha), one of the largest areas of this habitat in southwest Britain. Fifteen species of dragonfly and damselfly have been recorded, and plants such as Mare's-tail, Common Bladderwort, Flowering-rush, Bogbean and Marsh-marigold thrive here.

Species

The Bittern was the first of six former breeding birds to recolonise Britain this century, having last bred in 1886. In 1911 breeding was again recorded in Norfolk, since when the population has slowly increased, and there has been a gradual colonisation of sites in several other counties. Bitterns had been occasionally recorded in winter at Oxwich, but it was not until 1969 that a booming male was heard: what an exciting event! Subsequently, booming has been heard in several other years, with Bitterns now annual winter visitors, particularly during cold conditions which bring them in from the east. Grey Herons breed in Penrice Woods, close to Oxwich, and are always to be seen flying over, or wading in the shallows at the pool margins. Several scarce members of the heron family have been noted here, including Little Bittern and Purple Heron. Cormorants also come to fish from their colonies further west in Gower, and are often seen perched in the trees. Another scarce reedbed species, the Bearded Tit, was first recorded here in 1965 and in 1974 probably nested, as birds were still present in late July and a juvenile was caught and ringed; this species is now resident and several pairs breed, numbers being at a peak in late summer when up to 18 have been seen. Although rarely proved, it is almost certain that Water Rails nest here and they can certainly be heard throughout the summer months; their characteristic calls also seem to come from every part of the reedbeds throughout the winter, when a sizeable number must be present. Moorhens and, especially, Coots are much more obvious and are seen on the open water. Small numbers of Black-headed Gulls have nested in the past, and are still to be seen in all months. Although Kingfishers do not breed, they are regularly seen, especially during the late summer and autumn, when they move to coastal localities for the winter months. Marsh Harriers regularly pass this way on migration, and

Bearded Tit

sometimes one or two summer in Glamorgan; will a pair remain one day to grace the marsh? The populations of Sedge and Reed Warblers have evoked much study in recent years, an estimate in 1976 putting the population of the latter as high as ten pairs per acre (25 pairs per ha), making a total population of around 1,000 pairs. A Cetti's Warbler was seen here for the first time in 1977, after which birds were heard annually. Hopes that they might breed were realised in 1985 when two adults and three juveniles were seen; the breeding population is larger, as at least six males and five females were present.

Small numbers of Mallard and Teal breed, while Shoveler, Pochard and Tufted Duck may have done so. Shelduck broods are occasionally seen, while Garganeys are rare but regular passage migrants in the early spring. Green-winged Teals have also stayed here on several occasions. Wader records tend to be few, a lack of muddy margins being the main reason. Snipe breed and may be heard drumming in spring. The beach and dunes attract a small number of species, but sadly Ringed Plovers have ceased to breed.

Timing
Early mornings are by far the best, especially so during the summer months, when Oxwich village, car park and beach can be packed with visitors.

Access
The A4118 is the main road west from Swansea through south Gower. Leave this at SS502884 and head for Oxwich village; the road at one point cuts through the freshwater marsh, and for much of its length follows the boundary between marsh and sand dunes. There is a large

car park beside the Oxwich Reserve centre, and a footpath system from here through the dunes and along the edge of the saltmarsh. Oxwich Wood and Crawley and Nicholaston Woods are also well worth visiting, and contain marked footpaths.

Calendar

Resident Little Grebe, Cormorant, Grey Heron, Shelduck, Teal, Mallard, Pochard, Sparrowhawk, Buzzard, Water Rail, Moorhen, Coot, Snipe, Black-headed Gull, Cetti's Warbler, Bearded Tit, Reed Bunting.

December–February Bittern, Gadwall, Shoveler, Tufted Duck.

March–May Garganey in late March/early April, Ringed Plover, summer migrants arrive, from early April Swallows and Sand Martins over the marsh, by end of April Sedge and Reed Warblers in full residence and song.

June–July All breeding species present. First autumn passage commences in late July, with Green and Common Sandpipers and Kingfisher, a chance of terns in Oxwich Bay.

August–November Wader and tern passage during August and early part of September. Summer migrants leave, with last warblers present until mid-September, when large gatherings of Swallows and Sand Martins before their departure for winter quarters. Wintering ducks arrive and a chance of Bittern in November.

Habitat

From Mumbles Head to Port Talbot, the shoreline of Swansea Bay extends for over 11 miles (17.6 km), the whole length backed by the conurbation of Swansea and its suburbs, residential and holiday in the west, the docks and industry to the east. At first glance, perhaps not an area to excite the birdwatcher, but careful observations by dedicated local observers have revealed this as a site not to be missed. The tidal flats, especially in the west, extend up to 1 mile (1.6 km) from the shore, while the docklands should not be neglected as a birdwatching haunt.

Species

With some perception, an ornithologist early in 1973 was to write:

'There can be few more likely candidates for future addition to the British and Irish list than the Ring-billed Gull *Larus delawarensis*. It is abundant in North America, and . . . it winters on the Atlantic coast from New England to the Gulf of Mexico, a migratory pattern which would seem to render it liable to transatlantic vagrancy . . . it remains the only gull from the eastern Nearctic still to be recorded in Britain and Ireland.' (*British Birds* 66 : 115)

On 14 March that same year, a birdwatcher painstakingly examining a flock of Common Gulls, its close relative, noted a paler bird which was eventually identified as an adult Ring-billed Gull. This individual, the first record for Britain and Ireland, remained until the end of the month.

Ring-billed Gull

Imagine the surprise, however, when, barely three months later, at the same spot, a first-summer Ring-billed Gull was noted. This species has been recorded at Blackpill ever since, with up to nine adults in 1984. Not until 1977 were Ring-billed Gulls found elsewhere in Britain, but now they are regularly seen in a number of counties; there were no fewer than 194 in the three years from 1981, probably the result of a major population increase in North America. Will Ring-billed Gulls establish themselves as a breeding bird on this side of the Atlantic? Perhaps a pair or two already nest with Common Gulls on some remote Scottish lochan. Meanwhile, watchers at Blackpill in Swansea Bay continue to enjoy the sense of achievement when this bird is located.

Blackpill is certainly the place for gull-watching, with all the commoner species present throughout the year. The flock of Common Gulls may number several hundred even in midsummer, despite there being no large colonies closer than the Clyde region of Scotland. Mediterranean Gulls are now regular in their appearance here, mainly during the summer, while Little Gulls may be seen in virtually any month, either here or further west at Mumbles. Iceland and Glaucous Gulls have been recorded, while, rather surprisingly for a somewhat estuarine type of habitat, the Kittiwake can be seen in small numbers throughout the year. The first record of Whiskered Tern in Glamorgan was of two at Blackpill in May 1974. Black Terns have been seen on a number of occasions, Sandwich, Common, Arctic and Little Terns are regular on both spring and, especially, autumn passage, while a Caspian Tern was seen in August 1973.

The flats at Blackpill are a good haunt for waders, as well as for gulls and terns. Oystercatchers are present throughout the year and in midwinter up to 2,000 feed here, many frequenting the nearby Ashleigh Road playing-fields when the tide is in. Ringed Plover, Dunlin, Bar-tailed Godwit, Curlew and Redshank occur throughout the year, though in midsummer only a handful may be present. Dunlins are by far the most numerous, with up to 2,300 in January. Other waders regularly seen include Grey Plover, Knot, Sanderling, Black-tailed Godwit and Green-shank, while the Red-necked Phalarope has been recorded on several occasions.

Timing
It is essential to consult the tide tables and choose a visit for about two hours before or after high water. At these times the birds are close inshore, whereas at other times they disperse across the flats and viewing is then at long range, for the most part with a telescope.

Access
The A4067 follows the shore west from Swansea to Mumbles. Access is possible along most of its length by crossing the disused line of the old Mumbles railway, now the Swansea bike path.

Calendar

Resident Cormorant, Shelduck, Oystercatcher, Ringed Plover, Dunlin, Bar-tailed Godwit, Curlew, Redshank, Black-headed, Common, Lesser Black-backed, Herring and Great Black-backed Gulls, Kittiwake. In view of the number of records in many months of the year, one is in fact tempted to include the star, the Ring-billed Gull, in this section.

December–February Occasional divers and grebes offshore, Scaup, Goldeneye, Grey Plover, Knot, Sanderling, Greenshank, Turnstone.

March–May Whimbrel, Common Sandpiper, some tern passage.

June–July Wader numbers and gull numbers begin to increase as July progresses, the first southward-moving terns begin to put in an appearance.

August–November Autumn passage well under way, including Little Stint, Curlew Sandpiper, Ruff, Spotted Redshank, and as this tails off in late September winter visitors begin to arrive, including occasional Brent Goose, Wigeon, Teal, Pintail.

Habitat

At the southern extremity of Gower, beyond the great sweep of Rhossili Down, 632 feet (192 m) and with the village of Rhossili nestling at its foot, lies Worms Head. This narrow promontory is connected to the mainland by an extensive rocky causeway, revealed as the tide recedes, which allows access for several hours either side of low water. The head is some 37 acres (14.8 ha) in extent and comprises four small hills, rising like a dragon's serrated back (the name 'Worm' in Norse means dragon or serpent). Much of the headland is covered in Red Fescue, this providing ample food for the sheep which graze the table-top plateau of the Inner Worm. Other maritime plants include Spring Squill, Sea Beet, Golden and Rock Samphire, Tree-mallow, Rock Sea-lavender, Sea Stork's-bill and Buck's-horn Plantain.

Species

The seabird colonies are the most important feature and the one which attracts birdwatchers to this spot. Several species breed no further east along the shores of South Wales, the Kittiwake being the most numerous of these. It first nested here in 1943 and by 1976 the population had increased to 460 pairs, with a further 146 pairs at Devil's Truck near Mewslade; similar numbers are still present. Guillemots and Razorbills both nest, though as for the Kittiwake many of their sites are visible only from the sea. In 1982, counts revealed some 250 Guillemots and about 40 Razorbills.

Puffins are an exciting prospect here, as indeed they are wherever they nest. They were first recorded at Worms Head, in 1848, by the great Swansea naturalist Lewis Weston Dillwyn, who described them as breeding in Rabbit burrows. Rats caused a subsequent decline — how often we hear of the colonies suffering this fate — and as a result for many years only a handful of pairs survived, using cliff crevices; there is now much debate as to whether the occasional sighting of these birds means that a pair or two still nest. You will, however, have to search hard for a sight of the Puffins here.

The large gulls have had mixed fortunes. Lesser Black-backed Gulls, at one time nesting in small numbers, have now ceased, probably the result of increased visitor numbers and predation by Foxes which regularly cross to the head. Herring Gulls numbered up to 1,000 pairs in the early 1940s, but now only a small colony survives. Great Black-backed Gulls have followed the same pattern, with 25 pairs in 1941 but only a few at the present time. Other breeding species include several pairs of Fulmars, Shags, Meadow and Rock Pipits and Jackdaws.

Passage waders frequent the rocky causeway, and whatever the season, even at the height of the summer, you will find Oystercatchers and Turnstones there. From August onwards, look out also for Purple Sandpipers, a wader often overlooked as it generally occurs in small numbers well distributed over miles of rocky coast. Common Scoters, outliers from the immense flocks in Carmarthen Bay, often move close in under the Worm, and sometimes sizeable numbers congregate in Rhossili Bay. Eiders also wander here, though the main flock is at

Whiteford 8 miles (12.8 km) to the north. Worms Head ought to be a good vantage point for seawatching. In certain weather conditions, and particularly following strong southwest winds, Manx Shearwaters, Gannets, terns and auks get pushed high into Carmarthen Bay and are seen off the head. There have been no long-term systematic observations here, a challenge for some seawatcher to take up.

Timing

Visits are entirely dependent on the tide if you wish to cross from the mainland. Enquire in Rhossili as to times, or telephone the Coastguard if in any doubt. Cross as the tide begins to recede from the rocky causeway and you should then have several hours ashore. For those wishing to view from a distance, the cliffs opposite the head offer a fine vantage point.

Access

The B4247 ends in Rhossili village, where there is an ample car park. From here, a wide cliff path leads southwest to Rhossili Point, where the old Coastguard Lookout is now a small information kiosk. Nearby, a path descends to the rocky causeway, and once on the head itself there is a footpath to the most westerly point, though visitors are asked, in the interests of the seabird colonies, not to proceed to the outer section between mid-March and July. Worms Head and the whole 6 miles (9.6 km) of cliff stretching eastwards to Port-Eynon is a nature reserve managed by the Glamorgan Wildlife Trust, the National Trust and the Nature Conservancy Council, who all have holdings here. There is a coastal footpath, and this must be one of the best sections of cliff coast in the whole of southwest Britain.

Calendar

Resident Cormorant, Shag, Eider, Common Scoter, Kestrel, Peregrine, Oystercatcher, Turnstone, Lesser Black-backed, Herring and Great Black-backed Gulls, Rock Pipit, Stonechat, Jackdaw, Raven.

December–February Red-throated and Great Northern Divers, Purple Sandpiper. Fulmars and Kittiwakes return to their colonies and both Guillemots and Razorbills make occasional visits to the cliffs.

March–May Puffins arrive in early April and by early May all seabirds have commenced nesting. Passage migrants include Whimbrel, Common Sandpiper, Wheatear, Black Redstart and Ring Ouzel.

June–July Manx Shearwater, Gannet and occasional terns offshore. By end of period Guillemots and Razorbills have left the cliffs, having completed their breeding cycle.

August–November Puffins depart in early August, Kittiwakes a little later and Fulmars during early September. Seabird passage possible offshore until late September, when winter visitors begin to appear.

37 CRAIG YR ADERYN

Map 37
OS Map 124

Habitat

The Cormorant is sufficiently widespread on the Welsh coast and as a visitor to inland waters that it does not normally evoke great interest for the birdwatcher. One colony, however, merits mention, indeed a section of its own, for that at Craig yr Aderyn — 'Bird Rock' — near Tywyn in south Merioneth is unique. Prehistoric seas once flowed up the broad inlet of what is now the flat farmland bordering the Afon Dysynni, to the very foot of the rock which towers nearly 700 feet (213 m) above the valley. Nowadays Cardigan Bay is some 5 miles (8 km) distant, but still the Cormorants come to this ancestral crag, as they have probably done from the earliest of times.

Cormorant

Species

About 40 pairs of Cormorants regularly nest on Craig yr Aderyn. The colony has probably never been much larger, despite local tradition, as numbers are restricted by the availability of suitable ledges. Edward Lhuyd first described the colony in 1695, when he referred to 'corvorants, rock pigeons and hawks that breed on it'. William Catherall, in his *History of Wales* written in 1828, provides an early description of the rock and its seabird inhabitants:

> 'Craig Aderyn is a most picturesque and lofty rock, so called from the numerous birds which nightly retire among its crevices: the noise they make at nightfall is most hideously dissonant, and as the scenery around is extremely wild and romantic, the ideas engendered by such a clamour in the gloom of the evening in so dismal and desolate a spot are not the most soothing or agreeable. Towards twilight some large aquatic fowls from the neighbouring marsh may be seen majestically wending their way to this the place of nocturnal rest.'

Do not be put off by this, in places sombre, account. Craig yr Aderyn is well worth a visit, and you will be rewarded with spectacular views of Cormorants flighting to and fro high above your head. Look out also for Choughs, for all of the pairs nesting in Merioneth do so at inland sites and this is one; indeed, here they nest at one of the few natural inland sites in Wales, most pairs preferring quarries and mineshafts. There is a chance of birds of prey: Buzzard, Kestrel and even Peregrine.

Timing
No particular time. Outside the breeding season, however, the late afternoon and early evening, when, as William Catherall pointed out, the birds return to roost, may reveal most activity.

Access
Leave the A493 Tywyn to Dolgellau road at Bryncrug (SH609034) and follow the unclassified road along the east side of the Dysynni Valley. The road eventually passes directly below Craig yr Aderyn, from where views may be obtained looking up at the colony.

Calendar

Resident Cormorant, Buzzard, Kestrel, Peregrine, Skylark, Meadow Pipit, Magpie, Chough, Jackdaw, Raven, Carrion Crow, Chaffinch.

December–February Fieldfare, Redwing, Brambling.

March–May Summer migrants arrive, including Swallow, Wheatear, Redstart, Whinchat, Willow Warbler, Whitethroat.

June–July All residents and summer visitors present.

August–November Summer visitors depart, Swallows among the last with some in the area until early October, overlapping with the arrival of winter thrushes and the influx of finches.

Habitat

Although not so renowned for its birds as some other estuaries, the Mawddach deserves inclusion for it surely is the most beautiful estuary in Wales, if not in the whole of Britain. The Afon Mawddach, some 22 miles (35.2 km), is the longest river wholly within the Snowdonia National Park. Rising on high ground to the northeast, it plunges through the Coed y Brenin forest, gathering force with the addition of numerous tributaries, before it reaches the estuary and its wide sandflats surrounded by steep wooded hills. It is then a further 7 miles (11.2 km) before it gains the sea at Barmouth, squeezing through a narrow exit past a spit extending north from the southern shore. A little inland on the south side is Arthog Bog, alas a mere vestige of its former glory, for vast quantities of peat were extracted in days gone by to be burnt on the fires of Dolgellau and nearby villages. Gold has been mined in the hills around the Mawddach since Roman times, and there are numerous disused shafts and relics of former workings. Proposals have been made to extract gold from the sands of the estuary itself; fortunately these have not materialised, but they remain as yet another threat to a Welsh estuary. Some of the woodlands are of interest. The Royal Society for the Protection of Birds has a reserve of 114 acres (46 ha) at Coed Garth Gell, bounded on one side by a dramatic gorge; Sessile Oak and Birch are the commonest trees within the reserve, which is interspersed with heathy glades.

Species

Shelducks and Red-breasted Mergansers breed on or close to the estuary, and one of the sights during June and July is the broods of ducklings escorted by adult birds. Common Sandpipers breed on the upper estuary and along the tributary rivers. With few areas of suitable low-lying land, there is little scope for other waders to breed. Only small numbers of wildfowl and waders frequent the estuary, but most species can be seen and in due season include Oystercatcher, Ringed and Golden Plovers, Lapwing, Dunlin, Bar-tailed Godwit, Curlew and Redshank, with occasionally such birds as Curlew Sandpiper and Little Stint. Small numbers of terns move into the estuary in late summer as they travel south from colonies in Anglesey and Lancashire. Ospreys have occasionally been seen, on passage from nesting sites in Scotland. Most regular species occur in the surrounding woodlands and on the hills above, including Buzzard, all three woodpeckers, Tree Pipit, Whinchat, Redstart, Wood Warbler and Pied Flycatcher.

Timing

For visits to the estuary, tide tables should be consulted. The woodlands can be enjoyed at all times of day, though a spring visit is best made in the early morning, when bird song is at its peak.

Access

The RSPB and the North Wales Naturalists' Trust operate an information centre imaginatively situated in a long disused signal box beside the toll bridge at Penmaenpool (SH696185) and open daily from May to late September. Intending visitors should call here first for an update of bird news, while the upper floor provides an excellent vantage point for a section of the upper estuary. Using the old railway line, there is a walk along the whole section of the southern shore from Penmaenpool to Morfa Mawddach, from where you can cross to Barmouth by footbridge. The line east from Penmaenpool allows one to look at another section of estuary together with a small area of reedbeds and willow scrub. The northern shore is not so accessible save on the lower section at the approaches to Barmouth. Access to the RSPB reserve at Coed Garth Gell is by public footpath from SH687191, just west of the north side of the toll bridge, while excellent general views may be obtained from the New Precipice Walk, high above the upper reaches of the estuary, at SH705200.

Calendar

Resident Cormorant, Grey Heron, Mute Swan, Shelduck, Mallard, Red-breasted Merganser, Sparrowhawk, Buzzard, Kestrel, Oystercatcher, Ringed Plover, Herring and Great Black-backed Gulls, Tawny Owl, woodpeckers, Grey Wagtail, tit family, Nuthatch, Treecreeper, Jay, Raven, Greenfinch, Goldfinch, Chaffinch.

December–February Great Crested and Little Grebes, Wigeon, Teal, Goldeneye, Golden Plover, Lapwing, Dunlin, Snipe, Curlew, Green-shank, Turnstone, Black-headed and Common Gulls, Kingfisher, Dipper.

March–May Winter visitors depart. Whimbrel, Common Sandpiper, Sandwich Tern, Tree Pipit, Redstart, Sedge, Garden and Wood Warblers, Blackcap, Chiffchaff, Spotted and Pied Flycatchers.

June–July All resident and summer visitors present. First passage waders return, chance of terns particularly at estuary mouth.

August–November Summer visitors depart, wader numbers peak during mid-September and winter ducks begin to arrive shortly afterwards. In the woods tits band together, often joined by Goldcrests and Treecreepers. Winter visitors such as Fieldfare and Redwing from mid-October, Siskins and Redpolls possible in the valley.

39 MORFA HARLECH AND MORFA DYFFRYN

Habitat

Most spectacular of all the Welsh castles is that of Harlech, built on a 200-foot-high (61-m) spur of Lower Cambrian sandstone, an outlier of the Harlech Dome, between 1283 and 1289 by the master craftsmen of Edward I. Such a superb site, such fortifications, that in 1294 a mere 37 men defended the castle against the entire Welsh army. One can obtain few finer views of coastal Wales than from the now peaceful battlements, whose only sentinels are Feral Pigeons and Jackdaws: north to the sandhills and warrens of Morfa Harlech and Traeth Bach, north to the confluence of the Afon Dwyryd and Afon Glaslyn Estuaries, or south towards Shell Island and the equally great sandhills of Morfa Dyffryn. Both sites now include National Nature Reserves managed by the Nature Conservancy Council.

The Morfa Harlech NNR covers some 2,670 acres (1,080 ha) where wave action from the south has continually pushed shingle, silts and sands northwards, so that now a vast expanse of flatland has developed, fronting the original coast which ran to the northeast. Trapped between dunes and the high ground is a marshy area with prolific Sharp-flowered Rush, while the swamps contain Bogbean, Common Pondweed and Yellow Flag. The dunes have formed into a series of parallel ridges which curve towards the estuary. The new dunes close to the shore are dominated by Sand Couch, then, as one moves inland, by Marram and on the older dunes by a rich lichen and bryophyte flora with higher plants such as Portland Spurge, Lady's Bedstraw, Burnet Rose, Restharrow and Wild Thyme. Tucked among the dunes are botanically rich slacks with Creeping Willow, Variegated Horsetail, Silverweed, Marsh Helleborine, Early Marsh-orchid and Sharp Rush, this latter first recorded in Britain here in 1639. Travel 6 miles (9.6 km) south to Morfa Dyffryn and pass quickly through the holiday encampments of Shell Island to the 490 acres (198 ha) of the NNR. The dunes have much the same structure as Morfa Harlech, and once again the slacks provide the highlights, including Sea Centaury, Green-flowered Helleborine and Bee and Pyramidal Orchids.

Species

After the north shore of the Dyfi, the estuary at Traeth Bach is the most important in Merioneth, though it lacks the regular visits from the wild geese which are a feature of the Dyfi. Up to 3,000 birds winter here, the main species being Shelduck, Wigeon, Teal and Mallard together with waders such as Dunlin, Curlew and Redshank. There are small numbers of Pintails, Tufted Ducks and Goldeneyes. Red-breasted Mergansers were first proved nesting in Merioneth at Traeth Bach in 1957, and now about ten pairs nest and birds are recorded throughout the year. The marshes at Morfa Harlech are of interest, with Shelduck, Oystercatcher, Ringed Plover, Lapwing, Curlew, Redshank and Black-headed Gull all nesting. Small numbers of wildfowl come here in winter, including a regular flock of Whooper Swans, up to 30 in number, which tend to frequent the upper reaches of the estuary near Minffordd on the Caernarvonshire side. Red-throated Divers are regularly seen offshore, together with the occasional Great Northern Diver. Morfa Dyffryn is not so noted for its birds, only a small number of species breeding, though the shoreline is of interest in winter with Scaup, Eider, Common Scoter and Long-tailed Duck regularly seen offshore. In winter, birds such as Hen Harrier, Merlin, Peregrine and Short-eared Owl hunt over the sandhills.

Timing

When visiting the estuaries, consult the tide table as always. For the coastal hinterland time of day is less important, though best in the early morning, especially at Morfa Dyffryn, during the holiday season.

Access

Morfa Harlech Visits to the NNR are possible only on application for a permit to the NCC North Wales Regional Office. One can approach from Harlech by way of the car park at SH574317, where there is access to the shore. A footpath also leaves the A496 at SH574317, while further east another leaves the A496 at SH610362 and leads to Ynys Gifftan on the eastern boundary of the reserve.

Morfa Dyffryn Head for Shell Island, leaving the A496 at SH585267 in Llanbedr; good views out to sea may be obtained from Shell Island and from Llandanwg to the north. For the nature reserve, leave the road at SH568272 and continue south on foot. Alternatively, leave the A496 at SH586224 south of Dyffryn Ardudwy and drive to the beach car park; from here one can walk north along the shore.

Calendar

Resident Cormorant, Grey Heron, Mute Swan, Shelduck, Mallard, Red-breasted Merganser, Kestrel, Oystercatcher, Ringed Plover, Lapwing, Curlew, Redshank, Black-headed, Herring and Great Black-backed Gulls, Skylark, Meadow Pipit, Pied Wagtail, Reed Bunting.

December–February Red-throated and Great Northern Divers, Great Crested Grebe, Whooper Swan, Wigeon, Teal, Pintail, Tufted Duck, Scaup, Eider, Common Scoter, Goldeneye, Hen Harrier, Merlin, Peregrine, Short-eared Owl.

March–May Wheatear, Swallow and Sand Martin from late March, Cuckoo and smaller migrants such as Grasshopper and Sedge Warblers, Whitethroat, Spotted Flycatcher during April, also wader passage at the same time including Whimbrel and Common Sandpiper.

June–July Breeding species still present. Manx Shearwater occasionally seen offshore, also some terns. First autumn waders appear on estuary.

August–November Wader passage throughout early part of period, with a chance of scarce species such as Little Stint, Curlew Sandpiper, Ruff,

Black-tailed Godwit and Spotted Redshank. Winter ducks start arriving from late September, and a chance of seeing Whooper Swans from mid-November. Do not forget the sandhills for winter predators and possibility of birds such as Twite and Snow Bunting.

Habitat

The beautiful Vale of Ffestiniog effectively divides the main massif of Snowdonia from the Rhinog range to the south. The woodlands, especially those on the north side of the vale, are particularly important, and a major section of some 160 acres (65 ha) forms the Coedydd Maentwrog National Nature Reserve, extending for nearly 1½ miles (2.4 km) along the valley side. Most is made up of Sessile Oak over 100 years of age, with Birch, Rowan, Sycamore and Ash and also some Bracken areas. When the reserve was acquired Rhododendron had come to dominate one section, but this has subsequently been removed to allow native species to become re-established. At the eastern end, there are some wet heath areas between drier ridges. Several small streams and flushes cross the reserve, and these add further diversity and help with an impressive plant list. There is an extensive lichen flora on the trees, including several scarce species in the *Parmelia* and *Lobaria* groups. The flowering plants include Primrose, Selfheal, Lesser Celandine, Corn Mint, Purging Flax and Lady's Bedstraw. Red Squirrels have not been seen since 1971, and alas the Grey Squirrel is now abundant. Other mammals present include Fox, Badger, Weasel, Wood Mouse and Bank Vole. A small herd of wild goats, sometimes up to 20 strong, uses the woodlands from time to time.

Species

Hole-nesting birds have been further attracted to the woodlands by the provision of nestboxes, the most numerous of the occupants being the Pied Flycatcher. A main food source for this handsome summer migrant and indeed for other insectivorous species is the larvae of the Mottled Umber, a moth which in 1979 and 1980 reached plague proportions, stripping the oaks of up to 95 per cent of their foliage. Other species include several members of the tit family and the Redstart. All three woodpeckers are present, as are the Nuthatch and Treecreeper. Birds of prey include Sparrowhawk, Buzzard, Kestrel and Tawny Owl. Jays are common in the woodland, and there is usually a pair or two of Ravens. Does the Nightjar still cling on here? Sadly, this now seems doubtful, since it has disappeared from many former haunts. The small lake of Llyn Mair attracts Little Grebes, Grey Herons, Mute and Whooper Swans, Mallards, Pochards, Tufted Ducks, Goldeneyes, Moorhens and Coots.

Timing

Visits are best made in May or June, no particular time being best unless you wish to hear the dawn chorus.

Access

The A487 together with the B4410 pass through the valley, Llyn Mair being easily viewed from the latter. A nature trail (booklet available from the NCC North Wales Regional Office) commences at SH654414, and passes through the western end of the nature reserve. For the main block of woodland there is a public footpath from the entrance at SH659410.

Treecreeper

Attention should be drawn to the Ffestiniog Light Railway, which provides spectacular views of the valley and the surrounding hills, even if birdwatching opportunities may be limited.

Calendar

Resident Grey Heron, Mute Swan, Mallard, Sparrowhawk, Buzzard, Kestrel, Pheasant, Moorhen, Coot, Woodpigeon, Stock Dove, Tawny Owl, all three woodpeckers, Grey Wagtail, Goldcrest, tit family, Nuthatch, Treecreeper, Jay, Jackdaw, Raven, Chaffinch, Redpoll, Bullfinch.

December–February Little Grebe, Whooper Swan, Teal, Pochard, Tufted Duck, Goldeneye, Fieldfare, Redwing, Siskin.

March–May Winter visitors depart, though some ducks may remain well into April, summer visitors arrive and include Cuckoo, Tree Pipit, Redstart, Garden Warbler, Blackcap, Wood Warbler, Chiffchaff, Willow Warbler, Spotted and Pied Flycatchers.

June–July All residents and summer visitors present.

August–November Summer visitors have largely departed by early September, though chance of both Blackcap and Chiffchaff remaining to October and possibly even overwintering. Winter wildfowl start coming to Llyn Mair from late September, followed by Fieldfare and Redwing and possibly Brambling moving to the valley during late October.

Habitat

Situated just east of Pontypool, and separated from the valley of the Afon Lwyd to the west and the Usk to the east by ridges rising to about 500 feet (150 m), Llandegfedd Reservoir covers nearly 400 acres (162 ha) and was constructed in 1964 to supply water for Cardiff. The Sor Brook flows from the reservoir and joins the Usk at Caerleon, nearly 5 miles (8 km) to the south. The land surrounding the reservoir is mainly agricultural, with woodland on the steeper slopes.

Species

Llandegfedd Reservoir quickly established itself as the most important open freshwater site for birds in southeast Wales. A record of no fewer than three Black-throated Divers here on 7 January 1985 is particularly noteworthy; only a small number winter in Wales, mainly off the coast. Great Crested Grebes have nested twice, in 1972 and 1985, and are present throughout the year with the highest numbers, usually not exceeding 20, in midwinter. Both Slavonian and Black-necked Grebes have occurred here. A pair of Black-necked Grebes in summer plumage in May 1976 and a single bird in April 1985 were especially noteworthy and caused a few hearts to flutter. Cormorants, whose nearest colony is on Steep Holm, and Grey Herons regularly feed here, while Mute Swans nest. An increasing number of Bewick's Swans now come here in winter, with a maximum count of 68 in January 1985; most use the reservoir as a roost, flying 5 miles (8 km) northeast during the day to graze on the Olway Meadows. Winter duck numbers can be impressive, with Wigeon at over 1,000 strong being the most numerous, followed by up to 750 Teals and 600 Mallards. Pochards are the most numerous diving duck, with up to 500 recorded, its companion, the Tufted Duck, generally not exceeding 200 in number. Small parties of Goldeneyes visit the reservoir

Tufted Ducks

throughout the winter, and in 1984 three remained until 26 May. Goosanders have so far not bred in the county, though they have been seen displaying at one site so it can only be a matter of time; most that are seen at Llandegfedd are birds flighting in at dusk, presumably from the Usk, the highest number so far recorded being 51 in February 1985. As at other South Wales waters, the Ruddy Duck is now a regular visitor. The gathering of Coots can be noisily impressive, with over 200 in midwinter, while in 1970 1,000 were recorded; with few good marginal areas, it is not surprising that breeding is rather infrequent, the pair in 1985 being the first since 1976. Yellow Wagtails breed in the fields beside the reservoir, some five pairs in 1985, in which year a pair of the 'blue-headed' race was observed from mid-April until mid-August and four young were seen during July.

Waders recorded on passage include Oystercatcher, Little Ringed and Ringed Plovers, Green and Wood Sandpipers and Turnstone. Large numbers of Black-headed, Lesser Black-backed and Herring Gulls visit the reservoir, while a Mediterranean Gull was an unusual visitor on at least three occasions in 1985. Most remarkable was the third record of the Great Skua for Monmouthshire, a freshly dead but decapitated and partly eaten bird in October 1977. Usually it is the Great Skua that does the decapitating, so what was the story behind this? Terns pass through in small numbers in most autumns, but the 36 Black Terns in 1970 was an exceptional total for the county.

Timing

Not too critical, but early morning is the best, or, if you are hoping in winter to see returning Bewick's Swans or Goosanders, the late afternoon. Boating does take place, so there is always a chance of disturbance.

Access

There are walks along several sections of the shore, and access points from the various unclassified roads which pass by or close to the reservoir at SO332006, SO321002 and ST328986. A descriptive leaflet is available from Gwent County Council.

Calendar

Resident Great Crested Grebe, Cormorant, Grey Heron, Mute Swan, Mallard, Buzzard, Pied Wagtail, woodland passerines.

December–February Bewick's Swan, Wigeon, Teal, Pochard, Tufted Duck, Goldeneye, Red-breasted Merganser, Goosander, Ruddy Duck, Coot, Snipe, Black-headed, Common and Herring Gulls.

March–May Winter visitors depart, though some, especially Tufted Duck, remain until May. Summer passerines from early April onwards, when Swallows and Sand Martins start hawking over the water, being joined in May by Swifts, Yellow Wagtails from late April.

June–July Breeding species all present. Depending on water levels, returning waders such as Green Sandpiper may call.

August–November Tern and wader passage in August and September, from then on winter visitors begin to arrive, with Bewick's Swans in mid-November usually the last to be seen. Chance of Siskin and Redpoll in the Alders around the reservoir.

42 SEVERN ESTUARY AND GWENT LEVELS

Map 42
OS Map 171

Habitat

The estuary of the Severn in Monmouthshire varies in width from 2 miles (3.2 km) just below the Severn Bridge to some 11 miles (17.6 km) at the Glamorgan boundary 20 miles (32 km) to the southwest: a vast area with numerous mud- and sandbanks bearing such names, well known to mariners, as Middle Grounds, Welsh Grounds, Bedwin Sands and the Lady Bank, beneath which the Severn Tunnel runs. There is a single island, the Denny, a tiny rock some 50 feet (15 m) high. Behind the sea-walls and the tidal sluices which keep the Severn at bay lie the Caldicot Levels, and west of the River Usk the levels of Peterstone Wentlooge, together one of the largest remaining areas of unimproved wet grassland in lowland Britain. This is rich farmland for the most part, though there is some industry also, with an interlacing of ditches or 'reens'. Such an agricultural area means that only fragments of the once extensive fens remain. One is the Magor Nature Reserve of the Gwent Trust for Nature Conservation, a 59-acre (24-ha) site in which are preserved some old, unimproved pastures, ditches, pools and some scrub woodland; a hide overlooks the main pool. On the estuary and its guardian walls grow plants such as Thrift, Scurvygrass, Sea Aster, Sea Plantain, Glasswort and Common Cord-grass. The ditches intersecting the fields have a rich aquatic flora which includes common plants such as Common Reed, Common Pondweed, Water-plantain and Marsh-marigold. In a few spots, plants of restricted distribution, at least in Wales, still survive, among them Arrowhead, Floating Club-rush and the exquisite floating Frogbit. Dragonflies and damselflies are numerous in summer, and several scarce species have been recorded. Among the mammals Water Voles are numerous, though sadly the Otter is now but a memory.

The Severn, like a number of other estuaries in Britain, has been under consideration for development; there is a need for a second road crossing, the question being whether this should be by bridge or barrage. If a barrage is constructed, and it has been suggested that this could be as far west as a line from Aberthaw to Watchet, at least 80 per cent of the intertidal areas on which the waders are dependent for food will be lost. The resulting freshwater lake could, however, have benefits for wildfowl, though this will not compensate for the disappearance of the waders. Another, more controversial, plan is the reclamation of a large section of estuary westwards to the Usk Patch for use as an international airport, freshwater reservoir, docks and industrial development land. Again, most of the wader feeding areas would be lost. It is not just the feeding areas that are under threat, but also the roosting and resting sites beyond the sea-wall. As these are changed, as disturbance increases, so there is a continual decrease in the number of safe places the birds can use, and eventually a decline in numbers.

Species

The Severn is the seventh most important estuary in Britain, and about a third of the birds are dependent on the Monmouthshire shore. Over recent years, increasing numbers of Oystercatchers have used the Severn Estuary; formerly this was only a winter visitor in small numbers, but now several hundred are present for much of the year, and breeding has been reported from several sites. Ringed and Grey Plovers are also present throughout the year, though in midsummer numbers will drop to a mere handful of birds, usually fewer than ten and very difficult to locate. Lapwings still breed in some of the estuary-side fields, and by July the flocks total several thousand which resort to the intertidal zone to feed, returning inland when the flats are covered. Similar numbers of Knots are seen, while the Dunlin is the most numerous of all, with up to 20,000 in midwinter. Unlike on some other estuaries, the number of Black-tailed and Bar-tailed Godwits on the Severn is extremely small, most of the former occurring in the Peterstone Wentlooge area between April and October. Several hundred Curlews are present throughout the year, with the lowest numbers in May; they have long since ceased to nest in coastal Monmouthshire, though there are still a few pairs in the hills. Redshank numbers have declined and probably only a handful of pairs nest, while in midwinter numbers rise to about 800. Not surprisingly in view of the scarcity of rocky shores, Turnstone numbers are small, though the species is seen in all months. Other waders which occur occasionally, or on passage, include Sanderling, Little Stint, Curlew Sandpiper, Ruff, Jack Snipe, Whimbrel, Greenshank and Green and Common Sandpipers.

Shelducks breed, and several hundred are present throughout the year, with the lowest numbers in August and September. Mallards are also resident, and reach a peak during the early autumn, when up to 500 have been counted. Among the winter ducks, Wigeons begin to arrive in late September and rapidly reach a peak of up to 1,500 birds, most remaining until late February. A handful of Teals may be seen in August, by midwinter their numbers rising to around 500. An interesting development is the establishment of both Pochard and Tufted Duck as regular winter visitors to the estuary, with up to 100 of the former and as many as 600 of the latter. The Scaup also seems to be increasing, and in March 1985 no fewer than 56 were seen on the river in the Peterstone Wentlooge to St Bride's area. Common Scoters are reported in all months in extremely low numbers, usually fewer than ten, while scarce visitors include Eider, Long-tailed Duck and Velvet Scoter.

Manx Shearwaters, Storm Petrels, Gannets and Kittiwakes are regularly seen offshore in small numbers, especially in late summer. Skuas are also seen on passage at this time, while the sprinkling of spring occurrences is of interest, possibly none more so than the three Pomarine Skuas seen moving upriver on 6 May 1985, only the second county record. When last seen they were climbing high over the Severn Bridge, and from then on, hidden to view, presumably passed across England to the North Sea and so to their Arctic breeding grounds. Small numbers of terns occur in late summer, and there are records of several species of scarce gulls, Mediterranean, Little and Iceland Gulls all having been sighted in recent years. Most remarkable was a Little Auk caught in a tree in St Mary's Churchyard, Nash, on 9 October 1977, only the fourth record in the county of this wanderer from the coastal screes of Greenland; it was released at nearby Goldcliff and flew straight off over the estuary. Rock and Water Pipits regularly visit the coast in winter, but are probably missed by many observers intent on larger and more spectacular birds.

Yellow Wagtail

Breeding species of the hinterland include Water Rail, Moorhen, Snipe, Pied and Yellow Wagtails, Grasshopper, Sedge and Reed Warblers, Tree Sparrow and Reed Bunting. Passage migrants can be in large numbers, especially Swallows and martins, and in the autumn coasting Skylarks, Meadow Pipits, Fieldfares, Redwings, Starlings and Chaffinches. With any luck, you may find Snow Buntings on the sea-wall. Bitterns arrive in some winters, while the record of an American Bittern at Magor from late October to the end of December 1982 was particularly noteworthy; only about 60 have been recorded in Britain and this individual was watched by observers from far and wide.

Timing

Use of the tide tables is essential. When the tide is out, however, there may be passerine migration to observe as birds coast southwest in autumn, while at any season it is always worth spending time exploring the levels.

Access

Caldicot Level A footpath follows the sea-wall from Caldicot at ST476875 to Goldcliff at ST370829, east of the Usk Estuary. There are several access points from the unclassified road which wends its way across the eastern and western sections of the levels, at Magor Pill Farm (ST432856), Redwick Church (ST412840) and Whitson (ST383833).

Wentlooge Level The B4239 runs from Dyffryn on the outskirts of Newport to Rumney, Cardiff. Again, there are several access points leading to the coast, at St Bride's Wentlooge (ST295823), Peterstone Wentlooge (ST268801), and at Sluice Farm (ST253793) almost on the boundary with Glamorgan.

Calendar

Resident Cormorant, Grey Heron, Shelduck, Mallard, Sparrowhawk, Kestrel, Moorhen, Oystercatcher, Ringed Plover, Lapwing, Snipe, Redshank, Black-headed, Lesser Black-backed, Herring and Great Black-backed Gulls, Tawny Owl, Kingfisher, Green Woodpecker, Skylark, Meadow Pipit, Pied Wagtail, Mistle Thrush, Jackdaw, Carrion Crow, Starling, Tree Sparrow, Reed Bunting.

December–February Red-throated Diver, Great Crested Grebe, Bewick's Swan, Wigeon, Teal, Pintail, Pochard, Tufted Duck, Scaup, Common Scoter, Red-breasted Merganser, Hen Harrier, Peregrine, Coot, Ringed and Grey Plovers, Knot, Curlew, Turnstone, Common Gull, Short-eared Owl, Rock Pipit, Siskin, Redpoll, Snow Bunting.

March–May Winter visitors depart but some species, especially the waders, stay well into spring (a few stragglers may even summer), while passage birds during April include Sanderling, Whimbrel and Common Sandpiper. Wheatears on the sea-wall from late March, Swallow passage commences soon after, by end of April summer visitors such as Sedge and Reed Warblers, Whitethroat, and Lesser Whitethroat have arrived, in May Turtle Dove, Swift and Spotted Flycatcher.

June–July All summer residents present. Wader numbers show a steady increase on estuary as July proceeds, while most Shelducks depart on their moult migration.

August–November Wader numbers continue to increase and the first wintering ducks appear during September, by which time most summer visitors have left. Some seabird passage offshore during suitable weather on most days during late August and September, coasting movements of Skylarks, Meadow Pipits, autumn thrushes, Starling and finches from mid-October.

43 LAKE VYRNWY

Map 43
OS Map 125

Habitat

The Afon Vyrnwy flows eastwards from the southern edge of the Berwyns to join the Severn at its great bend beside the Breidden Hills. In the 1880s, Liverpool Corporation gradually acquired about 23,000 acres (9,310 ha) in the upper catchment, and in 1891 a magnificent dam was completed, impounding 1,300 million gallons (5,900 million litres) of water at about 850 feet (260 m) above sea level. Lake Vyrnwy, as the lake was quickly called, is the largest man-made lake in Wales, being nearly 5 miles (8 km) long and with a perimeter of 11 miles (17.6 km). Early in the present century, an extensive period of planting, mainly of conifers, was put in hand on the steep slopes above the water. Patches of deciduous woodland and scrub were retained, and here and there small patches of upland pasture. Climb out of the valley, and you encounter the real gem of Vyrnwy, the extensive heather and grass moorlands at the southwestern end of the Berwyn Range. Mammals on these uplands are generally few, though there can be large numbers of Short-tailed Voles and Pygmy Shrews, while even Moles reach on to the highest ground. Back in the woods, Red Squirrels still occur and there are Polecats and a large population of Badgers. Woodland plants include Oak and Beech Ferns, Wood-sorrel and Enchanter's-nightshade. The White-legged Damselfly, a species of streams and rivers, reaches its northern limit at Lake Vyrnwy.

Species

Pride of place among the small numbers of wildfowl which frequent Lake Vyrnwy must go to the Goosander. In the early 1950s a pair was present during the breeding season and could well have nested, though in this very under-recorded area it is not surprising that proof was not obtained for nearly a further 20 years, when ducklings were seen in 1970. Since then, small numbers have nested regularly and up to seven pairs are now present. In winter the lake may hold as many as 40 Goosanders, which from January onwards engage in their courtship displays. The preferred nest site is a spacious tree hole, and to ensure that sufficient are available specially designed nestboxes have been provided. One of the midsummer sights of Lake Vyrnwy is the broods of ducklings closely escorted by the female. The males depart during May, probably on a moult migration which takes them to Finnmark.

Other breeding waterbirds include up to seven pairs of Great Crested Grebes, though these are often unsuccessful owing to fluctuating water levels, nests being flooded, or left high and dry and so accessible to predators. Mallards and Teals also nest, and are joined in winter by Wigeons, Pochards, Tufted Ducks and Goldeneyes. Occasionally Common Scoters are seen, especially in late summer — a sign possibly of overland migration to winter quarters in southwest Wales? Whooper Swans regularly visit the lake in winter, up to 20 having been recorded. Common Sandpipers, Kingfishers, Grey Wagtails and Dippers all nest beside the lake or on the numerous feeder streams tumbling down from the surrounding hills. When the receding water of late summer leaves a suitable muddy margin at the northwestern end of the lake, waders stop briefly on passage: these have included Oystercatcher, Ringed Plover, Spotted Redshank, Greenshank and Green Sandpiper. Gulls are frequent visitors here, though none nests, and the pre-breeding-season flock of Black-headed Gulls is noteworthy, several thousand roosting here before departing to their colonies on the high moors of North Wales and northern England. Despite the distance from the sea, several species of tern, including Little Tern, have called briefly while on passage.

The woodlands hold as rich a variety of birds as one might encounter in woodlands anywhere in Wales. The Royal Society for the Protection of Birds, which has a nature reserve here, has carried out much woodland management, including the erection of nestboxes, to provide nest sites and a greater diversity of habitat. Both Sparrowhawks and Buzzards nest in the woodland, and there are usually several pairs of Tawny Owls and Long-eared Owls. The latter is a very local breeding species throughout much of Wales. It takes over the old nests of Sparrowhawks, Woodpigeons, Magpies and Carrion Crows for breeding, though the owls themselves are rarely seen; the best evidence for their presence is usually obtained early in the year, when the distinctive triple hoot call is heard, or when the young are in the nest, their call being reminiscent of an unoiled gate. Other notable woodland birds include Black Grouse, Woodcock, Great Spotted Woodpecker, Redstart, Wood Warbler, Firecrest, Pied Flycatcher, Siskin, Redpoll and Common Crossbill. The population of the latter rose to several hundred birds in the summer of

Long-eared Owl

1985, after a prolific cone crop the previous year; 12 months later, numbers had dropped and at times only a handful of birds could be located.

The high hills surrounding Lake Vyrnwy attract several raptors, including up to six pairs of Hen Harriers and in recent years four pairs of Merlins. Peregrines and Kestrels regularly hunt these uplands, while Short-eared Owls breed in some years and in the summer months can often be seen during the day. At the moorland edge where patches of Bracken, scrub and smaller trees occur, look out for Tree Pipit, Whinchat, Stonechat, Grasshopper Warbler and Whitethroat, all summer visitors to the area, for even the Stonechats move to lower ground at the end of the breeding season. Skylarks and Meadow Pipits are numerous right across the hills, and where rocky areas occur look out for Wheatear and Ring Ouzel. Red Grouse breed and so do Curlews, which with their bubbling call seem to be everywhere in the spring and early summer. Golden Plovers breed in small numbers, and in the spring their aerial displays are one of the sights and sounds of the moorland; during incubation and the early stages of fledging, the off-duty bird can usually be seen standing alert on a prominent hummock within the nesting territory.

Timing

Any time of the day, but it is really worth the effort to arrive early in the morning as you then seem to have the whole of the lakeside to yourself. Early morning is certainly preferable on the hills, as bird activity will be at its peak at this time. If it is Woodcock you hope to see, then a dawn or dusk arrival is essential.

Access

If coming from the east, leave the A495 about 12 miles (19.2 km) southwest of Oswestry at SJ193167, pass through Llanfyllin on to the B4393 and so to Llanwddyn near the southeast corner of the lake; the road continues on a shore-hugging circuit of the whole lake. If coming from Dolgellau, leave the A458 at SJ010112 near Llangadfan and follow the B4395 and then the B4393 to reach the lake. Two quite suberb minor roads leave the lake near its northern extremity and climb out of the valley and across the moors. The first leaves Pont Eunant (SH964225) and rises to some 1,600 feet (488 m) before dropping steeply into the upper reaches of the Dyfi. The other leaves the lake at SH965243, passes through the plantations bordering the Afon Nadroedd, and then across several miles of high ground before descending to Bala. There is an RSPB reception and information centre at SH017191, near the southern extremity of the lake, and a public hide on the northeast side which is open all the year. The whole reserve — lake, woodland and upland — extends over an incredible 17,320 acres (7,010 ha), of which 3,500 acres (1,417 ha) is prime heather moor, and is open at all times.

Calendar

Resident Great Crested Grebe, Grey Heron, Teal, Mallard, Goosander, Sparrowhawk, Buzzard, Kestrel, Peregrine, Red and Black Grouse, Pheasant, Moorhen, Coot, Black-headed Gull, Tawny, Long-eared and Short-eared Owls, Great Spotted Woodpecker, Grey and Pied Wagtails,

Dipper, Goldcrest, Firecrest, Carrion Crow, Raven, Chaffinch, Greenfinch, Siskin, Redpoll, Common Crossbill.

December–February Whooper Swan, Wigeon, Pochard, Tufted Duck, Goldeneye, Snow Bunting.

March–May Hen Harrier, Merlin, Golden Plover, Lapwing, Snipe, Woodcock, Curlew, Common Sandpiper, Cuckoo, Kingfisher, Redstart, Whinchat, Stonechat, Wheatear, Garden Warbler, Blackcap, Wood Warbler, Chiffchaff, Willow Warbler, Spotted and Pied Flycatchers.

June–July All summer residents present, a chance of passage waders at lakeside.

August–November Departure of summer visitors, Common Scoter and terns possible, while waders continue to call briefly if water level low. First winter ducks from late September, and from mid-October winter visitors such as Fieldfare and Redwing arrive.

Habitat

An extensive area of water meadows lines the banks of the River Severn downstream of Welshpool. The flooding in this area is not so extensive and prolonged as in former years, but nevertheless it still attracts wildfowl in winter and is worth watching at any time of the year.

Species

Canada Geese were introduced into Montgomeryshire, at Leighton, in 1860 and still thrive there today, with a flock of over 200 in late summer. Since those early days, they have spread to breed in many other localities in the east of the county. While one species has increased, another has declined. Not so many years ago, up to 400 White-fronted Geese wintered in the Severn Valley, centred on Leighton and nearby meadows; now barely a tenth of that number come, a sad event to chronicle. Occasionally other geese make brief visits, while a Barnacle Goose, perhaps a fugitive from some waterfowl collection, spent part of the summer of 1982 here. Small numbers of ducks occur in winter, but the Ruddy Duck in October 1982 was a surprise, even though, as told elsewhere, this species has colonised Anglesey and is spreading west through South Wales. Waders frequent the water meadows in winter, with Lapwings being the main species.

Timing

Early morning when the mist rises from the meadows, and before disturbance moves birds to other parts of the valley or on to the high ground, is the best.

Access

Leave Welshpool on the B4381 and turn south on the B4388 through Leighton; there is access to points overlooking the meadows at SJ239058 and SJ237050. The western side of the meadows is visible from a footpath which runs north from the A490 at SJ228042, parallel with the river, to Welshpool.

Calendar

Resident Little Grebe, Grey Heron, Mute Swan, Canada Goose, Mallard, Sparrowhawk, Buzzard, Pheasant, Moorhen, Stock Dove, Woodpigeon, Kingfisher, Skylark, Meadow Pipit, Grey and Pied Wagtails, Mistle Thrush, Great Tit, Carrion Crow, Raven, Greenfinch, Redpoll, Reed Bunting.

December–February Bewick's Swan, White-fronted Goose, Wigeon, Gadwall, Pintail, Shoveler, Goldeneye, Peregrine, Golden Plover, Lapwing, Jack Snipe, Snipe, Curlew, Redshank, large gulls, Dipper, Fieldfare, Redwing, Brambling, Siskin.

March–May Winter visitors depart. Passage of summer migrants, including Common Sandpiper and Yellow Wagtail.

June–July Resident species coming to end of breeding season, Canada Geese in flock, chance of waders on river.

August–November Summer migrants departing, though Swallows in evidence over the meadows until well into September. Passage waders likely, including Green and Wood Sandpipers and Greenshank. From early October onwards winter visitors arrive, though usually into November before geese are reported.

45 VYRNWY CONFLUENCE

Map 45
OS Map 126

Habitat

The Breidden Ridge rises in three peaks to 1,324 feet (404 m) and dominates the countryside on the Montgomeryshire-Shropshire border. This is a botanist's paradise, visited since the late seventeenth century by those searching for scarce plants such as the Western Spiked Speedwell, Sticky Catchfly and Rock Cinquefoil. For birdwatchers, the place to go in winter is the plain immediately to the north, for here, where the Severn makes a 90-degree turn to flow east, it is joined by the Vyrnwy, hurrying on the last stage of its journey from the Berwyns and the great reservoir to which it gives its name. In winter, especially after heavy rain or a thaw, the fields in the vicinity of the confluence flood and make an excellent temporary habitat.

Species

All three swans occur on the floods, while a number of White-fronted Geese, possibly the flock from Leighton, come here and Pink-footed Geese have occasionally been recorded. There is a nice range of ducks — in January 1982, numbers reached 500 Wigeons, 1,100 Teals, 420 Mallards and 42 Pintails — while smaller numbers of Shovelers, Pochards, Tufted Ducks, Goldeneyes and Goosanders are usually present. Waders are dominated by Lapwings, whose numbers may rise as high as 2,500, being joined by small numbers of Golden Plovers, Jack Snipe, Snipe, Curlews, Green and (surprisingly for midwinter) Common Sandpipers. Sparrowhawk, Merlin and Peregrine are regularly seen.

Dipper

Timing

Not critical, but as always the early morning, before the birds may be disturbed, has much to recommend it.

Access

Right on the border with Shropshire, indeed you will have to stray across at several points. Views may be obtained from the minor road which leaves the B4393 at Crewgreen (SJ327155) for Melverley (SJ333166), from where a road runs east towards Pentre (SJ366177). On the south side of the river a footpath leads north from Pentre Farm (SJ345156), though this will be under water at times in winter.

Calendar

Resident Grey Heron, Mute Swan, Mallard, Kestrel, Grey Partridge, Collared Dove, Grey and Pied Wagtails, Dipper, Wren, Dunnock, Robin, Blackbird, Song and Mistle Thrushes, Magpie, Jackdaw, Rook, Carrion Crow, Starling, House Sparrow, Chaffinch, Goldfinch, Reed Bunting.

December–February Cormorant, Bewick's and Whooper Swans, White-fronted Goose, Wigeon, Teal, Pintail, Shoveler, Pochard, Tufted Duck, Goldeneye, Goosander, Merlin, Peregrine, Coot, Golden Plover, Lapwing, Snipe, Curlew, Fieldfare, Redwing, Brambling, Siskin, Redpoll.

March–May Departure of winter visitors, though a few ducks may hang on until April depending on water levels. Summer visitors arrive, including Common Sandpiper and Yellow Wagtail.

June–July Green and Wood Sandpipers possible, by end of period usually several Common Sandpipers along river, having moved from breeding territories on the higher reaches (the occasional one remains for the winter). Kingfishers arrive at about this time, a species badly affected by recent hard winters so that at times its population in the county has been much reduced.

August–November Arrival of winter wildfowl and waders very dependent on water levels on the meadows. Usually good numbers of Fieldfares and Redwings from late October, when Siskin and Redpoll may feed in the riverside Alders.

46 MILFORD HAVEN WATERWAY

Habitat

From St Ann's Head to Haverfordwest by sea is 21 miles (33.6 km), from the broad waters of Milford Haven with its oil terminals, to the reaches of the Daucleddau, and finally along the twisting course of the Western and Eastern Cleddau Rivers between well-wooded banks to the upper reaches of the tidal limits. The numerous bays and creeks, together with the upper river, are fine areas for wildfowl and waders. For the most part the expanse of intertidal mud is limited, so that, unlike on the larger estuaries elsewhere in Wales, birds are generally not too distant even at low tide. There is an increasing use of the whole waterway by pleasure craft, though this has largely ceased by the time winter birds have arrived, while there are few summer residents to be disturbed. These activities do, however, pose a potential threat. Much of the Western Cleddau is a Regional Wildfowl Refuge designated in 1970, which means that no shooting can take place below high-water mark. Greater efforts need to be made to ensure that illegal shooting is eliminated, while further protected areas are needed on some of the lower reaches of the waterway. A footpath system around the upper part of the haven will provide access and encourage more visitors to previously secluded, rarely visited areas of the shore. Care is, however, taken to ensure that particularly sensitive areas are avoided during the winter months.

As in many other estuaries, large areas of saltings, in the case of Milford Haven just over 50 per cent, have been colonised by Common Cord-grass since it was first introduced here in the 1940s. The Marsh Pea, previously known from only one other site in Wales, was discovered in 1982 beside the Eastern Cleddau. Another interesting plant found in a few secluded estuarine marshes is the Marsh-mallow, the roots of which were used in former days to make sweets of the same name. Yellow Horned-poppy, a scarce plant in Wales, is found on the shingle bank at Dale; its unpleasant-smelling sap is considered a cure for bruises, hence the alternative name of Bruisewort. The woodlands on the steep, sometimes rocky slopes bordering parts of Milford Haven and its estuaries are of special interest to botanists. The Wild Service-tree or Wild Checker, found mainly in eastern England, is restricted in west Wales virtually to these estuarine woods; in autumn the few trees can easily be located by the bright red of the turning leaves, contrasting with the greens and yellows of the Sessile Oak.

The limestone bluff at the confluence of the Carew and Cresswell Rivers provides a rather special habitat. Stone has been quarried here for several hundred years, in the past most of it being transported by sea, using small vessels taken up narrow man-made creeks into the quarry workings for loading. Now the creeks are silted up, the haunt of Redshank and Common Sandpiper, and the quarries remain largely hidden by the scrub and woodland. Where the soil cover is thin and scrub has been unable to colonise, a rich flora has developed. Here one can find such plants as Hairy Rock-cress, Yellow-wort, Bee Orchid and Autumn Gentian. At Dale the hand of Man is also evident: a small lagoon, the result of gravel extraction for airfield construction during

World War II, provides an extra habitat. At Westfield Pill, near Neyland, a marina has been opened in the lower reaches; the upper section is hopefully to be designated a nature reserve, though at the time of writing whether this is to be a tidal lagoon or freshwater lake is still under discussion.

Species

Breeding species are few and far between: there is simply not a sufficient area of saltmarsh to provide space for birds such as Oystercatcher and Redshank. Countless generations of Grey Herons have nested in Slebech Park. Were they here when the Knights Hospitallers of St John of Jerusalem had their retreat here in the twelfth century? In recent years there have been up to 30 nests, the builders and their offspring always being much in evidence on the nearby estuaries. Canada Geese were introduced to Boulston beside the Western Cleddau over 30 years ago and have nested ever since, the flock usually numbering about 120 in late summer. The Shelduck is the only other breeding species, but its success seems to be low and the broods usually total no more than 60 ducklings; in winter there is a major influx and by January up to 1,400 are present, an important part of the population of western Britain.

Cormorants fish along the whole length of the estuary and small numbers gather to rest, to dry their wings, on the shingle ridge at the entrance to Sprinkle Pill. Great Crested Grebes winter in small numbers throughout the estuary, while Little Grebes winter on the lagoon at Dale and in the upper reaches; occasionally the rare grebes are seen. All three divers come into the entrance of Milford Haven, being most frequent in Dale Roads and Angle Bay and only occasional further upstream. Small parties of Brent Geese, at times only single individuals, are likely to pay infrequent visits at any time between October and March, both the light-breasted and dark-breasted races having been recorded. Up to 5,000 Wigeons winter, while Teals may reach 3,000, both totals being of national importance. Mallards by contrast barely reach 100, and small numbers of Pintails can be seen in midwinter. Goldeneyes frequent the river right to the upper limits of tidal waters, where as many as 50 may gather in small parties; certainly these are one of the sights of the estuary. Smaller numbers of Red-breasted Mergansers and scarce visitors such as Scaup, Eider, Long-tailed Duck and Smew are all recorded. A most unusual visitor on one occasion was a Black Guillemot flying downstream at Hook. Stragglers of several species of geese, perhaps attracted by the resident Canada Geese, have been seen on the estuary, including Pink-footed, White-fronted and Greylag Geese.

In Pembrokeshire, most Oystercatchers winter along the sea coast on the sandy beaches and rocky shores, but sometimes up to 300 or so can be found scattered throughout the lower part of Milford Haven. Small numbers of Ringed and Grey Plovers overwinter, the Gann at Dale and Angle Bay being the most likely places to see the latter, a most attractive wader from the high-Arctic tundras and one of the world's greatest migrants, occurring on all coasts to 40°S. Very small numbers of Knots and Sanderlings winter, and then only sporadically, contrasting with Dunlins which seem to be everywhere on the estuary and whose aggregate numbers on occasions reach 4,000. Careful ringing studies at Angle Bay show that the Pembrokeshire Dunlins come largely from

Arctic Europe, though birds en route to Iceland move through in spring. The other most numerous waders are Curlew and Redshank, both of which may exceed over 1,000 individuals at times. Greenshanks appear in small numbers — indeed, some 40 years ago it was on the Gann that this species began regularly to overwinter in Britain. Two other waders now seem regularly to overwinter on the Pembrokeshire estuaries, though you will have to search the creeks and narrow pills. These are the Green and Common Sandpipers, favourite sites for both being Westfield Pill and Castle Pill. Scarce waders which appear from time to time include Avocet, Little Stint, Curlew Sandpiper, Ruff and Wood Sandpiper. As on other estuaries in Wales, vagrant gulls are now very much a feature. Perhaps vagrant is the wrong word, for those who carefully study the flocks will be regularly rewarded with sightings of Mediterranean, Little and Ring-billed Gulls.

Timing

Timing is not so critical on the upper reaches as on many other estuaries. The river is narrow, and even at low tide only a limited area of foreshore close to the bank is available for feeding birds, so that observations can be made at reasonable ranges. On the lower reaches, and especially at Angle Bay, on the Gann and in the Pembroke River, the areas of intertidal mud and sand are much greater and observations need to be timed for the couple of hours or so either side of high water before the birds disperse.

Access

The Gann The B4327 Haverfordwest to Dale road passes close to the shore at SM808067, where there is a small car park. From here, excellent views can be obtained across the flats, and at times Turnstones feed on the beach within a few yards of the car. It is possible to walk northeast below the shingle ridge separating the lagoon from the estuary, and so obtain good views of both. Beyond is an area of saltings and the sinuous, narrow, high-banked course of the Gann River, haunt of winter Greenshanks.

Sandy Haven Access at Sandy Haven (SM855074) or near Sandy Haven Chapel (SM857086).

Castle Pill Access at Black Bridge on the B4325 Milford Haven to Neyland road at SM916061, or in Pill (SM914056).

Llanstadwell The tiny creek and ridge at SM958050 is easily viewed from the car; the first Ring-billed Gull for Pembrokeshire was here for eight days in 1985.

Western Cleddau At the time of writing, the Pembrokeshire Coast National Park Authority is in the process of developing a footpath to follow much of the perimeter of the upper reaches of the Milford Haven Waterway. Currently access is best at Lower Hook Quay (SM990121), from where one can walk west along the shore to Little Milford (SM967119) where a road comes close to the river, or southeast to Sprinkle Pill. The extreme upper reaches are easily viewed from the

Fortunes Frolic footpath which follows close to the eastern bank, leaving Haverfordwest near the old gasworks at SM957154.

Eastern Cleddau The road runs to the shore at Picton Ferry (SN010123) and directly opposite on the south bank at Landshipping (SN013118). It is always well worth visiting the very head of the estuary at Blackpool Mill (SN060145): not much in the way of estuarine birds here, but always a chance of Kingfisher, Grey Wagtail and Dipper whatever the season.

West Williamston There is a small car park at SN033058, from where one can walk to the estuary and then northwest to the point where the Carew and Cresswell Rivers meet.

Pembroke River On the north bank there is easy access to the shore at East Pennar (SM962022).

Angle Bay Access is possible from Angle village by walking east along the south side of the bay from near Angle Hall (SM868027); or from Kilpaison, for which you leave the B4320 Pembroke to Angle road at SM908008 on the unclassified road for Rhoscrowther, and after nearly 1 mile (1.6 km) turn left at SM904015 for Angle Bay.

Calendar

Resident Cormorant, Grey Heron, Mute Swan, Canada Goose, Shelduck, Mallard, Oystercatcher, Lesser Black-backed, Herring and Great Black-backed Gulls.

December–February Red-throated Diver, Little and Great Crested Grebes, Wigeon, Teal, Pintail, Scaup, Goldeneye, Red-breasted Merganser, Ringed and Grey Plovers, Lapwing, Dunlin, Snipe, Bar-tailed Godwit, Curlew, Redshank, Greenshank, Turnstone, Black-headed and Common Gulls, Kingfisher.

March–May Departure of winter visitors, but Red-breasted Mergansers may remain until May, as do small numbers of all waders. Passage migrants on estuaries include Sanderling, Whimbrel and Common Sandpiper.

June–July Residents all present, but Shelducks virtually disappear by end of period when most undertake moult migration. First returning waders, with Lapwing and Curlew numbers rising rapidly during July.

August–November Occasional parties of Brent Geese from late October. Mallard numbers increase during September, soon followed by Wigeon, Teal and other winter ducks including Pintail. Wader movement throughout August and September, both passage and winter visitors including those which occur in only small numbers in this far southwest corner of Wales, such as Little Stint, Curlew Sandpiper, Ruff, Black-tailed Godwit and Spotted Redshank.

47 PEMBROKESHIRE ISLANDS

Maps 47(i), 47(ii),
47(iii) and 47(iv)
OS Map 157

Habitat

In 1927 a young man from Monmouthshire took a lease on the island of Skokholm, where he lived for the next 14 years with his wife and daughter, earning a livelihood from farming, fishing and writing. His name was R. M. Lockley, and his researches into the then unknown life histories of several seabirds, most notably Manx Shearwater, Storm Petrel and Puffin, his founding in 1933 of the first bird observatory in Britain, and his books about the island and about island life, soon ensured that Skokholm and the other islands of the Pembrokeshire coast became probably the best known of all nature conservation sites in Wales, and among the best known in Britain. So, attention was first drawn to the wealth of seabirds, the wild flowers, the seals, the magic of small islands. It is therefore not surprising that many people have followed in the footsteps of R. M. Lockley and his pioneer friends and come to Skokholm and Skomer, to continue the studies commenced over 50 years ago and for the sheer pleasure of seeing the abundant wildlife.

The interest aroused, and the information gained, have resulted in three of the four islands becoming nature reserves. Lonely Grassholm is owned by the Royal Society for the Protection of Birds, while both Skokholm and Skomer are held on lease and managed by the West Wales Trust for Nature Conservation. Grassholm is a mere 22 acres (8.9 ha) in extent, while Skomer, largest of the islands off the Welsh coast, is 720 acres (291 ha), Skokholm is a third of the size at 240 acres (97 ha), and privately owned Ramsey is 650 acres (263 ha) in extent. Only on Ramsey does any farming still continue. The once extensive farms on Skokholm and Skomer have long since ceased to operate, though the relics from those days — the buildings, the field walls, even some of the machinery used — are clear for everyone to see.

Ramsey has two hills: Carn Llundain, rising to 450 feet (137 m), and the slightly lower Carn Ysgubor brood over the high western cliffs and several spectacular inlets and caves such as those of Aber Mawr and Ogof Dafydd. On the low eastern plateau is a series of fields, several ponds and short valleys, and to the south an expanse of heather and Bracken. A feature of Ramsey that makes it unique among Welsh islands is its satellites — islets — some large and some small: Ynys Berry to the south; while to the west a whole chain, the Bishops and Clerks, four main islets and numerous rocks and reefs, which, in the words of Pembrokeshire's Elizabethan historian George Owen, 'preach deadly doctrine to their winter audience and are commendable in nothing but for their good residence, these all yelde store of gulls in the tyme of the year'.

Move south across St Brides Bay and Skomer is reached, separated from the nearest point on the mainland by Middleholm (Midland Island) and the 600-yard (550-m) width of Jack Sound. Skomer has been a National Nature Reserve since 1959, but 13 years before that, in 1946, it was the scene of the establishment for the summer of a field centre, one of the first in Britain. This was based at the old farm in the centre of the island, but unfortunately was badly damaged in a storm in 1954 and never repaired. It still stands, a gaunt sentinel on the skyline, a monument to generations of island farmers who have tilled the soil here since the Iron Age, possibly since Bronze Age times. There is ample evidence of occupation by these early people, including hut sites, burial cairns, animal pounds and the outlines of ancient field boundaries.

Nearly 3 miles (4.8 km) across Broad Sound from Skomer is Skokholm, a gentle island of mainly low sandstone cliffs and with far less cover than its larger northern neighbours. This is the place to be in the aftermath of a full westerly gale, when long swells crash into aptly named Mad Bay, sending plumes of spray high across the island; then back for tea with other island visitors, in the buildings now run as a hostel for visiting naturalists, and to talk over the birds of the day, both those seen and those hoped for.

The islands are not only bird islands, for there is a wealth of other wildlife. Ramsey and Skomer are the headquarters for the Grey Seal in southwest Britain, with over 400 pups born each autumn. Visit the islands in the spring and you will be staggered by the spectacle of wild flowers, especially Bluebells, which on Skomer seem to cover not only large areas of the island plateau, but also most of the more sheltered cliff slopes. Red Campion dominates many areas, Foxgloves in some years stand in stately profusion along the field boundaries, and then on the south and west slopes the truly maritime plants, the Thrift, Sea Campion and Scentless Mayweed, grow. There are unusual plants, perhaps none more so than Yellow-eyed-grass, a North American species formerly known in Britain and Ireland only from a meadow near Wexford Harbour. Suddenly it occurred in a spring flush on the west cliffs of Skomer — was it brought here by migratory wildfowl? Clinging to an eastern cliff on Ramsey is a maritime subspecies of Juniper, known elsewhere from only a few bushes on three other cliffs in Pembrokeshire, remnants from before the Ice Age when, according to the pollen record, Juniper was widespread in west Wales. Rabbits seem to be everywhere on Ramsey, Skokholm and Skomer, but it is a pity that Ramsey has Brown Rats; fortunately these rodents are absent from the other islands, where consequently large colonies of burrow-nesting seabirds thrive. There is one special mammal, the Skomer Vole, a unique island race found only on Skomer and closely related to the Bank Vole which occurs throughout mainland Britain.

Species

Without hesitation, one can say that the Manx Shearwater must have pride of place in any account of the birds of the Pembrokeshire islands. About 100,000 pairs nest on Skomer and perhaps a third of that number on Skokholm. Wherever you go on either island you will see burrows, and you can be sure that many will contain Manx Shearwaters. If you are able to cross only as a day visitor, then you are unlikely to see a Manx Shearwater save for a few distant birds flighting far offshore. You must arrange to spend at least a night on Skomer, or better still a week on Skokholm, where on The Knoll, the high ground sheltering the buildings, Manx Shearwaters occupy ancestral burrows. It is not too fanciful to suggest that descendants of 'Adam' and 'Ada', the first two Manx Shearwaters studied by R. M. Lockley, still come to this spot. Ringing has shown that many Manx Shearwaters return to the same colonies in which they were reared; it has also revealed that these are long-lived birds, many reaching 20 years of age, while one Skokholm resident captured in 1976 had been first ringed as a full-grown bird in 1946.

The best time of year to visit a Manx Shearwater colony is in late August or early September when the young are departing. Stand on a quiet night close to the immense colonies above Skomer's North Haven, or hard by the lighthouse on Skokholm, and everywhere can be heard the soft flapping of wings as young birds, having just emerged from the burrow, exercise for the first time. The young do this for several nights before setting off to the cliff edge and their first flight. By morning the only evidence of all this nocturnal activity is the soft grey down at burrow entrances, or blown to be caught on Bracken already scorched by the first late-summer gale. The adults have already left, and both they and the young make rapid journeys to winter quarters off the east coast of South America — Brazil, Uruguay and Argentina. Some make remarkable journeys, though none more so than a bird ringed on Skokholm on the last day of August 1965 and recovered 16 days later near São Francisco do Sul, Brazil, having travelled some 6,000 miles (9,600 km), an average of 375 miles (600 km) per day. A few wander further in the southern hemisphere: there have been sight records in Australasian waters, and a bird ringed as a nestling on Skokholm in September 1960 was found dead on a beach at the eastern end of the Great Australian Bight in November 1961. Manx Shearwaters regularly occur off the eastern seaboard of North America from Newfoundland to New England, and in 1973 were found breeding for the first time on Penikese Island off Massachusetts, followed in 1976 by breeding on islands off Newfoundland, where a bird ringed six years previously on Skokholm was found. One wonders whether all these colonists came from Pembrokeshire.

Imagine the surprise of observers on Skomer in June 1981 when, on investigating a strange call heard from among boulders at night, they discovered a Little Shearwater. It remained until 10 July, and even more surprisingly returned the following year. The nearest colonies are in Madeira and possibly the Azores, but, as Little Shearwaters are regularly seen offshore in British waters, and since the Skomer individual was clearly prospecting, birdwatchers should be aware that another species could well colonise one of our offshore islands.

The number of Storm Petrels on Skokholm is estimated at about 6,000 pairs, with probably less than 1,000 pairs on Skomer. On Skokholm many nest in crevices in the old field walls and others in boulder slopes, one of the largest colonies being immediately north of the lighthouse where, in the bowl running down to the sea, hundreds nest among the scree. By day all is quiet save for the calls of a few pairs of Herring Gulls and the resident Rock Pipits. Return at night and sit quietly among the boulders, listen intently, and from the crevices you will hear the harsh purring song with frequent guttural hiccoughs, once described as 'like a fairy being sick'. As Storm Petrels become active at dusk, you can watch them flying over the colony in the twilight or on moonlit nights. During May and June you may be fortunate enough to see the circular aerial display chases, one bird in hot pursuit of the other over their particular section of the colony.

All visitors to the Pembrokeshire islands hope to see Puffins, but two points to bear in mind are that there are none on Ramsey and that by mid-August all will have departed from their colonies on Skokholm and

Skomer. They arrive back at the islands in late March, and for the next month are of erratic occurrence at the colonies. On some days they will be present, on others all will have vanished back out to sea, something which is disappointing for island visitors in April. Towards the end of this month the single egg is laid in a burrow, occasionally in a rock crevice, on the slopes above the cliffs. As half the population is from then on incubating underground, and many of the remainder are out at sea before coming to take their turn, the month of May can also be a disappointing time for would-be Puffin-watchers: comparatively few birds will be evident during the day, though large numbers will land during the evening and remain until about dusk. All changes from early June, when the eggs hatch and the parent birds commence seven weeks' hard labour, being tasked to catch large quantities of sand-eels and other small fry with which to feed the single chick. With good fortune, they will dodge the waiting Herring Gulls and Jackdaws hoping to wrest their catch and will reach the safety of the burrow; those less fortunate will have to return to sea to seek a replacement meal and then try again. Peak numbers of Puffins occur at the colonies in late July, the breeding population being supplemented by non-breeders prospecting for nesting sites which will be used in subsequent years. A cloudy, even rainy day will help ensure that maximum numbers are ashore from the late morning onwards.

Although Guillemots and Razorbills nest on all four islands, the numbers of the former on Skokholm are rather few, usually about 100 pairs. This is due to an almost complete lack of suitable ledges, and it is for this reason that no Kittiwakes nest there. One of the most dramatic of all seabird cliffs in Britain is The Wick on Skomer: a great chasm, the result of much geological grinding and slipping millions of years ago, leaving a 200-foot (60-m) vertical basalt cliff opposite which are steep slabs below slopes in which Puffins nest. The cliff seems to be filled for much of its length by Kittiwakes, Guillemots and Razorbills, from the lowest ledges to the very top where Herring Gulls and more Puffins nest. A vast avian city from which throughout the summer months there is a continual clamour, the screaming cries of Kittiwakes, the trumpeting notes of Guillemots, in a welter of excitement as the birds bow to one another in greeting, or fence with pointed bills — and, if you listen hard, the deep burring resonance of Razorbills. Everywhere there are birds flying to and fro. Kittiwakes low down, like a myriad dancing flock of snowflakes. The torpedo-shaped bodies and rapidly whirring wings of Guillemots and Razorbills. Early in the season, look out for the quite delightful 'butterfly' display flight of the latter as they leave the ledges with wings beaten in a slow accentuated motion. One other seabird nests here, and in the updraughts along the cliff face it shows effortless, astonishing prowess: the perfect glider, the Fulmar. At the inner end of The Wick is a single high ledge — you cannot miss it — within the safe recess of which Fulmars have nested for over a quarter of a century. Some will sit tight, incubating or later brooding a small chick. Others come and go, swooping down, or soaring just below the clifftop with only the occasional twist of the wings to maintain momentum, sometimes steering with their feet, and then, when one lands, comes the greeting ceremony, a loud, often prolonged cackling by both of the pair.

One seabird deserves a special mention, for, although Gannets can be seen off most parts of the Welsh coast, there is only one colony in the Principality, on lonely Grassholm, 8 miles (12.8 km) from the nearest point on the Pembrokeshire mainland. Gannets have nested on Grass-holm since at least 1860, when the number was about 20 pairs. They now number some 29,000 pairs, and there is currently no sign of the increase waning; the rate is such that immigrants from other western colonies, Little Skellig off Co. Kerry and Ailsa Craig in the Clyde, may well have contributed to the increase. Whatever the reason, the Gannets continue to flourish, occupying the whole of the northern part of Grass-holm and in recent years, as they have extended southwards, the central ridge. Originally this ridge was the vantage point overlooking the colony, but now it is occupied by serried ranks of Gannets which stare down the slope as visitors approach to the line of white posts erected by the RSPB (to avoid causing disturbance, no-one should venture beyond this line).

Gannets

The islands, especially Ramsey and Skomer with their wide range of habitats, support a rich number of birds other than seabirds, from wildfowl, waders and raptors to small passerines. Mallards nest, and each year family parties from Skomer attempt the passage to the main-land, the ducklings quite often being lost on route to the depredations of Great Black-backed Gulls. Oystercatchers, Lapwings and Curlews all nest; for the latter two species the islands are their remaining stronghold in Pembrokeshire, both having declined drastically on the mainland in the wake of drainage of the damp fields and moors in which they previously nested. The Buzzard, Kestrel, Peregrine and Little Owl all nest, the latter a regular predator on Storm Petrels, the evidence being plain for all to see in the pellets collected from its roosting sites. Perhaps this is why there are so few petrels on Skomer when compared to Skokholm? Visitors to Ramsey and to Skomer in spring and early summer should look out for Short-eared Owls; several pairs breed, and the adults regularly hunt during daytime, at times seeming oblivious to man for they often pass quite close when quartering the Bracken areas looking for voles. There are several possibly unexpected species on these treeless offshore islands, such as the Woodpigeons which nest on the ground, the Magpies in low bramble bushes and the Carrion Crows on the tops of the old field walls. There are numerous small passerines, including Pied Wagtail, Wren, Dunnock, Blackbird, Sedge Warbler, Whitethroat and Reed Bunting.

Several species of duck, mainly Wigeon, Teal and Mallard, frequent the island ponds in winter. One striking newcomer has been the Barnacle Goose: a flock of 26 arrived on Skomer in mid-November 1981, numbers increased to 39, and the last did not leave until 9 May the following year. Since then the geese have returned each winter, grazing in the fields, roosting on the North Pond, and from time to time flighting to fields on the Marloes Peninsula, and especially the Marloes Mere Nature Reserve. So, although you cannot get to Skomer in winter, you do have a chance of seeing the only wintering flock of Barnacle Geese in Wales.

Barnacle Geese

Some birds from the nearby mainland are very infrequent visitors to the islands. There are few records of woodpeckers, perhaps not surprisingly in view of the absence of trees. In most autumns small numbers of Blue and Great Tits appear, occasionally joined by other members of their family including Long-tailed Tits; such an apparently fragile bird of thick hedgerows seems especially out of place on an island. Rooks are almost as scarce, while a Grey Partridge on Skomer in 1986 was only the second record for the island. The House Sparrow and Tree Sparrow are rare visitors, though surprisingly, especially in the case of the latter, both have nested on Skomer in the past. Grey Herons are equally remarkable visitors, but never more so than in August 1981 when ten were seen flying west from Skokholm. Where were they going? To Ireland, or, as the *Pembrokeshire Bird Report* pondered, to an impending disaster in the Atlantic?

Bird-ringing was carried out on Skokholm from 1933 to 1940 and again from 1946 to 1976, the results helping to elucidate many questions regarding the movements of birds and the fortunes of our seabird populations. It was not long before it became apparent that rare vagrants regularly occurred on the Pembrokeshire islands. A mouth-watering list over the years includes several which were first records for Britain, species such as Olive-backed Pipit, Olive-backed Thrush and Olivaceous and Bonelli's Warblers. Many others were the first for Wales, and of these one can perhaps mention Lesser Golden Plover, Little Swift, Pied Wheatear, Savi's and Sardinian Warblers, Red-eyed Vireo, Rustic Bunting and Northern Oriole. Other scarce visitors have included Semipalmated and Upland Sandpipers, Scops Owl, Red-throated Pipit, Barred Warbler Serin and Scarlet Rosefinch. There are also the ones that 'got away', the bird which vanished before a full description could be obtained. Did it have a wingbar? What colour were its legs? What were these and the other vital details without which the description will not be accepted by the County Bird Recorder and the Rare Birds Committees? Each island warden has had this experience, perhaps none more frustrating than on Skomer in October 1961, when a fleeting glimpse was had of what was most probably a Blackburnian Warbler, a summer visitor to eastern North America which winters from Central America south to Peru. This species had not previously been recorded in Europe, nor has one been seen since.

Timing

As a day visitor, one is of course wholly dependent on the departure of boats. Usually the earliest you can reach the islands will be 10.30 hours, and most visitors will have left by 17.00. To see all aspects of the islands and their wildlife, a night ashore is essential. A night on Skomer, better still several nights there, or a week on Skokholm should be arranged. You will then have ample time to explore the island at leisure, to see the evening gatherings of Puffins, whose numbers after about 18.00 are far in excess of those seen earlier in the day, then of course, at dusk, the first Storm Petrels, and when it is really dark the awakening of the vast Manx Shearwater colonies. These avian riches no birdwatcher should forgo by failing to arrange to stay on one or other of the islands.

Access

Grassholm The weather is all important, not so much for the crossing from Martinshaven, which takes 1–1½ hours depending on the tide, but for the landing, which needs calm weather with no swell. Landings are permitted only after 15 June so as to avoid disturbance. The boat (number of passengers limited to 12) does, however, make regular circumnavigations from April onwards, and these afford fine views of the Gannet colony and the haul-out of Grey Seals, as well as a chance of seeing Manx Shearwaters on the voyage out, especially if it is during the evening. Full details of sailings are available from Dale Sailing Company, Dale, Haverfordwest (tel: Dale 349). For trips to Grassholm arranged by the Pembrokeshire Coast National Park Authority in the Dale Sailing Company boat, ring either the Company or the National Park (tel: Haverfordwest 4591). For general information concerning Grassholm, contact the RSPB Wales Office.

Ramsey Open April to mid-September, a boat crossing daily, weather permitting, from the lifeboat station at St Justinian; a landing fee is payable. The several boat trips daily around the island from St Justinian provide excellent opportunities for seeing the spectacular western cliffs of the island. An information board at the top of the lifeboat-station steps or the information centre in the Memorial Hall, St David's, should be consulted for up-to-date information on both landings and circumnavigations.

Skokholm Full-board accommodation for up to 15 visitors is available on a weekly basis from late March to mid-September. Certain weeks are course weeks on such subjects as 'Seabirds', 'Bird Migration' and 'Wildlife Photography'. Enquiries and bookings to the WWTNC Office. The only day visits are on Mondays, weather permitting, from the beginning of June until late August. Places on the boat must be booked with the Pembrokeshire Coast National Park Office, from whom full details are available. A landing fee is payable on arrival.

Skomer Open daily, weather permitting, except on Mondays (other than Bank Holidays), from the beginning of April to mid-September. When Easter falls in March, the island opens earlier as appropriate. Please note that the island is usually closed for a few days in early June, and enquiries about this should be made with the WWTNC or Dale Sailing Company. The first crossing is at 10.00 hours and there are further crossings at about 11.00 and 12.00, though these later times are subject to revision depending on the number of visitors wishing to cross. A landing fee is payable on arrival. Visitors return to the mainland during the late afternoon. The same boat also makes trips around the island during the early afternoon. Enquiries about crossings to the island should be made with the Dale Sailing Company. There is a limited amount of self-catering accommodation for up to six visitors on Skomer and enquiries and bookings should be made with the WWTNC, to whom general enquiries regarding the island should also be made.

Calendar

Resident Cormorant, Shag, Mallard, Common Scoter likely offshore throughout year (part of a small flock in St Brides Bay), Buzzard, Kestrel, Peregrine, Pheasant, Oystercatcher, Turnstone, Herring and Great Black-backed Gulls, Stock Dove, Woodpigeon, Little and Short-eared Owls, Skylark, Meadow and Rock Pipits, Wren, Pied Wagtail, Dunnock, Stonechat (though in hard weather may desert islands, and as a consequence not breed for several years), Blackbird, Song Thrush, Magpie, Chough, Jackdaw, Carrion Crow, Raven, Starling, Linnet, Reed Bunting.

December–February Red-throated and Great Northern Divers, Fulmars arrive early January, Gannets shortly afterwards, Barnacle Goose, Wigeon, Teal, Shoveler, Merlin, occasional Hen Harrier. Kittiwakes at cliffs from early February, while Guillemots and Razorbills make infrequent visits throughout period. All resident species much reduced in numbers, and in hard weather may desert the islands altogether.

March–May Manx Shearwaters arrive early March, Storm Petrels late April. Lapwings and Curlews arrive, as do the large numbers of Lesser Black-backed Gulls on Skokholm and Skomer. First Puffins usually seen in late March and the first landings take place within a few days.

Guillemots and Razorbills make more frequent and longer visits to cliffs, though will not be fully resident until the eggs are laid in early May. Passage migrants include Corncrake, Whimbrel, Common Sandpiper, Turtle Dove, Cuckoo, Swift, Hoopoe, Sand Martin, Swallow, House Martin, Black Redstart, Redstart, Whinchat, Wheatear, Ring Ouzel, most warblers, while Sedge Warbler and Whitethroat remain to breed, Spotted and Pied Flycatchers.

June–July Grey Heron and Black-headed Gull from late July, Guillemots and Razorbills have all completed their breeding cycle by end of period and their colonies are once more deserted.

August–November Wigeon, Teal, Water Rail, wader passage especially when the ponds are low in August and early September, Snipe resident throughout winter, Black-headed and Common Gulls, Kittiwakes leave cliffs during late August but small numbers offshore for most of period, tern passage during August and early September. Puffins depart by mid-August, Tawny and Barn Owls sometimes take up temporary residence during the autumn. Sand Martin, Swallow, Yellow and Pied Wagtail passage during early September, Robins arrive during August and take up their winter territories, main warbler passage finishes by mid-September though Blackcaps may be seen until November. Fieldfare, Redwing, Mistle Thrush, Goldcrest, Blue and Great Tits, Chaffinch, Goldfinch and Greenfinch during late autumn.

48 PENGELLI FOREST

Map 48
OS Map 145

Habitat

The largest block of ancient woodland remaining in west Wales, the forest extends for 162 acres (66 ha), a third of its size in the sixteenth century. Then it was known as a 'greate woode', a source of much timber, of grazing for horses, cattle and sheep, a place where large numbers of Woodcock were taken in winter, a place where honey was collected from the nests of wild bees in summer. Over the intervening 350 years or so, the wood has shrunk as agricultural development has nibbled at the perimeter, though fortunately the main block remains, possibly owing to the presence of several steep-sided ravines which make access difficult in parts. Despite purchasing the woodland, the Forestry Commission did not proceed with a programme of conversion to conifers, and in 1979 this body entered into an agreement with the West Wales Trust for Nature Conservation. The Trust has subsequently carried out a range of woodland management tasks to assist in providing a greater variety of habitats for birds.

Pengelli Forest may be divided broadly into two main habitats. Closest to the entrance on the west side is Pant Teg, mainly Sessile Oak and Birch woodland on steep slopes. Proceed through this and you reach a large area where Birch, Alder and Ash, along with Oak, are dominant on poorly drained boulder-clay soil with a thick ground cover. Other trees of note here include Aspen, Goat Willow, Wild Cherry and, most interesting of all, three trees of the Midland Hawthorn, at this its only known station in west Wales — was its arrival here bird-aided? Woodland plants found in the forest include Golden-saxifrage, Early Dog-violet, Wood Anemone, Common Cow-wheat, Moschatel and Wood Sage. The range of mammals present includes Badger, Grey Squirrel, Polecat and Dormouse, this last species being particularly scarce in southwest Wales though undoubtedly overlooked. A recent arrival, though up to now with only one brief sighting plus footprints, is the Muntjac Deer. A woodland butterfly of note is the White-letter Hairstreak; its food plant the Wych Elm still survives here, having so far escaped the ravages of Dutch Elm disease. This is a butterfly which prefers the tops of trees, around which it flights on sunny afternoons, descending to more reasonable heights only to seek nectar sources such as bramble blossom.

Species

All the typical woodland birds can be seen, Sparrowhawks, Buzzards and Tawny Owls being the birds of prey which nest in or close to the forest. In an even-aged woodland with few natural nest holes, the provision of nestboxes was an early task undertaken by the WWTNC management team. The timing was perfect, for it coincided with the recent westwards extension in range of Pied Flycatchers, which first nested here in 1984; their numbers have increased in subsequent years and will presumably continue to do so as more nestboxes are erected. Other occupiers of the nestboxes include Redstarts, and Great, Blue, Coal and Marsh Tits. The woodland warblers such as Garden Warbler, Blackcap, Wood Warbler, Chiffchaff and Willow Warbler are all present.

Woodcock still come in winter, though alas not in the numbers there must have been in Elizabethan times.

Timing

Not material, unless it is the dawn chorus you wish to hear in May and the early part of June.

Access

Leave the A487 Cardigan to Fishguard road at SN105390, just east of Felindre Farchog, by the unclassified road which follows the foot of the hill, wends its way around the great Iron Age mound of Castell Henllys, crosses a stream by means of a ford, and eventually skirts the western boundary of the forest. Cars may be parked close to the access gate, from where a series of footpaths leads through a large section of woodland. A leaflet is available from the WWTNC.

Calendar

Resident Sparrowhawk, Buzzard, Kestrel, Pheasant, Stock Dove, Woodpigeon, Tawny Owl, Green and Great Spotted Woodpeckers, Wren, Dunnock, Robin, Blackbird, Song and Mistle Thrushes, Goldcrest, tit family, Nuthatch, Treecreeper, Jay, Magpie, Jackdaw, Carrion Crow, Raven, Chaffinch, Greenfinch, Goldfinch, Bullfinch.

December–February Mallard, Woodcock, Grey Wagtail, Dipper, Redwing, Fieldfare, Brambling.

March–May Summer visitors arrive, including Cuckoo, Redstart, Whitethroat, Garden Warbler, Blackcap, Wood Warbler, Chiffchaff, Willow Warbler, Spotted and Pied Flycatchers.

June–July All residents and summer visitors present, many young birds about, though by end of period the forest will fall strangely silent, save for the buzz of numerous insects and the calls of young Buzzards overhead.

August–November Summer visitors depart by early September, though the occasional Blackcap and Chiffchaff may remain until October and one or two may even overwinter. Woodcock arrive late October, shortly after the first Fieldfares and Redwings.

49 ST DAVID'S COMMONS

Map 49
OS Map 157

Habitat

The oceanic heaths of Anglesey, the Lleyn and Pembrokeshire have a character all of their own, occupying as they do low-lying land on windswept coastal peninsulas. The best example in Britain is the mosaic of heathland largely to the northeast of St David's, fragments — though some are large — set in a rich agricultural landscape of early potatoes and dairy herds. To the naturalist, the heaths contain riches and treasures for those able to search and with an eye for some of the diminutive plants and insects found there. On the drier sections there is Heather, Bell Heather and Western Gorse, and where the ground is wetter Cross-leaved Heath with its pale pink flowers is dominant. In the fens Purple Moor-grass grows in hummocks which make walking difficult, though these do not compare with those of the appropriately named Greater Tussock-sedge. Willow scrub has developed in some sections, while the presence of open water such as that on Trefeiddan and at Dowrog Pool adds a further dimension to these exciting areas. To extend the amount of open water available, the West Wales Trust for Nature Conservation with the assistance of the Welsh Water Authority has dug a number of new pools and pits on its Dowrog Common Nature Reserve. Scenically, the commons are best from early summer onwards, first with masses of Heath Spotted-orchids in a variety of hues from white to lilac. Look out also for the Lesser Butterfly-orchid, especially in the firebreaks beside the road which crosses Dowrog. As the summer proceeds, there are the pinks and purples of the three heathers and the saffron of the Western Gorse. For the specialist, such plants as Yellow Centaury, Pale Dog-violet, Wavy St John's-wort, Three-lobed Crowfoot and Pillwort will cause great excitement; the latter, a species of fern, is endangered throughout Europe, and is now listed as a *Red Data Book* species by the International Union for the Conservation of Nature. The Marsh Fritillary occurs, its larvae feeding on the leaves of Devil's-bit Scabious and hibernating at the base of the plant in communal silk cocoons. Dragonflies and damselflies are numerous throughout the summer, from the largest such as the Emperor and the Golden-ringed Dragonflies to the Small Red and Scarce Blue-tailed Damselflies.

Species

Montagu's Harriers nested here until the early 1960s, and the occasional bird is still seen on passage in most years, sometimes staying for a few days, sufficient to quicken the pulse of local birdwatchers hoping that a pair will again take up residence. Sparrowhawks, Buzzards and Kestrels breed in the willow scrub and are normally not too difficult to see. The wintering Hen Harriers which come to the St David's Peninsula are one of the main attractions, with up to eight going to roost in willows on Dowrog. They are likely to be seen quartering any of the commons during the day, and some hang on until April before moving north. Will a pair remain to breed? Other winter raptors include regular Merlins, Peregrines and Short-eared Owls, the latter having possibly nested in 1983.

Stonechats, Grasshopper and Sedge Warblers, Whitethroats and Reed Buntings are among the small number of passerines which breed. There are always several pairs of Mallards, together with Moorhen and Coot, while Water Rails probably remain to nest on occasions, though this is a really difficult species to prove, one heard rather than seen.

Winter wildfowl numbers are small but always include occasional parties of Bewick's and Whooper Swans, 32 of the former in January 1985 being especially noteworthy. The Mallard flock increases during the autumn, to be joined by small numbers of Wigeons and Teals, occasionally Shovelers and Pintails. Garganeys are almost annual in their appearance at Trefeiddan Pool during the early spring. The absence of muddy margins at the pools means that wader numbers are small, something that could be improved upon by management. Those that have been noted include Jack Snipe, Dunlin, Greenshank and Green Sandpiper, while Snipe are present right through the winter. Unusual visitors have included Little Bittern, Spotted Crake and Savi's Warbler.

Timing

Not critical here. If, however, you wish to look for Hen Harriers going to roost, then visit in the late afternoon, though for the less hardy on a cold winter's day it is possible to watch from the car.

Access

Dowrog Common An unclassified road leaves the A487 St David's to Fishguard road at SM782268 and crosses the common; there is a small car park close to the western boundary at SM772277. Follow the pony tracks across the common.

Trefeiddan Pool Easily viewed from the unclassified road which runs from St David's to the lifeboat station at St Justinian, the best point being on the side road at SM735253.

Tretio Common An unclassified road leaves the A487 St David's to Fishguard road at Carnhedryn Uchaf and crosses the common. This area is not so well watched as the previous two sites and also lacks any open water, but nevertheless is well worth a visit.

Vachelich Moor Also called the St David's Airfield Common as it is directly north of the now largely disused St David's Airfield. Access is difficult and there is a rubbish tip on the north side, but one can certainly watch for harriers from either SM782325 where a public footpath crosses the common, or from the road at SM796265.

Calendar

Resident Mallard, Sparrowhawk, Buzzard, Kestrel, Pheasant, Water Rail in some years, Moorhen, Coot, Woodpigeon, Little Owl, Skylark, Meadow Pipit, Pied Wagtail, Dunnock, Robin, Blackbird, Magpie, Carrion Crow, Raven, Linnet, Reed Bunting.

December–February Bewick's and Whooper Swans, Wigeon, Teal, Shoveler, Merlin, Peregrine, Water Rail, Jack Snipe, Snipe, Short-eared Owl.

March–May Garganey, Cuckoo, Swallows and Sand Martins over the pools, Wheatear on passage, Grasshopper and Sedge Warblers, Whitethroat.

June–July All residents and summer visitors present.

August–November Chance of passage waders during August and early September, winter visitors including Hen Harriers from mid-October.

Habitat

A line of Carboniferous limestone cliffs extends westwards from the vicinity of Stackpole Quay for some 11 miles (17.6 km) to just beyond Linney Head, the most southwesterly point in Pembrokeshire. The coastal scenery for the whole distance is superb, with numerous bays, narrow inlets, sea caves, stacks, blow holes and natural arches. At only a few points on the Castlemartin Peninsula, mainly secluded bays to which access is prohibited, is the cliff line broken. The two exceptions are the sandy beaches, much loved by holidaymakers, of Barrafundle and Broad Haven. The latter lies at the entrance to the drowned inlets of the Bosherston Lakes, a main central pool and three connecting arms. These shallow lakes were created in the eighteenth and nineteenth centuries by the construction of dams at strategic points across what were formerly marshy valleys. The only visible outflow is across Broad Haven beach, but infra-red photographs interestingly show a considerable upwelling of fresh water close to Church Rock just offshore. The lakes are one of the finest lowland freshwater systems in southern Britain and are noted for their rich aquatic flora, most striking being the large expanse of White Water-lilies, a spectacle which draws large numbers of people throughout the summer months.

Most of the coastal vegetation is short maritime turf, but the clifftops support a number of scarce plants. These include an endemic sea-lavender so rare that it has no English name, Small Restharrow, Hoary Rock-rose and the recently discovered Goldilocks. At Stackpole Warren the high Rabbit population has created grassland communities noted for their lichens, and also a flora resembling that of parts of the East Anglian Breckland. As one moves east through the area the amount of clifftop scrub, usually Common Gorse, becomes more abundant, and in really sheltered spots small groups of trees add further diversity.

The National Trust owns the former Stackpole Estate, though alas the fine house of the Cawdors was demolished in 1967 before the Trust took over. Fortunately the rare Greater Horseshoe Bat was able to find new breeding quarters in the nearby stable block, this being one of only about half-a-dozen colonies in Britain. Rich feeding areas for the bats over the nearby Range, and a variety of winter hibernation sites in caves and man-made caverns, enable the bats to survive. Much of the area of nature conservation interest at Stackpole is a National Nature Reserve, and the Nature Conservancy Council employs a warden there. The Army took over virtually the whole of the Castlemartin Peninsula as a tank gunnery range in the period immediately prior to the last war. The years have not diminished in any way the need for such training areas, though it means that the coast, especially the far west, is not readily accessible.

Species

Despite the length of coastline, the seabirds are restricted mainly to the vicinity of Stackpole Head and to Stack Rocks. The latter are often referred to as the Elegug Stacks, after the local name for the Guillemot. The Stacks, of which there is one large and three small, lie just off the

149

mainland and must constitute one of the best places in the country to see cliff-nesting birds at close quarters. They hold the largest number of Guillemots and Razorbills on the mainland coast of South Wales. If you are unable to visit one of the island colonies, then this is the place to come; the cliff edge is within a few yards of the car park. The Guillemots are mostly on top of the Main Stack, with a smaller group on the Green Bridge Stack. In places, especially on the former, the birds are packed so tight that there hardly seems room for more to land. Even so, the colonies were once considerably larger, judging by the evidence of postcard views and of other photographs taken earlier in the century. In 1986 some 3,553 Guillemots were present, together with 480 Razorbills many of which nest in crevices and holes, both on the Stacks and on the coast opposite. Some 490 pairs of Kittiwakes occupy the lowest levels, and, if you look closely, several pairs of Shags. The liberal whitewash of droppings is often the only clue to the latter's presence, as incubating birds sit tight in gloomy recesses. Fulmars nest here, as do Herring Gulls, a few pairs of Lesser Black-backed Gulls, and on the top of at least two stacks usually a pair of Great Black-backed Gulls. Just east of the Stacks is an especially dramatic seabird colony, not in terms of numbers but because of its geological splendour. This is The Cauldron, an aptly named giant blow hole and natural arch through which Kittiwakes, Guillemots and Razorbills fly to reach their nest sites: an awesome spectacle as the sea surges through the arch in times of storm, though the seabirds, often nesting within a few feet of high-water mark, apparently seem unconcerned.

Puffin

There are rather few seabirds on the coast eastwards to St Govan's and beyond. It is, however, worth looking for the small numbers in the vicinity of The Castle and Mewsford Point. Keep an eye out for Puffins, for the occasional pair probably nests in these cliffs but is easily overlooked. They can normally be seen at Stackpole Head, where about a dozen pairs nest, though even here careful searching among the birds on the water and flying up to the colony will be necessary. The Kittiwakes, Guillemots and Razorbills are not so easily viewed at Stackpole as at Stack Rocks, but nevertheless the colony is well worth a visit. If you have a choice, make your way here during May, when the clifftop is a carpet of blue, the Spring Squill in full flower.

Peregrines now nest at several places along the cliffs, while there is usually a pair or two of Kestrels. In winter, Hen Harriers are frequent visitors to the Range and the sand dunes in the far west. The large number of sheep which graze on the Range during the winter non-firing period is a major factor in encouraging the small population of Choughs, several pairs of which nest. The close-cropped turf, and the sheep dung, is ideal for ants, beetles and other invertebrates on which the Choughs feed. In frosty weather they often resort to the sand dunes, and even to the seaweed debris at the top of the storm beaches.

Bosherston Lakes have few breeding wildfowl but provide instead a wintering site of local importance for a range of species. Coots predominate and up to 300 may be present in midwinter, with smaller numbers of Pochards and Tufted Ducks. Since males of both these duck species have remained in recent summers, might we anticipate breeding in the not too distant future? Although only in small numbers, Gadwall, Scaup, Goldeneye and Goosander are regular visitors. The list of scarce wildfowl seen in recent years is impressive and includes Garganey, Red-crested Pochard, Ferruginous Duck and Velvet Scoter. In February 1967, great excitement was caused when a male Ring-necked Duck was present from 12 February to 8 March, only the eighth record for Britain. Small numbers now regularly winter in this country, though hopes that they may begin to breed have so far not been realised, something not helped by a scarcity of females (though are these overlooked, at least by human eye, among the flocks of Tufted Ducks?). There have been several further records from Bosherston since the first in 1967. Bitterns now occur each winter, especially during periods of hard weather, with up to five being present during the cold spell of 1981/2. Water Rails are regularly heard from the reedbeds, though generally only in winter. An immature Lesser Yellowlegs in October 1984 was especially noteworthy, while other scarce visitors have included Black Tern and Firecrest.

Timing

This is not critical, but an early-morning visit to such places as Stack Rocks is always most pleasant: the clifftop should be your own, and the seabird city on the Stacks will seem especially boisterous.

Access

Leave Pembroke and travel south on the B4319.

Stack Rocks Turn south off the B4319 just west of Merrion Barracks, but please note that the road across the Range is for much of the year open only at weekends, on Bank Holidays and on some evenings. It is closed when firing takes place, and then the gate is shut and red flags fly. The times of firing are published weekly in the local papers and displayed in Bosherston Post Office. Excellent general views of the Range, and of the tank activity, may be obtained from the viewing point at SR929978, close to aptly named Cold Comfort on the hill to the west of the hamlet of Warren.

Range West This is a live firing Range covering the whole area west of the Stack Rocks road and is closed to visitors. The only means of access is by joining one of the Pembrokeshire Coast National Park Authority guided walks, which take place on certain Sundays throughout the year. This involves a 7-mile (11.2-km) coastal walk from Stack Rocks to Linney Head, one of the loneliest coastlines in Wales. There are few breeding seabirds on this section, but visitors have a good chance of seeing Chough, Raven and occasionally Peregrine.

Range East The Range to the east of the Stack Rocks road is open only along the coastal footpath from Stacks Rocks to the car park at St Govan's Chapel (SR966930), under the same arrangements as for Stack Rocks.

St Govan's Head Turn off the B4319 for Bosherston and continue through the village and so to the coast. When visiting the chapel tucked into a steep cleft in the cliff, look out for the cliff-nesting House Martins. Access is possible eastwards to St Govan's Head, a fine vantage point for observing seabirds, mostly Manx Shearwaters and Gannets from the nearby islands. It could, however, prove to be of interest during spring and autumn for observing other seabirds, but as yet has received little attention. Patient pioneering is clearly required.

Bosherston Ponds Park in the car park close to Bosherston Church, and then follow the footpaths to and around the ponds, crossing by means of a footbridge to reach the coastal footpaths at Broad Haven beach.

Broad Haven On the southern outskirts of Bosherston, a road bears east to a large car park directly above the beach.

Stackpole Head Follow the signs on the unclassified road from Pembroke to Stackpole village, and then to the National Trust car park at Stackpole Quay (SR992957), from where the coastal footpath leads to the head past the delightful Barrafundle beach.

Calendar

Resident Cormorant, Shag, Mute Swan, Mallard, Kestrel, Peregrine, Moorhen, Coot, Oystercatcher, Kingfisher, Rock Pipit, Stonechat, Chough, Jackdaw, Raven.

December–February Red-throated and Great Northern Divers, Little and Great Crested Grebes, Fulmars return to the cliffs in early January, Bittern, Wigeon, Gadwall, Pochard, Tufted Duck, Scaup, Goldeneye, Goosander, Lapwing, Golden Plover, Curlew. Guillemots and Razorbills return sporadically to the cliffs throughout whole period, though on many occasions if you are not there shortly after dawn they will have returned to sea again. Kittiwakes take up residence during February.

March–May Manx Shearwater and Gannet appear offshore. Puffins return at end of March. First summer migrants arrive, usually Swallow, Sand Martin, Black Redstart, Wheatear and Ring Ouzel by end of March, chance of Garganey at Bosherston.

June–July Breeding seabirds all present. On occasions large movements of Manx Shearwaters and Gannets to and from the Bristol Channel, chance of passage terns during late July.

August–November Guillemot, Razorbill and Puffin all depart by early August, Kittiwakes by end of month and Fulmars during early September. Wildfowl begin to appear during September, and in October large numbers of Golden Plover and Lapwing may feed on the Range. Chance of Hen Harrier, while late summer migrants may include Wheatear.

51 STRUMBLE HEAD

Map 51
OS Map 157

Habitat

Pembrokeshire is a county of fine headlands, with Strumble Head the most outstanding seawatch site on the coast of Wales. It compares with the classic points of St Ives and Portland Bill in southern England. The head rises to about 100 feet (30 m), mainly as steep grass- and heather-covered slopes with rock outcrops. This is the western end of the Pencaer Peninsula, a 3-mile (4.8-km) run of coastline protecting Fishguard Bay to the east. A lighthouse has stood on the rocky islet of Ynys Meicel since 1908, but the keepers who once crossed the narrow footbridge have been absent for several years, for Strumble is now an automatic station, the light never ceasing to flash by day or by night. Just beyond Ynys Meicel is the slightly larger Carreg Onnen, and from here the coast runs south for 5 miles (8 km) before turning southwest for the 11 miles (17.6 km) to St David's Head. In spring and early summer the cliffs on or close to Strumble Head are alive with colour — the flowers of Thrift, Spring Squill, Sea Campion and Scurvygrass, together with some surprises such as Primroses in sheltered spots and Cowslips which seem to thrive in the clifftop grassland.

Species

Save for Herring Gulls on Carreg Onnen and Fulmars towards Pen Brush, there are no breeding seabirds at Strumble Head. Choughs breed on this coastline and one does not usually have to go very far before seeing a pair. There are usually Ravens about, Kestrels hover over the cliffsides, and the occasional Peregrine will sweep by. Stonechats, Linnets and Yellowhammers frequent the clifftop scrub, being joined in summer by Grasshopper Warblers and Whitethroats, and in the stream hollows even the occasional Sedge Warbler.

It is, however, as a spot for observing migration, especially the passage of seabirds, that Strumble Head is noted. In the early 1960s, birdwatchers commenced in a concerted way what quickly became known as seawatching, the essential ingredients being a prominent headland, much patience, and good binoculars supplemented if possible by a telescope. Headlands such as that just west of St Ives in Cornwall, Portland Bill in Dorset, St Catherine's Point on the Isle of Wight, Spurn Point at the mouth of the Humber, and several in Ireland, most notably Cape Clear, Co. Cork, became synonymous with large passages of seabirds and the arrival of scarce species, some previously hardly ever recorded in British waters. In 1963 and 1964 some seawatches were carried out at St David's Head, to be followed shortly afterwards by the first pioneering watches at Strumble Head. Ten years or more were to elapse before birdwatchers began to carry out almost day-by-day watches during the late summer and autumn, with casual watches at other times. Now a wealth of information has been collected, though as yet little has been published in detail, and this reveals at times tremendous passages of some seabirds, together with an exciting range of scarce species. Most movement naturally takes place from late August until early October, but whatever the time of year Strumble Head is always well worth a visit.

With the colonies on Skokholm and Skomer some 25 miles (40 km) away, Manx Shearwaters pass daily right through the summer months, the evening passage being as striking as that soon after dawn. These are birds on regular feeding movements which take them north through St George's Channel and well into the Irish Sea. As September proceeds so the feeding movements cease, but Manx Shearwaters are still to be seen, now genuine passage birds, many probably from the colonies in the Inner Hebrides. The last may not be seen until mid-November, with remarkable stragglers until late December — does this mean that some do not overwinter in the South Atlantic? Each year, a few examples of the Balearic race of the Manx Shearwater are seen: this has brownish-black upperparts, compared with the grey-black of the Manx Shearwater, and as its name suggests breeds on the Balearic and other islands in the western Mediterranean. Sooty Shearwaters are regular, with a never-to-be-forgotten movement on 1 September 1985 when no fewer than 237 passed during the day. A few Great Shearwaters are seen annually, having moved into the North Atlantic from the giant colonies on Tristan da Cunha. Cory's Shearwaters are similar in their occurrence, even though they breed on islands as close as those off the coasts of Portugal and in the Azores. The Little Shearwater is now seen annually. Is this because more move north, or because of the increased skill of observers — and more of them come to that? Each October a few Leach's Petrels pass, but Storm Petrels, although breeding on the Pembrokeshire islands, are rarely seen. A Wilson's Petrel in 1986 was only the twelfth for Britain and Ireland.

Manx Shearwaters

Gannets may be observed almost throughout the year, and only in winter do the numbers tail right off. An albino on 15 September 1985 was a memorable experience for all concerned. Cormorants and Shags, birds from local colonies, are regular offshore whatever the season or time of day; there seems little evidence of any passage movement. Divers feed in the tide-race off the head throughout the winter, the Red-throated Diver being the most frequent. Small parties of Whooper Swans are seen in late autumn in most years, but of all wildfowl the Common Scoter is the most regular, passing in all months with the lowest numbers in late winter and spring. Small numbers or individuals of several other species have been noted, including Wigeon, Pochard, Tufted Duck, Velvet Scoter, Goldeneye and Red-breasted Merganser. Passage waders noted include Knot, Bar-tailed Godwit, Whimbrel, Curlew, Spotted Redshank, Redshank, Green Sandpiper and Grey Phalarope. A good deal of wader movement takes place at night, and at Strumble Head birds have been seen flying through the lighthouse beams, or heard calling in the darkness overhead, a further dimension to one's watching and one which also helps ensure that you are there at dawn.

One of the most exciting events to have taken place at Strumble Head was the sighting in the autumn of 1986 of a South Polar Skua. This species breeds on many coasts and islands in Antarctic and sub-Antarctic seas, and rarely wanders into the northern hemisphere. Great Skuas pass regularly each autumn, 469 having been recorded on 44 days between 28 July and 17 November 1985; nearly a third of that total was on a single day, an indication of the importance of the right weather conditions. Slightly larger numbers of Arctic Skuas passed during the same period, together with about 100 Pomarine Skuas, while Long-tailed Skuas are much less frequent, only nine being recorded during 1985. The 75 Little Gulls seen on 10 November 1985 was a remarkable total, as most which pass are single birds. Small numbers of Sabine's Gulls are seen each autumn, birds moving from Arctic breeding grounds to winter quarters in the mid-Atlantic. Kittiwakes are always offshore and at times immense passages have been observed, for example the 19,000 seen passing west in seven hours on 17 October 1983 and 18,000 in eleven hours on 20 October 1984. There is a regular late-summer movement of terns, though most have left by early October. A Gull-billed Tern on 30 July 1985 was especially noteworthy. From mid-September onwards, large numbers of Guillemots and Razorbills flight southwards through St George's Channel, many passing close to Strumble Head, while small numbers fish in the tide-races. Occasionally Black Guillemots, Little Auks and Puffins are seen.

When seabird passage has died away, or when you need a change, then it is always well worth searching the sheltered valleys to the east and west for small migrants. Among the highlights are the bands of tits and Goldcrests which work their way so actively along the cliffs in autumn. Rare visitors are seen occasionally, though a Pallid Swift on two successive days in November 1984 was exceptional, and on a strange date for a bird that breeds in northwest Africa eastwards across the Mediterranean to Iran; it seems likely that it moved northwards during an unusual incursion of southerly air, as several were reported elsewhere in Britain at this time. Other rarities have included Siberian Stonechat and Pallas's and Yellow-browed Warblers. In the early part of September, large numbers of Sand Martins and Swallows flight in from the sea and then follow the coast to the southwest, to be followed from mid-October by at times immense passages of Skylarks, Meadow Pipits, thrushes, Starlings and finches, which are a special feature of late-autumn watches at Strumble Head. Should the weather be unfavourable to passage movement, then retire to Fishguard Harbour 4 miles (6.4 km) away; in due season there are divers, grebes, seaducks and waders, while a recent highlight was a Ross's Gull in February 1981.

Timing

It is essential that one arrives at dawn to catch the main movements, both in numbers and in species, though it is always worth watching whatever the time of day. Much depends on the weather situation, the ideal being gale-force southwesterly winds which, on veering northwesterly and decreasing, have the effect of releasing large numbers of birds previously held back in the Irish Sea.

Access

An unclassified road is well signed from Fishguard Harbour and terminates at Strumble Head, where there is ample car-parking at SM895414. This allows watching from the car, but better still is the large former War Department building just below, which provides some degree of shelter, though beware: it is a popular spot, and up to 40 birdwatchers have been known to gather there on 'good' mornings during the early autumn.

Calendar

Resident Fulmar, Gannet, Cormorant, Shag, Common Scoter, Buzzard, Kestrel, Peregrine, Oystercatcher, Lesser Black-backed, Herring and Great Black-backed Gulls, Rock Pipit, Stonechat, Linnet, Yellowhammer.

December–February Red-throated and Great Northern Divers, Wigeon, Scaup, Eider, Velvet Scoter, Goldeneye, Merlin, Purple Sandpiper, Turnstone, Black-headed and Common Gulls, Guillemot, Razorbill.

March–May Possible returning Arctic and Great Skuas, small numbers of terns, mostly Sandwich Tern, from early April. On land a range of summer visitors likely to be seen includes Whimbrel, Common Sandpiper, Cuckoo, Wheatear, Ring Ouzel, warblers and Spotted Flycatcher, while passing Sand Martins and Swallows with the occasional House Martin seen throughout April and May.

June–July The few breeding species in evidence, while some local movements of Manx Shearwaters and Gannets offshore. The first terns begin to reappear by end of July.

August–November This is the time to be at Strumble Head, and if you are able to spend a reasonable period there you should observe among others Cory's, Great, Sooty and Manx Shearwaters, also the Balearic race of Manx Shearwater, Leach's Petrel, Wigeon, Eider, Velvet Scoter, Ringed Plover, Knot, Dunlin, Black-tailed and Bar-tailed Godwits, Whimbrel, Curlew, Turnstone, Pomarine, Arctic, Long-tailed and Great Skuas, Little and Sabine's Gulls, Kittiwake, Sandwich, Common and Arctic Terns, Guillemot, Razorbill, Puffin. Swallow and Sand Martin, and from mid-October Skylark, Meadow Pipit, thrushes, Starling, finches.

Habitat

The lonely uplands on the Cardiganshire-Radnorshire border give rise to numerous streams which chatter down steep valleys to feed the Claerwen and Elan Rivers, tributaries of the Wye. Here a group of five reservoirs has been built: Craig Goch, Penygarreg, Garreg-ddu, Caban-coch and Claerwen, the last two on the border with Breconshire. The reservoirs supply water to Birmingham and the West Midlands, and are a renowned tourist attraction in central Wales. All can be viewed easily from public roads. Some coniferous plantations surround the lower reservoirs, but as one proceeds up the valleys these are left behind and the uplands, which rise to 1,800 feet (550 m) at Bryn Eithiniog, are largely sheep-grazed moor.

Species

It is surprising to report that the first records of Bewick's and Whooper Swans in Radnorshire were as recently as 1962, when small parties of both species were seen on the Elan Reservoirs. Both are now regular visitors in small numbers to the county, the Whooper Swan in particular being seen annually at the reservoirs, though generally only as a single family party. Diving ducks occur in small numbers, mostly Pochard, Tufted Duck, Goldeneye and Red-breasted Merganser, scarce visitors having included Ferruginous Duck, Common Scoter and Smew. Goosander numbers build up in the late winter and may total 40 birds by March; they first nested in the county in 1972, when nine young were seen in the Elan Valley. Who would have thought it possible to record the Herring Gull anywhere in Britain as a scarce passage migrant? Yet this is its status in Radnorshire, only 15 having been recorded between 1952 and 1984, a third of these at the Elan Reservoirs. Not so surprising is the scarcity of Kittiwake records: indeed there is just one, but the fact that it was of a flock of 14 adult birds in mid-May 1976, when they really should have been at their cliff breeding colonies, makes it even more remarkable and just goes to show the continuing mystery and excitement of birdwatching. Common Terns very occasionally arrive at the reservoirs while on late-summer passage. If the water levels are low at this time it is worth looking for migrant waders, and there are usually Common Sandpipers about as they breed along the shore. Although the Osprey has yet to be recorded here, it now seems to be a regular, if uncommon, spring and autumn passage migrant along the Wye, so that it is surely only a matter of time before one is seen hunting over the reservoirs.

The uplands to the west of the Elan Valley contain small numbers of breeding Golden Plovers, Lapwings, Dunlins, Snipe, Curlews and Redshanks. Other upland breeding birds include Tree Pipit, Whinchat, Stonechat, Wheatear, Ring Ouzel, Linnet and Reed Bunting. In winter, Hen Harriers and Merlins take up residence, the latter having formerly nested here. Scarce visitors have included Rough-legged Buzzard Roller and Dotterel.

Timing

This is not critical, though early morning is by far the best and should enable you to avoid the large number of visitors to the reservoir sides.

Common Sandpiper

Even at the peak of the holiday season, however, if you make a short walk away from the roadside you seem to have the hills to yourself.

Access

Well signed from Rhayader, with an unclassified road terminating at a car park below the Claerwen Reservoir. In the Elan Valley, the road follows the shoreline of the reservoirs save for the upper reaches of Penygarreg and the whole of Craig Goch. From the head of the Craig Goch Reservoir you have a choice: return the way you have come; turn east over Penrhiw-wen to Rhayader; or turn west on up the valley and eventually over the hills to Cwmystwyth in Cardiganshire. If you wish to explore the tops, take the ancient trackway on foot southwest from SN897716 for 4 miles (6.4 km) to the head of the Claerwen Reservoir.

Calendar

Resident Mallard, Goosander, Red Kite, Buzzard, Kestrel, Peregrine, Red Grouse, Coot, Snipe, Skylark, Meadow Pipit, Grey and Pied Wagtails, Dipper, Stonechat, Mistle Thrush and Reed Bunting.

December–February Whooper Swan, Pochard, Tufted Duck, Goldeneye, Red-breasted Merganser, Hen Harrier, Merlin.

March–May Upland waders arrive by end of March, including Golden Plover, Lapwing, Dunlin, Snipe, Curlew, Redshank, Common Sandpipers return to reservoirs during April. Other summer visitors include Cuckoo, Tree Pipit, Wheatear, Whinchat, Ring Ouzel.

June–July All residents and summer visitors present, though the upland waders have largely departed by late July.

August–November Chance of passage waders, even terns, at the reservoirs during August and early part of September, following which winter ducks begin to appear, Whooper Swans from early November onwards. Probably Snow Bunting on the high ground at this time — but who goes to look?

Habitat

The Wye forms the boundary between Radnorshire and Breconshire, and shortly after Erwood the river at last squeezes from its gorge to commence a meandering course across the water meadows to the west, and then to the east, of Glasbury. The remnants of long-disused channels can still clearly be seen, while there are several pools which retain water in all but the driest summers.

Species

This is probably the best spot in the county for wildfowl and waders, which share both banks of the river and so two counties. Up to ten Little Grebes winter here, and are occasionally joined by Great Crested Grebes. Although barely 20 pairs of Grey Herons nest in Radnorshire, they are often to be seen feeding on this section of river or flying past. Several pairs of Mute Swans breed, while in late summer a flock of up to 60 may congregate. Bewick's Swans now winter annually, with up to 40 recorded on occasions, but Whooper Swans are less frequent for this species prefers upland lakes and reservoirs. Canada Geese barely ever breed in Radnorshire, but during the winter a flock moves in from Herefordshire to feed on the pastures around Glasbury. Normally the Wigeon flock is up to 40 strong, but cold weather further east results in a rapid rise in numbers. Teals frequent the meanders, but the most numerous duck is the Mallard, with flocks of up to 200 having been reported. Goldeneyes are regular throughout the winter, while hard weather brings Pochard and Tufted Duck and occasionally Scaup and Long-tailed Duck. Common Scoter and Garganey have been recorded on several occasions. Goosanders are regularly seen, with family parties totalling up to 100 females and ducklings having been recorded along the course of the Wye during the summer of 1986.

The first record of the Little Ringed Plover for Radnorshire was of one on the Wye at Glasbury in May 1985. Will this species eventually colonise gravel banks on the river? Ringed Plovers are occasionally seen, while the meadows attract several hundred Golden Plovers and Lapwings during the winter, together with a few Curlews. Other waders seen include Redshank, Greenshank and Green and Wood Sandpipers, while Common Sandpipers breed and occasionally overwinter. The Great Black-backed Gull is a regular but scarce winter visitor to the Glasbury area, having been recorded only once elsewhere in the county. Among breeding species, look out for Yellow Wagtails.

Timing

Not critical here, though as elsewhere early-morning visits are much to be preferred.

Access

The A438, A4079 and B4350 roads all give good general views. On foot, you can walk north from the bridge at Hay-on-Wye for nearly 2 miles (3.2 km) following a section of the Offa's Dyke Path. To the southwest of the town, the Wye Valley Long Distance Footpath follows the river for nearly 2 miles (3.2 km) before returning to the B4350 at SO203421.

Calendar

Resident Grey Heron, Mute Swan, Mallard, Goosander, Moorhen, Coot, Kingfisher, Grey and Pied Wagtails, Dipper, Reed Bunting.

December–February Little and Great Crested Grebes, Bewick's and Whooper Swans, Wigeon, Teal, Pintail, Shoveler, Pochard, Tufted Duck, Goldeneye, Golden Plover, Lapwing, Curlew, Great Black-backed Gull.

March–May Common Sandpiper and Yellow Wagtail arrive in mid-April, by which time water levels are dropping and wintering species have departed.

June–July The few breeding species are present, Mute Swan numbers rise, chance of passage waders during late July.

August–November Passage waders likely until well into September, including Ringed Plover, Dunlin, Redshank, Greenshank, Green and Wood Sandpipers. As autumn proceeds the winter ducks arrive, followed by Bewick's Swans during November.

54 MAELIENYDD

Map 54
OS Map 148

Habitat

Extending northeast from the Ithon Valley is the ridge of Maelienydd, rising to 1,400 feet (427 m) at its highest point but much being no more than 950 feet (290 m) in altitude. This is one of the few reasonably sized areas of upland rough grazing remaining in Radnorshire, a bonus feature being the presence of several small pools and adjoining marshy areas. Habitats such as this have been rapidly disappearing as improvements for agriculture have taken place, and in addition to Maelienydd only those at Penybont Common and Rhosgoch now remain.

Species

Teals possibly nest here though this is difficult to prove, but there are usually a few at the pools, where they are joined by Mallards. Red Kites sometimes hunt over these uplands, though Buzzards, and during the winter Hen Harriers, are more likely to be seen. Perhaps the most exciting record for Maelienydd is that of the Stone-curlew seen on 20 August 1980, the first noted for the county, though likely rarely to be repeated. Good numbers of Golden Plovers occur in winter, but sadly there seem to be no recent breeding records. Large flocks of Lapwings gather each autumn, when up to 1,000 birds have been recorded. Waders noted at the pools include Little Stint, Curlew Sandpiper, Dunlin, Black-tailed and Bar-tailed Godwits, Spotted Redshank, Redshank and Greenshank. Among the few passerines, look out for Whinchat, Stonechat and Wheatear.

Timing

Not critical, but early morning is best.

Access

Two unclassified roads cross Maelienydd. To join these, leave the A483 Newtown to Llandrindod Wells road at Llanbister (SO107735) or at Llanddewi Ystradenni (SO108686); several footpaths provide access on to the upland.

Calendar

Resident Teal, Mallard, Red Kite, Buzzard, Moorhen, Lapwing, Skylark, Meadow Pipit, Stonechat, Mistle Thrush, Carrion Crow, Raven, Linnet, Reed Bunting.

December–February Hen Harrier, Merlin, Peregrine, Golden Plover, Snipe.

March–May Cuckoo, Tree Pipit, Whinchat, Wheatear, Whitethroat are among the summer visitors, while Swallows are not infrequent flighting over the high ground.

June–July All residents and summer visitors present. In hot weather, large numbers of Swifts may hunt for insects high over the uplands.

August–November Summer visitors depart, Wheatears may remain until late September, even early October in some years. Passage waders throughout August and September, Ringed Plover, Dunlin, Curlew and Green Sandpiper being the most frequently recorded. From mid-October winter visitors include Fieldfare and Redwing, possibility of Snow Bunting.

Habitat

During a three-year survey of over 100 western oak woodlands, the Royal Society for the Protection of Birds identified several in the Upper Wye Valley as being among the best for birds. Since then, the RSPB has acquired three woodlands and an upland area close by, part of a policy of establishing major reserves by the gradual acquisition of at times quite small parcels of land containing key habitats. The woodlands here are on the steep valley sides close to where the Elan joins the Wye south of Rhayader. The river forms the boundary with Breconshire, and some of the reserve, including Carn Gafallt, is to the west and therefore in the neighbouring county. At present, the holding comprises the woodlands of Dyffryn (54 acres/22 ha), Cwm (18 acres/7.3 ha), Glanllyn (100 acres/40 ha) and the heather-dominated plateau of Carn Gafallt (643 acres/260 ha). There is a rich flora, while the woodland butterflies recorded include Purple Hairstreak, and Pearl-bordered, Small Pearl-bordered and Silver-washed Fritillaries.

Species

All woodland birds of western Britain are to be found here, with many populations, particularly those of Redstart, Wood Warbler and Pied Flycatcher, at a high level. Other species include Blackcap, Chiffchaff, Willow Warbler, Spotted Flycatcher and Willow Tit. Ravens breed in the woodland, and are regularly seen flying along the valley sides or across the uplands. Siskins breed in the valley, and there are usually Redpolls about also. Leave the woods behind, and on the approaches to the plateau the birds encountered include Tree Pipit and Whinchat. At least eight species of raptor are seen here, including Red Kite, Sparrowhawk, Buzzard, Kestrel and Peregrine. The river, too, is a special feature, with Goosander, Common Sandpiper, Kingfisher, Grey Wagtail and Dipper.

Timing

Not critical, but a dawn visit in May or early June must be the aim of every reader.

Access

Access to Dyffryn Wood is possible at all times from a lay-by at SN980672 on the A470 just south of Rhayader. The road closely follows the river through the gorge and provides possibilities for observation at several points. Carn Gafallt is also open at all times; footpaths climb from the minor road between Llanwrthwl and Elan Village.

Calendar

Resident Goosander, Red Kite, Sparrowhawk, Buzzard, Kestrel, Peregrine, Red Grouse, Pheasant, Woodcock, Stock Dove, Woodpigeon, Tawny Owl, Kingfisher, Green and Great Spotted Woodpeckers, Skylark, Meadow Pipit, Grey and Pied Wagtails, Dipper, Wren, Dunnock, Robin, Blackbird, Song and Mistle Thrushes, Goldcrest, Long-tailed, Marsh,

Pied Flycatcher

Willow, Coal, Blue and Great Tits, Nuthatch, Treecreeper, Jay, Raven, Chaffinch, Greenfinch, Goldfinch, Siskin, Redpoll, Yellowhammer.

December–February Fieldfare, Redwing, Brambling.

March–May Chiffchaff the first summer visitor to arrive, usually before end of March, other arrivals as April proceeds are Common Sandpiper, Cuckoo, Tree Pipit, Redstart, Whinchat, Garden Warbler, Wood Warbler, Willow Warbler, Spotted and Pied Flycatchers. Male Goosanders depart during May.

June–July Goosander broods on river. All residents and summer visitors about, though many not very evident by end of July.

August–November Gradual and largely unnoticed departure of summer migrants. Fieldfare and Redwing together with a few Bramblings from mid-October. Resident tits, often joined by Goldcrests and Treecreepers, forage in bands through the woods, so some areas temporarily devoid of birds while in another spot they seem to be everywhere — just one of the attractions of the winter woodlands.

ADDITIONAL SITES

Although Wales is a small country, in birdwatching terms it is large and in addition to the 55 main sites described in detail there are numerous other bird watching areas deserving attention, some of which are listed below.

Site and Grid Reference	Habitat	Main Bird Interest	Peak Season
Anglesey			
Alaw Estuary SH300814	Estuary	Wildfowl and waders	Late summer to early spring
Carmel Head SH297931	Coastal headland	Seabird passage; a Slender-billed Gull in August 1985, if accepted, will be the first for Wales	All year, but especially late summer/early autumn
Inland Sea SH275795	Estuary	Terns and waders	April to September
Penrhos SH276804	Woodland, marsh and estuary	Woodland species, while the marsh and estuary attract a range of wildfowl and waders	All year
Soldiers Point SH237837	Edge of harbour	Seabirds, divers, grebes, chance of scarce migrants; an Isabelline Shrike in 1985 was the first for Wales	Late summer to spring
Breconshire			
Brechfa Pool SO119377	Small pool	Bewick's Swan, Wigeon, Teal, Mallard, passage waders	Late summer to early spring
Craig Cerrig Gleisiad SN965220	Sandstone crags, cliffs and gullies	Buzzard, Peregrine, Red Grouse, Ring Ouzel	Summer
Craig y Cilau SO189158	Limestone escarpment and wood-land	Buzzard, Kestrel, woodland birds, Raven	Summer

166

Site and Grid Reference	Habitat	Main Bird Interest	Peak Season
Dderw Pool SO142376	Two small pools	Winter wildfowl and passage waders	Late summer to early spring
Llwyn-On SO005110	Reservoir	Whooper Swan, Teal, Pochard, Tufted Duck	Winter
Priory Groves SO049295	Woodland	Woodland birds, plus Grey Wagtail and Dipper on river	All year
Pwll Gwy Rhoc SO184153	Upland pool	Passage waders, upland birds	Late summer

Caernarvonshire

Site and Grid Reference	Habitat	Main Bird Interest	Peak Season
Aberdaron Bay SH173263	Coastal bay and headland	Winter divers and grebes, passage seabirds; migrants have included Subalpine Warbler and Lesser Grey Shrike	Late summer to spring
Conwy Estuary SH775790	Estuary and coastal sands	Small numbers of ducks, large numbers of waders	Late summer to spring
Fforyd Bay SH450600	Estuary	Wildfowl and waders, chance of Snow Bunting	Late summer to early spring
Gwydr Forest SH770589	Extensive conifer plantations plus broadleaved areas and open moorland	Buzzard, Black Grouse, Woodcock, Common Crossbill, Siskin	All year, but especially spring/early summer
Pencilan Head SH294230	Coastal cliffs	Seabirds, Peregrine, Stonechat, Chough	April to September
Penrhyn Glas SH336439	Coastal cliffs	Seabirds, Stonechat, Chough, Raven	April to September

Cardiganshire

Site and Grid Reference	Habitat	Main Bird Interest	Peak Season
Coed Cwm Ddu SN309429	Woodland and river	Woodland birds, plus Grey Wagtail and Dipper	All year

Site and Grid Reference	Habitat	Main Bird Interest	Peak Season
Cwm Clettwr SN670920	Woodland in steep-sided valley	Woodland birds, including Sparrowhawk and Pied Flycatcher	All year, but, best in spring
Falcondale SN569499	Small lowland lake	Great Crested Grebe, Mallard, Shoveler, Coot	All year
Llyn Eiddwen SN607674	Upland lake	Whooper Swan, small numbers of other wildfowl	˙Winter and early spring
Llyn Oerfa SN728798	Upland lake	Whooper Swan, occasional other wildfowl	Winter
Old Warren Hill SN613787	Woodland	Woodland birds, including Pied Flycatcher	All year
Pen Deri SN550732	Cliffs and cliff woodland	Cormorant, Shag, Peregrine, Chough, Raven	All year

Carmarthenshire

Site and Grid Reference	Habitat	Main Bird Interest	Peak Season
Brechfa Forest SN525303	Coniferous woodland and river valleys	Buzzard, Great Spotted Woodpecker plus river birds	All year
Lledi Reservoirs SN515040	Two small reservoirs	Great Crested Grebe, small numbers of winter wildfowl	All year
Llyn Pencarreg SN536456	Kettle-hole lake	Winter wildfowl, occasional passage waders and terns	Late summer to early spring
Llyn-y-Fan Fach SN803217	Glacial lake below high crags	Peregrine, Red Grouse, Common Sandpiper, Ring Ouzel	Summer
Old Castle Pond SN500003	Town pond	Coot, Moorhen and Reed Warbler breed, winter wildfowl	All year

Site and Grid Reference	Habitat	Main Bird Interest	Peak Season
Pendine SN234079	Sea coast with some cliffs to west	Common Scoter all year, much larger numbers in winter, when joined by other species; a White Stork ringed in Germany was an outstanding visitor	All year, but especially winter
Poor Man's Wood SN785355	Woodland	All common woodland species, including Wood Warbler	All year

Denbighshire

Site and Grid Reference	Habitat	Main Bird Interest	Peak Season
Ceiriog Valley SJ158329	Woodland, moor and river valley	Red and Black Grouse, Short-eared Owl, Kingfisher, woodland birds	Spring and early summer
Llyn Gweryd SJ173550	Upland lake	Black-headed Gull breeds, winter wildfowl	All year
Tanat Valley SJ155243	River valley	Buzzard, Common Sandpiper, Kingfisher, Dipper	Summer
World's End SJ233478	Upland	Red Grouse, Ring Ouzel, Raven	Summer
Wrexham Gravel Pits SJ346536	Gravel pits	Canada Goose, Pochard, Tufted Duck, Goldeneye	Winter

Flintshire

Site and Grid Reference	Habitat	Main Bird Interest	Peak Season
Clwyd Estuary SJ005794	Narrow estuary	Wildfowl and waders, Dunlin especially numerous	Winter
Cilcain SJ166642	Reservoirs	Teal, Mallard, Merlin, Red Grouse	Summer
Connah's Quay SJ275715	CEGB power station reserve	Wildfowl and waders	All year
Llyn Helyg SJ115773	Lowland lake	Great Crested Grebe and winter wildfowl	All year

Site and Grid Reference	Habitat	Main Bird Interest	Peak Season
Glamorgan			
Aberthaw ST036662	Estuary and lagoons	Waders and gulls	Late summer to spring
Broad Pool SS510910	Pool and adjacent wet heath	Lapwing, Snipe, Redshank; Bewick's Swan in winter	All year
Craig-y-llyn SN905038	Upland lake and crags	Peregrine, Ring Ouzel, Raven	All year
Cyfartha Castle SO040072	Lake	Wildfowl	Winter
Eglwys Nunydd SS795840	Industrial reservoir	Winter wildfowl, passage waders, occasional terns	All year, but best in winter
Lisvane ST190822	Reservoir	Mainly winter wild-fowl, but is noted for Tufted Duck which gather to moult from late summer	All year, but especially in winter
Llanishen ST186816	Reservoir	As for Lisvane, but more prone to disturbance from waterborne activities	Winter
Neath Estuary SS723929	Estuary and sandy beach	Waders and some wildfowl; a Sociable Plover in October 1984 was the first for Wales	Late summer to early spring
Merionethshire			
Aber Dysynni SH561032	Sea coast	Seabirds on passage, divers and grebes	Late summer to spring
Bala Lake SH902321	Largest natural fresh-water site in Wales	Occasional waders and passage terns, winter wildfowl	All year
Broadwater SH580025	Estuarine pool	Whooper Swan, Wigeon, Teal, waders	Late summer to early spring
Cader Idris SH712130	High upland with crags and cliffs	Wheatear, Ring Ouzel, Raven	Summer

Site and Grid Reference	Habitat	Main Bird Interest	Peak Season
Coed y Brenin SH771527	Coniferous woodlands and river valley	Common Sandpiper, Kingfisher, Dipper, Redpoll, Siskin	All year
Llyn Trawsfynydd SH697384	Reservoir and adjacent woodland	Common Sandpiper, breeding gulls and Common Terns, winter wildfowl and woodland species	All year
Tal-y-llyn SH716100	Lake	Great Crested Grebe, Common Sandpiper, winter ducks, occasional passage waders and terns	All year

Monmouthshire

Site and Grid Reference	Habitat	Main Bird Interest	Peak Season
Blorenge SO260109	Heather moor	Merlin, Red Grouse, Whinchat, Wheatear	All year
Five Locks ST287968	Disused canal	Kingfisher, Redpoll, Siskin	All year
Llanthony Valley SO255315	Remote valley and upland	Buzzard, Peregrine, Red Grouse, Dipper, Wood Warbler	All year
Lower Wye ST526973	River valley with fine woodlands	Woodland birds including Pied Flycatcher, some estuary and river species	All year
Strawberry Cottage SO315214	Woodland	Redstart, Pied Flycatcher, tit family, Nuthatch	All year
Sugar Loaf SO268168	Upland	Buzzard, Kestrel, Whinchat, Wheatear	Summer
Wentwood ST430933	Reservoir and woodland	Wildfowl and woodland species	Winter

Montgomeryshire

Site and Grid Reference	Habitat	Main Bird Interest	Peak Season
Clywedog SN896878	Reservoir	Wildfowl, including Red-breasted Merganser, occasional passage waders and terns	Late summer to early spring

Site and Grid Reference	Habitat	Main Bird Interest	Peak Season
Glaslyn Moors SN825945	Heather moor	Hen Harrier, Merlin, Red Grouse, Golden Plover	All year
Llyn Du SJ174127	Lake	Great Crested Grebe and Coot breed, passage waders, winter wildfowl	All year
Llyn Mawr SO008971	Upland lake	Wildfowl include a small flock of White-fronted Geese	Winter

Pembrokeshire

Site and Grid Reference	Habitat	Main Bird Interest	Peak Season
Broad Haven SM860136	Sea coast	Fulmar, Peregrine, Chough, winter divers, grebes and Common Scoter, terns in late summer	All year
Dinas Head SN005414	Fine coastal headland	Peregrine, Chough, seabirds, Stonechat	All year
Fishguard Harbour SM951382	Open water, rocky and sandy shores	Red-throated Diver, Great Crested Grebe, small numbers of waders; check the gull flocks carefully	Winter to spring
Gwaun Valley SN046350	Valley woods and river	Buzzard, Sparrow-hawk, Grey Wagtail, Dipper, woodland species include Redstart	All year
Llys-y-fran SN037243	Reservoir	Wildfowl, with Pochard and Tufted Duck the main species	Late summer to early spring
Marloes Mere SM776083	Rushy pasture	Wildfowl include Wales' only flock of Barnacle Geese	Autumn to spring
Nevern SN060396	Estuary	Wildfowl and waders	Late summer to spring

Radnorshire

Site and Grid Reference	Habitat	Main Bird Interest	Peak Season
Llandrindod Wells Lake SO063605	Town lake	Wildfowl	Winter

Site and Grid Reference	Habitat	Main Bird Interest	Peak Season
Llyn Heilyn SO167581	Pool beside A481	Wildfowl, with occasional passage waders	Late summer to early spring
Pencerrig Lake SO045542	Small lake	Breeding Tufted Duck, winter wildfowl	All year
Radnor Forest SO197645	Uplands and coniferous woodlands	Merlin, Red Grouse, Golden Plover, Siskin	All year
Rhosgoch SO195485	Marsh and pool	Breeding species include Curlew, Sedge Warbler and Reed Bunting	All year

COUNTY AVIFAUNAS, RECORDERS, REPORTS, SOCIETIES AND OTHER USEFUL ADDRESSES

For a short general background to the history of bird-recording in Wales readers are recommended to consult the paper by Christine Johnson, 'County Bird Recording in Wales', in *Nature in Wales* (1983) 2: 57–62, together with a follow-up letter in the same journal (1985) 4: 122–123. In some counties more than one avifauna has been published, for instance, in the case of Pembrokeshire, one in 1894 and a second in 1949. Only the most recent and informative accounts of the counties are listed here, but as readers can see many are out of date, some lamentably so, and there is an urgent need for new ones to be published. This situation cannot be a result of a shortage of records, or of the necessary information, but rather stems from the herculean efforts which are needed to sift in some cases nearly half a century of records into a digest suitable for publication. The effort will, however, be well worthwhile; the readers await, and such work can only stimulate further interest in and investigation of birds in Wales.

Unlike in Scotland and Ireland, there has never been a 'Birds of Wales', but one is currently in preparation by Roger Lovegrove and Graham Williams, both of the RSPB's Wales Office. It is eagerly awaited, though patience is required; the task is huge, but the eventual publication will surely be a landmark in Welsh ornithology.

Anglesey No avifauna ever published for this county. Why has this omission been allowed to be perpetuated?

Breconshire Massey, M. E. 1976. *Birds of Breconshire*. Brecon. See also Radnorshire.

Caernarvonshire Hope Jones, P., and Dare, P. J. 1976. *Birds of Caernarvonshire*. Cambrian Ornithological Society, Colwyn Bay.

Cardiganshire Ingram, G. C. S., Salmon, H. M., and Condry, W. M. 1966. *The Birds of Cardiganshire*. West Wales Naturalists' Trust, Haverfordwest.

Carmarthenshire Ingram, G. C. S., and Salmon, H. M. 1954. *A Hand List of the Birds of Carmarthenshire*. West Wales Field Society, Haverfordwest.

Denbighshire Hope Jones, P., and Roberts, J. L. 1983. *Birds of Denbighshire. Nature in Wales* new series 2 : 56–65.

Flintshire Done, C., Birch, J. E., Birch, R. R., Birkwell, J. M., Stokes, E. J., and Walton, G. F. 1968. *The Birds of Flintshire*. Flintshire Ornithological Society, Rhyl.

Glamorgan Heathcote, A., Griffin, D., and Salmon, H. M. 1967. *The Birds of Glamorgan.* Cardiff Naturalists' Society, Cardiff. Also: Salmon, H. M. 1974. *A Supplement to the Birds of Glamorgan.* Cardiff Naturalists' Society, Cardiff.

Merionethshire Hope Jones, P. 1974. *Birds of Merioneth.* Cambrian Ornithological Society, Colwyn Bay.

Monmouthshire Ferns, P. N., Hamar, H. W., Humphreys, P. N., *et al.* 1977. *The Birds of Gwent.* Gwent Ornithological Society, Pontypool.

Montgomeryshire No avifauna published for this county.

Pembrokeshire Ingram, G. C. S., Lockley, R. M., and Salmon, H. M. 1949. *The Birds of Pembrokeshire.* West Wales Field Society, Haverfordwest.

Radnorshire Peers, M. 1985. *Birds of Radnorshire and Mid Powys.* Llangammarch Wells. Includes a ten-page supplement covering North Breconshire.

In addition to the county avifaunas, reference must be made to the islands, with lists being published for:

Bardsey Roberts, P. 1985. *The Birds of Bardsey.* Bardsey Bird and Field Observatory, Bardsey.

Skokholm 1983. *Birds of Skokholm.* West Wales Trust for Nature Conservation, Haverfordwest.

County bird recorders
If you are birdwatching in Wales, please do not forget to send your records to the relevant recorder listed below. Records of common species, as well as of the less common and the rare vagrants, are always needed. Please share your pleasurable hours of watching with others, in the knowledge that your observations are of interest and assistance in allowing us to learn more about the birds of Wales.

Anglesey T. Gravett, Tyddyn Llan, Eglwsbach, Colwyn Bay, Clwyd, LL28 5TY.

Breconshire Martin Peers, Gorsebank, Llangammarch Wells, Powys.

Caernarvonshire As for Anglesey.

Cardiganshire P. E. Davis, Felindre, Aberarth, Aberaeron, Dyfed, SA46 0LP.

Carmarthenshire D. H. V. Roberts, 6 Ger-y-Coed, Pontiets, Llanelli, Dyfed, SA15 5UN.

Denbighshire As for Anglesey.

Flintshire R. Birch, 8 Thornberry Close, Saughall, Cheshire.

Glamorgan (Mid) J. R. Smith, 15 Milton Drive, Bridgend, Mid Glamorgan, CF31 4QE.

Glamorgan (South) R. C. Smith, 29 Marlborough Close, Llantwit Fardre, Mid Glamorgan, CF28 2NP.

Glamorgan (West) H. E. Grenfell, The Woods, 14 Bryn Terrace, Mumbles, Swansea, West Glamorgan, SA3 4HD.

Merionethshire F. A. Curie, Ty Clyd, Alyn Road, Fairbourne, Gwynedd, LL38 2LZ.

Monmouthshire B. J. Gregory, Monmouth School, Monmouth, Gwent, NP5 3XP.

Montgomeryshire R. G. Burton, RSPB Wales Office, Frolic Street, Newtown, Powys, SY16 1AP.

Pembrokeshire J. W. Donovan, The Burren, Dingle Lane, Crundale, Haverfordwest, Dyfed.

Radnorshire A. J. Smith, Tree Cottage, Holme Marsh, near Lyonshall, Kington, Herefordshire, HR5 3JS.

County bird reports

From 1967 a 'Welsh Bird Report', ably compiled by P. E. Davis and P. Hope Jones, was published in the journal *Nature in Wales*. Unfortunately it was not possible to continue beyond 1976, and regretfully no other means has subsequently been found to publish such an annual report. Most of Wales is, however, covered by county reports, the situation in 1987 being as follows.

Anglesey The bird report for Gwynedd covers the counties of Anglesey, Caernarvon and Merioneth, together with Denbigh which, just to add a little confusion, lies in Clwyd. Available from Dr G. L. McLeod, 21 Benarth Court, Glan Conwy, Colwyn Bay, Clwyd, LL28 5ED.

Breconshire No report currently published.

Caernarvonshire See Anglesey.

Cardiganshire Bi-annual report available from West Wales Trust for Nature Conservation, 7 Market Street, Haverfordwest, Dyfed, SA61 1NF.

Carmarthenshire Annual reports available as for Cardiganshire.

Denbighshire See Anglesey.

Flintshire No report currently published.

Glamorgan Annual report for Mid and South Glamorgan from D. H. Binstead, 37 Penhill Road, Llandaff, Cardiff, CF1 9PR. *Gower Birds,* the annual report of the Gower Ornithological Society, now includes records for the whole of West Glamorgan (in earlier years it dealt only with Gower): available from R. H. Davies, 203 Penybanc Road, Ammanford, Dyfed, SA18 3QP.

Merionethshire See Anglesey.

Monmouthshire The 'Gwent Bird Report' is published annually and is available from D. H. Wood, 17 Castle Park Road, Newport, Gwent.

Montgomeryshire Most recent report available is that for 1982, which may be obtained from the Montgomery Trust for Nature Conservation, 8 Severn Square, Newtown, Powys, SY16 2AG.

Pembrokeshire Annual report available as for Cardiganshire.

Radnorshire Bird records for Radnorshire are published along with those for Hereford in the annual report of the Herefordshire Ornithological Club, available from Mrs J. M. Bromley, The Garth, Kington, Herefordshire, HR5 3BA.

In addition to the county reports, the following will also be of interest:

Bardsey The annual report for the Observatory contains the systematic bird list and is available from R. G. Loxton, Department of Zoology, University of Leeds, Leeds, LS2 9JT.

Skokholm and Skomer A joint report for the two islands is published in the winter issue of the 'Friends of Skokholm and Skomer Bulletin', available from the West Wales Trust for Nature Conservation, 7 Market Street, Haverfordwest, Dyfed, SA61 1NF.

Nature in Wales First published in 1955 by the then West Wales Field Society, the journal *Nature in Wales* was later shared with the North Wales Naturalists' Trust and publication continued until 1983, when the National Museum of Wales took over the responsibility of the journal, subsequently publishing to date nine issues, of which seven have been double issues. Although covering all aspects of natural history, the ornithological content over the years has been high, and no serious student of the birds of Wales should neglect to consult back numbers as well as current issues. Copies of most back issues are available from the West Wales Trust for Nature Conservation.

Bird clubs and societies

Anglesey The Cambrian Ornithological Society covers the counties of Anglesey, Caernarvon, Denbigh and Merioneth. Dr G. L. McLeod, 21 Benarth Court, Glan Conwy, Colwyn Bay, Clwyd, LL28 5ED.

Breconshire Brecknock Naturalists' Trust, Lion House, 7 Lion Street, Brecon, Powys.

Caernarvonshire See Anglesey.

Cardiganshire West Wales Trust for Nature Conservation, 7 Market Street, Haverfordwest, Dyfed, SA61 1NF.

Carmarthenshire As for Cardiganshire. In the extreme southeast of the county the Llanelli Naturalists' Society is active: Secretary, Richard Pryce, Rhyd Deg, Maes-y-Bont, Llanelli, Dyfed, SA14 7HG.

Denbighshire Clwyd Ornithological Society, Mrs Carolyn Gradwell, 48 Fordd Pentre, Carmel, Holywell, Clwyd, CH7 1PZ. Wrexham Birdwatchers' Society, Miss Merion T. Williams, 10 Lake View, Gresford, Wrexham, Clwyd, LL12 8PU.

Flintshire Clwyd Ornithological Society, as for Denbighshire. Deeside Naturalists' Society, R. A. Roberts, 38 Kelsterton Road, Connah's Quay, Clwyd, CH5 4BJ.

Glamorgan Cardiff Naturalists' Society, Stephen Howe, Department of Geology, National Museum of Wales, Cardiff, CF1 3NP. For West Glamorgan, Gower Ornithological Society, R. H. Davies, 203 Penybanc Road, Ammanford, Dyfed, SA18 3QP.

Merionethshire See Anglesey.

Monmouthshire Gwent Ornithological Society, Mrs E. Titcombe, 20 High Cross Drive, Newport, NP1 9AM.

Montgomeryshire Montgomery Field Society, Mrs M. Richards, Cartref, Y Cefn, Trewern, Welshpool, SY21 8SZ.

Pembrokeshire As for Cardiganshire.

Radnorshire Herefordshire and Radnorshire Ornithological Club, Mrs J. M. Bromley, The Garth, Kington, HR5 3BA.

Nature Conservation Trusts

Brecknock Naturalists' Trust Lion House, 7 Lion House, Brecon, Powys.

Glamorgan Wildlife Trust Nature Centre, Fountain Road, Tonddu, Bridgend, Mid Glamorgan, CF32 0EH.

Gwent Trust for Nature Conservation 16 White Swan Court, Monmouth, NP5 3NY.

Montgomeryshire Trust for Nature Conservation 8 Severn Square, Newtown, Powys, SY16 2AG.

North Wales Naturalists' Trust 376 High Street, Bangor, Gwynedd, LL57 1YE.

Radnorshire Wildlife Trust Gwalia Annexe, Ithon Road, Llandrindod Wells, Powys, LB1 6AA.

West Wales Trust for Nature Conservation 7 Market Street, Haverfordwest, Dyfed, SA61 1NF.

Pembrokeshire Coast National Park County Offices, St Thomas's Green, Haverfordwest, Dyfed, SA61 1QZ.

Royal Society for the Protection of Birds (Wales) Frolic Street, Newtown, Powys, SY16 1AP.

Snowdonia National Park Penrhyndeudraeth, Gwynedd, LL48 6LS.

Welsh Water Authority Cambrian Way, Brecon, Powys, LD3 7HP.

Woodland Trust Autumn Park, Grantham, Lincolnshire, NG31 6LL.

Other useful addresses

Brecon Beacons National Park 7 Glamorgan Street, Brecon, Powys, LD3 7DP.

British Trust for Ornithology Beech Grove, Tring, Hertfordshire, HP23 5NR.

Council for National Parks 45 Shelton Street, London, WC2H 9HJ.

Forestry Commission North Wales Office, Victoria House, Victoria Terrace, Aberystwyth, Dyfed, SY23 2DQ; South Wales Office, Churchill House, Churchill Way, Cardiff, CF1 4TU.

National Trust North Wales Office, Trinity Square, Llandudno, Gwynedd; South Wales Office, The Kings Arms, Bridge Street, Llandeilo, Dyfed, SA16 9BN.

Nature Conservancy Council Dyfed/Powys Regional Office, Plas Gogerddan, Aberystwyth, Dyfed, SY23 3EB; North Wales Regional Office, Plas Penrhos, Ffordd Penrhos, Bangor, Gwynedd, LL57 2LQ; South Wales Regional Office, 43 The Parade, Roath, Cardiff, CF2 3UH.

ALPHABETICAL LIST OF SPECIES WITH WELSH AND SCIENTIFIC NAMES

This list includes all bird species mentioned in the text. The Welsh names are based on those in *Rhestr o Adar Cymru*, compiled by P. Hope Jones and E. V. Breeze Jones and published by the National Museum of Wales in 1973.

English	Welsh	Scientific
Albatross, Black-browed	Albatros Aelldu	*Diomedea melanophris*
Auk, Little	Carfil Bach	*Alle alle*
Avocet	Cambig	*Recurvirostra avosetta*
Bee-eater	Gwybedog y Gwenyn	*Merops apiaster*
Bittern	Aderyn y Bwn	*Botaurus stellaris*
American	Aderyn-bwn America	*Botaurus lentiginosus*
Little	Aderyn-bwn Lleiaf	*Ixobrychus minutus*
Blackbird	Mwyalchen	*Turdus merula*
Blackcap	Telor Penddu	*Sylvia atricapilla*
Bluethroat, Red-spotted	Bronlas Smotyn Coch	*Luscinia svecica*
Brambling	Pinc y Mynydd	*Fringilla montifringilla*
Bullfinch	Coch y Berllan	*Pyrrhula pyrrhula*
Bunting, Black-headed	Bras Penddu	*Emberiza melanocephala*
Cirl	Bras Ffrainc	*Emberiza cirlus*
Corn	Bras yr Ŷd	*Miliaria calandra*
Lapland	Bras y Gogledd	*Calcarius lapponicus*
Little	Bras Lleiaf	*Emberiza pusilla*
Ortolan	Bras y Gerdi	*Emberiza hortulana*
Reed	Bras y Cyrs	*Emberiza schoeniclus*
Rock	Bras y Graig	*Emberiza cia*
Rustic	Bras Gwledig	*Emberiza rustica*
Snow	Bras yr Eira	*Plectrophenax nivalis*
Yellow-breasted	Bras Bronfelen	*Emberiza aureola*
Buzzard	Bwncath	*Buteo buteo*
Honey	Bod y Mêl	*Pernis apivorus*
Rough-legged	Bod Bacsiog	*Buteo lagopus*
Cape Pigeon	Colomen y Penrhyn	*Daption capense*
Chaffinch	Ji-binc	*Fringilla coelebs*
Chiffchaff	Siff-saff	*Phylloscopus collybita*
Chough	Brân Goesgoch	*Pyrrhocorax pyrrhocorax*
Coot	Cwtiar	*Fulica atra*
Cormorant	Mulfran	*Phalacrocorax carbo*
Corncrake	Rhegen-yr-Ŷd	*Crex crex*
Crake, Spotted	Rhegen Fraith	*Porzana porzana*
Crane	Garan	*Grus grus*
Cream-coloured Courser	Rhedwr y Twyni	*Cursorius cursor*
Crossbill, Common	Gylfin Groes	*Loxia curvirostra*
Crow, Carrion	Brân Dyddyn	*Corvus corone*
Hooded	Mae'r Frân Lwyd	*Corvus corone cornix*
Cuckoo	Cog	*Cuculus canorus*
Curlew	Gylfinir	*Numenius arquata*
Eskimo	Gylfinir Eskimo	*Numenius borealis*
Dipper	Bronwen y Dwr	*Cinclus cinclus*
Diver, Black-throated	Trochydd Gyddfddu	*Gavia arctica*
Great Northern	Trochydd Mawr	*Gavia immer*
Red-throated	Trochydd Gyddfgoch	*Gavia stellata*
Dotterel	Hutan y Mynydd	*Charadrius morinellus*
Dove, Collared	Turtur Dorchog	*Streptopelia decaocto*

Rock (Feral Pigeon)	Colomen y Graig	*Columba livia*
Stock	Colomen Wyllt	*Columba oenas*
Turtle	Turtur	*Streptopelia turtur*
Dowitcher, Long-billed	Giach Gylfin-hir	*Limnodromus scolopaceus*
Duck, Black	Hwyaden Ddu	*Anas rubripes*
Ferruginous	Hwyaden Lygadwen	*Aythya nyroca*
Long-tailed	Hwyaden Gynffon-hir	*Clangula hyemalis*
Ring-necked	Hwyaden Dorchog	*Aythya collaris*
Ruddy	Hwyaden Goch	*Oxyura jamaicensis*
Tufted	Hwyaden Gopog	*Aythya fuligula*
Dunlin	Pibydd y Mawn	*Calidris alpina*
Dunnock	Llwyd y Gwrych	*Prunella modularis*
Eagle, Golden	Eryr Euraid	*Aquila chrysaetos*
Egret, Little	Creyr Bach	*Egretta garzetta*
Eider	Hwyaden Fwythblu	*Somateria mollissima*
Falcon, Red-footed	Cudyll Troedgoch	*Falco vespertinus*
Fieldfare	Socan Eira	*Turdus pilaris*
Firecrest	Dryw Penfflamgoch	*Regulus ignicapillus*
Flycatcher, Collared	Gwybedog Torchog	*Ficedula albicollis*
Pied	Gwybedog Brith	*Ficedula hypoleuca*
Red-breasted	Gwybedog Brongoch	*Ficedula parva*
Spotted	Gwybedog Mannog	*Muscicapa striata*
Fulmar	Aderyn-Drycin y Graig	*Fulmarus glacialis*
Gadwall	Hwyaden Lwyd	*Anas strepera*
Gannet	Hugan	*Sula bassana*
Garganey	Hwyaden Addfain	*Anas querquedula*
Godwit, Bar-tailed	Rhostog Gynffonfrith	*Limosa lapponica*
Black-tailed	Rhostog Gynffonddu	*Limosa limosa*
Goldcrest	Dryw Eurben	*Regulus regulus*
Goldeneye	Hwyaden Lygad-aur	*Bucephala clangula*
Goldfinch	Nico	*Carduelis carduelis*
Goosander	Hwyaden Ddanheddog	*Mergus merganser*
Goose, Barnacle	Gŵydd Wyran	*Branta leucopsis*
Bean	Gŵydd y Llafur	*Anser fabalis*
Brent	Gŵydd Ddu	*Branta bernicla*
Canada	Gŵydd Canada	*Branta canadensis*
Greylag	Gŵydd Wyllt	*Anser anser*
Lesser White fronted	Gŵydd Dalcen-wen Leiaf	*Anser erythropus*
Pink-footed	Gŵydd Droedbinc	*Anser brachyrhynchus*
White-fronted	Gŵydd Dalcen-wen	*Anser albifrons*
Goshawk	Gwalch Marth	*Accipiter gentilis*
Grebe, Black-necked	Gwyach Yddddu	*Podiceps nigricollis*
Great Crested	Gwyach Fawr Gopog	*Podiceps cristatus*
Little	Gwyach Fach	*Tachybaptus ruficollis*
Pied-billed	Gwyach Gylfinfraith	*Podilymbus podiceps*
Red-necked	Gwyach Yddfgoch	*Podiceps grisegena*
Slavonian	Gwyach Gorniog	*Podiceps auritus*
Greenfinch	Llinos Werdd	*Carduelis chloris*
Greenshank	Pibydd Coeswerdd	*Tringa nebularia*
Grosbeak, Rose-breasted	Gylfindew Brongoch	*Pheucticus ludovicianus*
Grouse, Black	Grugiar Ddu	*Lyrurus tetrix*
Red	Grugiar	*Lagopus lagopus*
Guillemot	Gwylog	*Uria aalge*
Black	Gwylog Ddu	*Cepphus grylle*
Gull, Black-headed	Gwylan Benddu	*Larus ridibundus*
Bonaparte's	Gwylan Bonaparte	*Larus philadelphia*
Common	Gwylan y Gweunydd	*Larus canus*
Glaucous	Gwylan y Gogledd	*Larus hyperboreus*

Great Black-backed	Gwylan Gefnddu Fwyaf	*Larus marinus*
Herring	Gwylan y Penwaig	*Larus argentatus*
Iceland	Gwylan yr Arctig	*Larus glaucoides*
Lesser Black-backed	Gwylan Gefnddu Leiaf	*Larus fuscus*
Little	Gwylan Fechan	*Larus minutus*
Mediterranean	Gwylan Mor y Canoldir	*Larus melanocephalus*
Ring-billed	Gwylan Fodrwybig	*Larus delawarensis*
Ross's	Gwylan Ross	*Rhodostethia rosea*
Sabine's	Gwylan Sabine	*Larus sabini*
Slender-billed	Gwylan Bigfain	*Larus genei*
Harrier, Hen	Bod Tinwen	*Circus cyaneus*
Marsh	Bod y Gwerni	*Circus aeruginosus*
Montagu's	Bod Montagu	*Circus pygargus*
Hawfinch	Gyfinbraff	*Coccothraustes coccothraustes*
Heron, Grey	Crëyr Glas	*Ardea cinerea*
Night	Crëyr y Nos	*Nycticorax nycticorax*
Purple	Crëyr Porffor	*Ardea purpurea*
Hobby	Hebog yr Ehedydd	*Falco subbuteo*
Hoopoe	Copog	*Upupa epops*
Jackdaw	Jac-y-do	*Corvus monedula*
Jay	Ysgrech y Coed	*Garrulus glandarius*
Junco, Slate-coloured	Jynco Llwyd	*Junco hyemalis*
Kestrel	Cudyll Coch	*Falco tinnunculus*
Killdeer	Cwtiad Torchog Mawr	*Charadrius vociferus*
Kingfisher	Glas y Dorlan	*Alcedo atthis*
Kite, Black	Barcud Du	*Milvus migrans*
Red	Barcud	*Milvus milvus*
Kittiwake	Gwylan Goesddu	*Rissa tridactyla*
Knot	Pibydd yr Aber	*Calidris canutus*
Lapwing	Cornchwiglen	*Vanellus vanellus*
Lark, Shore	Ehedydd y Traeth	*Eremophila alpestris*
Linnet	Llinos	*Carduelis cannabina*
Magpie	Pioden	*Pica pica*
Mallard	Hwyaden Wyllt	*Anas platyrhynchos*
Mandarin	Hwyaden Gribog	*Aix galericulata*
Martin, House	Gwennol y Bondo	*Delichon urbica*
Sand	Gwennol y Glennydd	*Riparia riparia*
Merganser, Red-breasted	Hwyaden Frongoch	*Mergus serrator*
Merlin	Cudyll Bach	*Falco columbarius*
Moorhen	Iâr Ddŵr	*Gallinula chloropus*
Nightingale	Eos	*Luscinia megarhynchos*
Thrush	Eos Fronfraith	*Luscinia luscinia*
Nightjar	Troellwr Mawr	*Caprimulgus europaeus*
Nuthatch	Delor y Cnau	*Sitta europaea*
Oriole, Golden	Euryn	*Oriolus oriolus*
Northern	Euryn y Gogledd	*Icterus galbula*
Osprey	Gwalch y Pysgod	*Pandion haliaetus*
Ouzel, Ring	Mwyalchen y Mynydd	*Turdus torquatus*
Owl, Barn	Tylluan Wen	*Tyto alba*
Little	Tylluan Fach	*Athene noctua*
Long-eared	Tylluan Gorniog	*Asio otus*
Scops	Tylluan Scops	*Otus scops*
Short-eared	Tylluan Glustiog	*Asio flammeus*
Tawny	Tylluan Frech	*Strix aluco*
Oystercatcher	Pioden y Môr	*Haematopus ostralegus*
Partridge, Grey	Petrisen	*Perdix perdix*
Red-legged	Petrisen Goesgoch	*Alectoris rufa*
Parakeet, Ring-necked	Paracit Torchog	*Psittacula krameri*

Pelican, White	Pelican Gwyn	*Pelecanus onocrotalus*
Peregrine	Hebog Tramor	*Falco peregrinus*
Petrel, Collared	Pedryn Torchog	*Pterodroma leucoptera*
Leach's	Pedryn Gynffon-fforchog	*Oceanodroma leucorrhoa*
Storm	Pedryn Drycin	*Hydrobates pelagicus*
Wilson's	Pedryn Wilson	*Oceanites oceanicus*
Phalarope, Grey	Llydandroed Llwyd	*Phalaropus fulicarius*
Red-necked	Llydandroed Gyddfgoch	*Phalaropus lobatus*
Wilson's	Llydandroed Wilson	*Phalaropus tricolor*
Pheasant	Ffesant	*Phasianus colchicus*
Golden	Ffesant Euraid	*Chrysolophus pictus*
Pintail	Hwyaden Lostfain	*Anas acuta*
Pipit, Meadow	Corhedydd y Waun	*Anthus pratensis*
Olive-backed	Corhedydd Cefnwyrdd	*Anthus hodgsoni*
Red-throated	Corhedydd Gyddfgoch	*Anthus cervinus*
Richard's	Corhedydd Richard	*Anthus novaeseelandiae*
Rock	Corhedydd y Graig	*Anthus petrosus*
Tawny	Corhedydd Melyn	*Anthus campestris*
Tree	Corhedydd y Coed	*Anthus trivialis*
Water	Corhedydd y Dwr	*Anthus spinoletta*
Plover, Golden	Cwtiad Aur	*Pluvialis apricaria*
Grey	Cwtiad Llwyd	*Pluvialis squatarola*
Kentish	Cwtiad Caint	*Charadrius alexandrinus*
Lesser Golden	Corgwtiad Aur	*Pluvialis dominica*
Little Ringed	Cwtiad Torchog Bach	*Charadrius dubius*
Ringed	Cwtiad Torchog	*Charadrius hiaticula*
Sociable	Cwtiad Heidiol	*Chettusia gregaria*
Pochard	Hwyaden Bengoch	*Aythya ferina*
Red-crested	Hwyaden Gribgoch	*Netta rufina*
Puffin	Pâl	*Fratercula arctica*
Quail	Sofliar	*Coturnix coturnix*
Rail, Water	Rhegen y Dŵr	*Rallus aquaticus*
Sora	Rhegen Sora	*Porzana carolina*
Raven	Cigfran	*Corvus corax*
Razorbill	Llurs	*Alca torda*
Redpoll	Llinos Bengoch	*Carduelis flammea*
Redshank	Pibydd Coesgoch	*Tringa totanus*
Spotted	Pibydd Coesgoch Mannog	*Tringa erythropus*
Redstart	Tingoch	*Phoenicurus phoenicurus*
Black	Tingoch Du	*Phoenicurus ochruros*
Redwing	Coch dan-aden	*Turdus iliacus*
Robin	Robin Goch	*Erithacus rubecula*
Roller	Rholydd	*Coracias garrulus*
Rook	Ydfran	*Corvus frugilegus*
Rosefinch, Scarlet	Llinos Goch	*Carpodacus erythrinus*
Ruff	Pibydd Torchog	*Philomachus pugnax*
Sanderling	Pibydd y Twyod	*Calidris alba*
Sandpiper, Baird's	Pibydd Baird	*Calidris bairdii*
Broad-billed	Pibydd Llydanbig	*Limicola falcinellus*
Buff-breasted	Pibydd Bronllwyd	*Tryngites subruficollis*
Common	Pibydd y Dorlan	*Actitis hypoleucos*
Curlew	Pibydd Cambig	*Calidris ferruginea*
Green	Pibydd Gwyrdd	*Tringa ochropus*
Pectoral	Pibydd Cain	*Calidris melanotos*
Purple	Pibydd Du	*Calidris maritima*
Semipalmated	Pibydd Llwyd	*Calidris pusilla*
Spotted	Pibydd Brych	*Actitis macularia*

Upland	Pibydd Cynffonir	*Bartramia longicauda*
White-rumped	Pibydd Tinwen	*Calidris fuscicollis*
Wood	Pibydd y Graean	*Tringa glareola*
Scaup	Hwyaden Benddu	*Aythya marila*
Scoter, Common	Môr-hwyaden Ddu	*Melanitta nigra*
Surf	Môr-hwyaden yr Ewyn	*Melanitta perspicillata*
Velvet	Môr-hwyaden y Gogledd	*Melanitta fusca*
Serin	Llinos Frech	*Serinus serinus*
Shag	Mulfran Werdd	*Phalacrocorax aristotelis*
Shearwater, Balearic	Aderyn-Drycin Balearic	*Puffinus puffinus mauretanicus*
Cory's	Aderyn-Drycin Cory	*Calonectris diomedea*
Great	Aderyn-Drycin Mawr	*Puffinus gravis*
Little	Aderyn-Drycin Bach	*Puffinus assimilis*
Manx	Aderyn-Drycin Manaw	*Puffinus puffinus*
Sooty	Aderyn-Drycin Du	*Puffinus griseus*
Shelduck	Hwyaden yr Eithin	*Tadorna tadorna*
Ruddy	Hwyaden Goch Yr Eithin	*Tadorna ferruginea*
Shoveler	Hwyaden Lydanbig	*Anas clypeata*
Shrike, Great Grey	Cigydd Mawr	*Lanius excubitor*
Isabelline	Cigydd Gwelw	*Lanius isabellinus*
Lesser Grey	Cigydd Glas	*Lanius minor*
Red-backed	Cigydd Cefngoch	*Lanius collurio*
Woodchat	Cigydd Pengoch	*Lanius senator*
Siskin	Pila Gwyrdd	*Carduelis spinus*
Skua, Arctic	Sgiwen y Gogledd	*Stercorarius parasiticus*
Great	Sgiwen Fawr	*Stercorarius skua*
Long-tailed	Sgiwen Lostfain	*Stercorarius longicaudus*
Pomarine	Sgiwen Frech	*Stercorarius pomarinus*
South Polar	Sgiwen Pegwn y De	*Stercorarius maccormicki*
Skylark	Ehedydd	*Alauda arvensis*
Smew	Lleian Wen	*Mergus albellus*
Snipe	Gïach Gyffredin	*Gallinago gallinago*
Jack	Gïach Fach	*Lymnocryptes minimus*
Sparrow, House	Aderyn y To	*Passer domesticus*
Song	Llwyd Persain	*Melospiza melodia*
Tree	Golfan y Mynydd	*Passer montanus*
White-throated	Llwyd Gyddfwyn	*Zonotrichia albicollis*
Sparrowhawk	Gwalch Glas	*Accipiter nisus*
Spoonbill	Llwybig	*Platalea leucorodia*
Starling	Drudwen	*Sturnus vulgaris*
Stilt, Black-winged	Hirgoes	*Himantopus himantopus*
Stint, Little	Pibydd Bach	*Calidris minuta*
Temminck's	Pibydd Temminck	*Calidris temminckii*
Stonechat	Clochdar y Cerrig	*Saxicola torquata*
Siberian	Clochdar Siberia	*Saxicola torquata maura/ stejnegeri*
Stone-curlew	Rhedwr y Moelydd	*Burhinus oedicnemus*
Stork, White	Ciconia Gwyn	*Ciconia ciconia*
Swallow	Gwennol	*Hirundo rustica*
Swan, Bewick's	Alorch Bewick	*Cygnus columbianus bewickii*
Mute	Alorch Dof	*Cygnus olor*
Whooper	Alorch y Gogledd	*Cygnus cygnus*
Swift	Gwennol Ddu	*Apus apus*
Alpine	Gwennol Ddu'r Alpau	*Apus melba*
Little	Gwennol Ddu Fach	*Apus affinis*
Pallid	Gwennol Ddu Welw	*Apus pallidus*

Tanager, Summer	Euryn yr Haf	*Piranga rubra*
Teal	Corhwyaden	*Anas crecca*
Green-winged	Corhwyaden Asgell Werdd	*Anas crecca carolinensis*
Tern, Arctic	Morwennol y Gogledd	*Sterna paradisaea*
Black	Corswennol Ddu	*Chlidonias niger*
Caspian	Morwennol Fwyaf	*Sterna caspia*
Common	Morwennol Gyffredin	*Sterna hirundo*
Gull-billed	Morwennol Ylfinbraff	*Gelochelidon nilotica*
Little	Morwennol Fechan	*Sterna albifrons*
Roseate	Morwennol Wridog	*Sterna dougallii*
Royal	Morwennol Fawr	*Sterna maxima*
Sandwich	Morwennol Bigddu	*Sterna sandvicensis*
Whiskered	Corswennol Farfog	*Chlidonias hybridus*
White-winged Black	Corswennol Adeinwen	*Chlidonias leucopterus*
Thrush, Gray-cheeked	Bronfraith Fochlwyd	*Catharus minimus*
Mistle	Brych y Coed	*Turdus viscivorus*
Rock	Brych y Graig	*Monticola saxatilis*
Song	Bronfraith	*Turdus philomelos*
Olive-backed	Corfonfraith	*Catharus ustulata*
Tit, Bearded	Titw Barfog	*Panurus biarmicus*
Blue	Titw Tomas Las	*Parus caeruleus*
Coal	Titw Penddu	*Parus ater*
Great	Titw Mawr	*Parus major*
Long-tailed	Titw Gynffon-hir	*Aegithalos caudatus*
Marsh	Titw'r Wern	*Parus palustris*
Penduline	Titw Pendil	*Remiz pendulinus*
Willow	Titw'r Helyg	*Parus montanus*
Treecreeper	Dringwr Bach	*Certhia familiaris*
Turnstone	Cwtiad y Traeth	*Arenaria interpres*
Twite	Llinos y Mynydd	*Carduelis flavirostris*
Vireo, Red-eyed	Telor Melyn	*Vireo olivaceus*
Wagtail, Blue-headed	Siglen Benlas	*Motacilla flava flava*
Grey	Siglen Lwyd	*Motacilla cinerea*
Pied	Siglen Fraith	*Motacilla alba*
Yellow	Siglen Felen	*Motacilla flava flavissima*
Warbler, Aquatic	Telor y Dwr	*Acrocephalus paludicola*
Barred	Telor Rhesog	*Sylvia nisoria*
Blackburnian	Telor Blackburnian	*Dendroica fusca*
Blackpoll	Telor Tinwen	*Dendroica striata*
Bonelli's	Telor Bonelli	*Phylloscopus bonelli*
Cetti's	Telor Cetti	*Cettia cetti*
Dartford	Telor Dartford	*Sylvia undata*
Dusky	Telor Tywyll	*Phylloscopus fuscatus*
Garden	Telor yr Ardd	*Sylvia borin*
Grasshopper	Troellwr Bach	*Locustella naevia*
Great Reed	Telor Mawr y Cyrs	*Acrocephalus arundinaceus*
Icterine	Telor Aur	*Hippolais icterina*
Melodious	Telor Pêr	*Hippolais polyglotta*
Olivaceous	Telor Llwyd	*Hippolais pallida*
Pallas's	Telor Pallas	*Phylloscopus proregulus*
Reed	Telor y Cyrs	*Acrocephalus scirpaceus*
River	Telor yr Afon	*Locustella fluviatilis*
Sardinian	Telor Sardinia	*Sylvia melanocephala*
Savi's	Telor Savi	*Locustella luscinioides*
Sedge	Telor yr Hesg	*Acrocephalus schoenobaenus*
Subalpine	Telor Brongoch	*Sylvia cantillans*
Willow	Telor yr Helyg	*Phylloscopus trochilus*
Wood	Telor y Coed	*Phylloscopus sibilatrix*

Yellow	Telor Melyn	*Dendroica petechia*
Yellow-browed	Telor Aelfelen	*Phylloscopus inornatus*
Wheatear	Tinwen y Garn	*Oenanthe oenanthe*
Black-eared	Tinwen Clustiog Du	*Oenanthe hispanica*
Pied	Tinwen Fraith	*Oenanthe pleschanka*
Whimbrel	Coegyfinir	*Numenius phaeopus*
Little	Coegyfinir Bach	*Numenius minutus*
Whinchat	Crec yr Eithin	*Saxicola rubetra*
Whitethroat	Llwydfron	*Sylvia communis*
Lesser	Llwydfron Fach	*Sylvia curruca*
Wigeon	Chwiwell	*Anas penelope*
American	Chwiwell America	*Anas americana*
Woodcock	Cyffylog	*Scolopax rusticola*
Woodlark	Ehedydd y Coed	*Lullula arborea*
Woodpecker,		
Great Spotted	Cnocell Fraith Fwyaf	*Dendrocopos major*
Green	Cnocell Werdd	*Picus viridis*
Lesser Spotted	Cnocell Fraith Leiaf	*Dendrocopos minor*
Woodpigeon	Ysguthan	*Columba palumbus*
Wren	Dryw	*Troglodytes troglodytes*
Wryneck	Pengam	*Jynx torquilla*
Yellowhammer	Bras Melyn	*Emberiza citrinella*
Yellowlegs, Lesser	Melyngoes Bach	*Tringa flavipes*
Greater	Melyngoes Mawr	*Tringa melanoleuca*

MAPS

Key to Sites

1. Anglesey Lakes
2. Cemlyn Lagoon
3. Newborough Warren
4. Point Lynas
5. Puffin Island and the Penmon Peninsula
6. South Stack Cliffs
7. Llangorse Lake
8. Nant Irfon
9. Talybont Reservoir
10. Bardsey Island
11. Coed Aber
12. Great Orme
13(i). Snowdonia (northeast)
13(ii). Snowdonia (central)
14. Traeth Lavan
15. Aberystwyth and the Rheidol Valley
16. Cors Caron
17. Dyfi Estuary
18(i). South Cardiganshire Coast (New Quay)
18(ii). South Cardiganshire Coast (Lochtyn Peninsula)
18(iii). South Cardiganshire Coast (Teifi Estuary and Cardigan Island)
19. Burry Inlet (north) and Loughor Estuary
20(i). Lower Tywi Valley (east)
20(ii). Talley Lakes
21. Taf, Tywi and Gwendraeth Estuaries
22. Upper Tywi Valley
23. Berwyn Range
24. Mynydd Hiraethog
25. Rhos-on-Sea
26. Dee Estuary
27. Point of Air
28. Shotton Pools
29. Burry Inlet (south) and Whiteford
30. Cwm Clydach
31. Flat Holm
32. Kenfig Dunes and Pool
33. Lavernock Point
34. Oxwich
35. Swansea Bay
36. Worms Head
37. Craig yr Aderyn
38. Mawddach Estuary
39(i). Morfa Harlech
39(ii). Morfa Dyffryn
40. Vale of Ffestiniog
41. Llandegfedd Reservoir
42. Severn Estuary and Gwent Levels
43. Lake Vyrnwy
44. Leighton Flats
45. Vyrnwy Confluence
46(i). Milford Haven Waterway (Cleddau Rivers)
46(ii). Milford Haven Waterway (Angle Bay)
46(iii). Milford Haven Waterway (Dale Roads)
47(i). Grassholm
47(ii). Ramsey Island
47(iii). Skokholm
47(iv). Skomer Island
48. Pengelli Forest
49. St David's Commons
50. Stackpole and Castlemartin
51. Strumble Head
52. Elan Valley Reservoirs
53. Glasbury
54. Maelienydd
55. Wye-Elan Woods

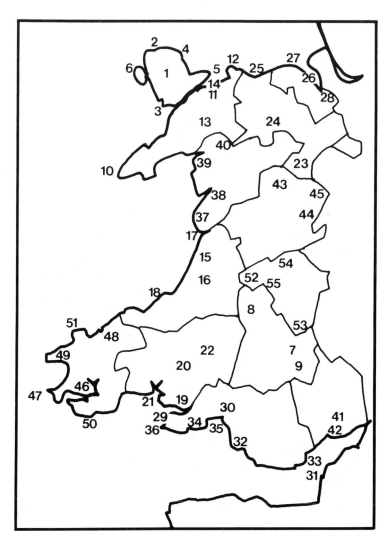

Key to Maps

═══ Roads	☙ ☙ ☙ Marsh/saltings
----- Pathway	▦ Mud
⊬⊶⊩ Railways & stations	⁞⁞⁞ Rocky shore
🅿 Parking	⟋⟋⟍ Cliffs/steep slopes
𝒊 Information centres	♠ ♠ Conifers
⤳ Rivers & streams	☙☙ Deciduous
⌂ Lighthouse	≋≋≋ Water/lakes
▦ Gannetry	

Map 1: Anglesey Lakes

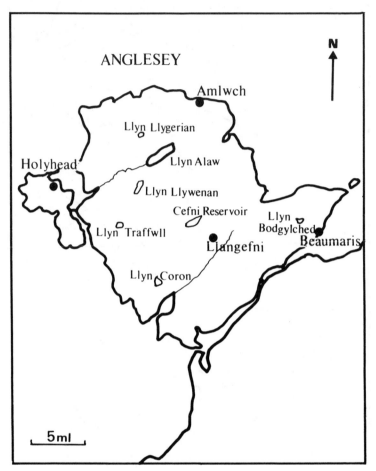

Map 2: Cemlyn Lagoon

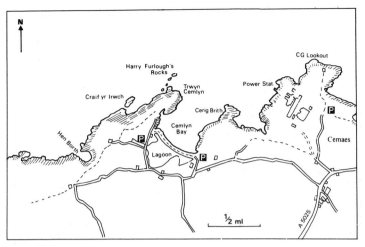

Map 3: Newborough Warren

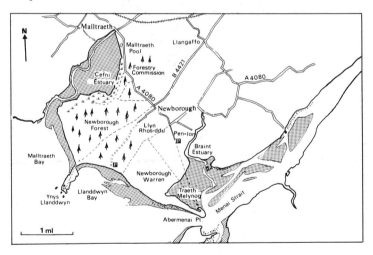

Map 4: Point Lynas

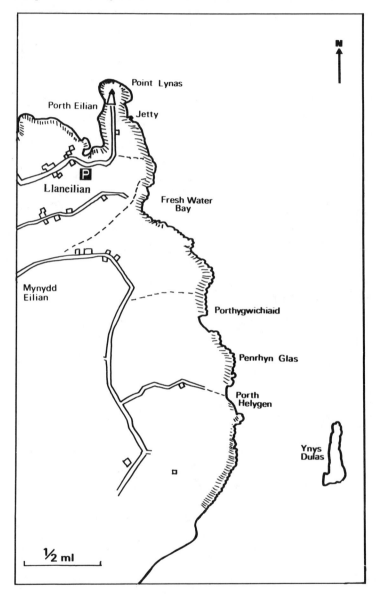

Map 5: Puffin Island and the Penmon Peninsula

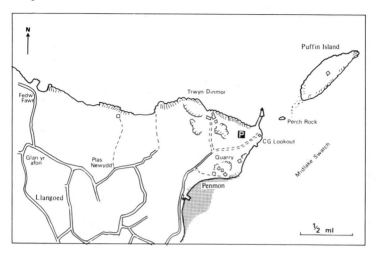

Map 6: South Stack Cliffs

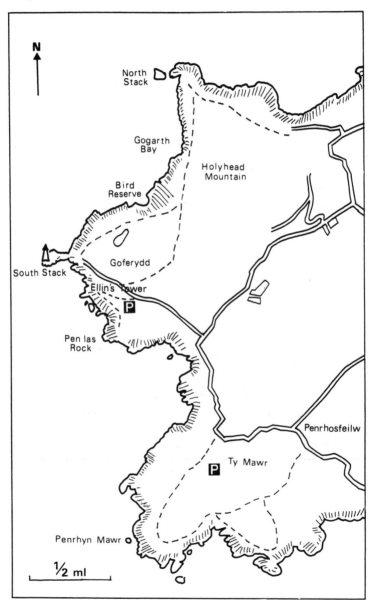

Map 7: Llangorse Lake

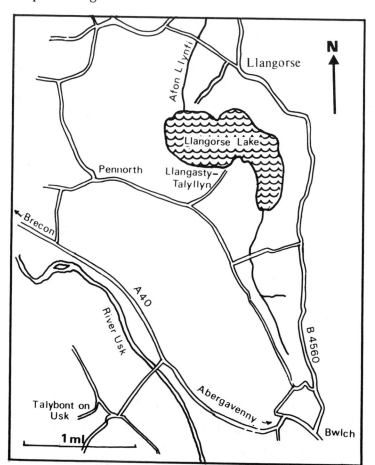

Map 8: Nant Irfon

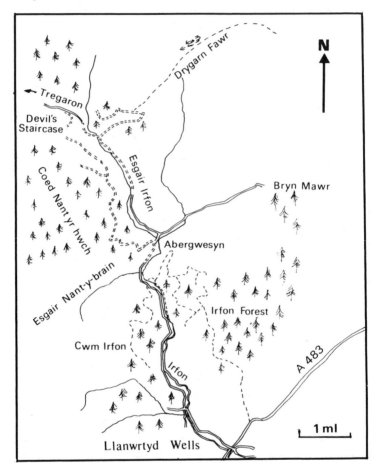

Map 9: Talybont Reservoir

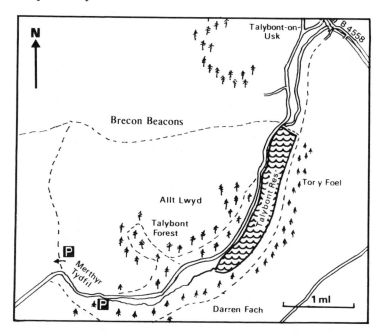

Map 10: Bardsey Island

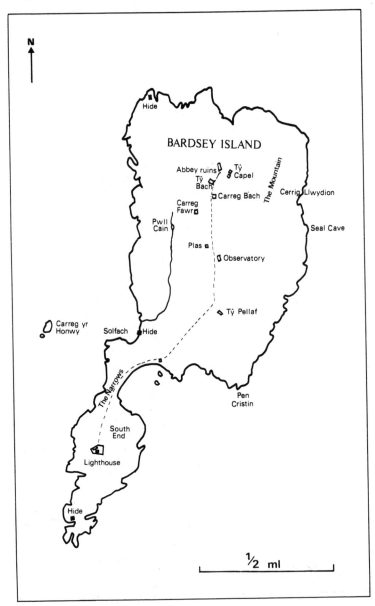

Map 11: Coed Aber

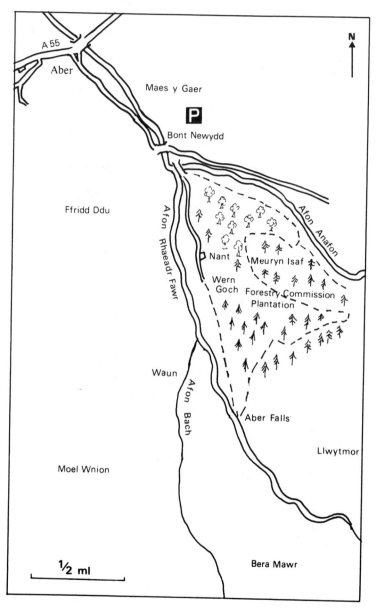

Map 12: Great Orme

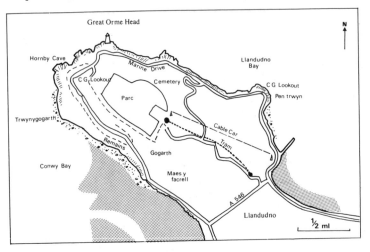

Map 13(i): Snowdonia (northeast)

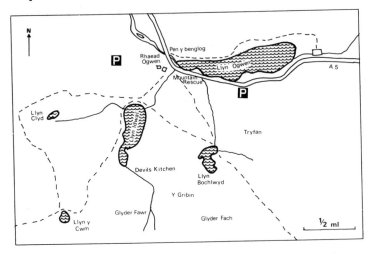

Map 13(ii): Snowdonia (central)

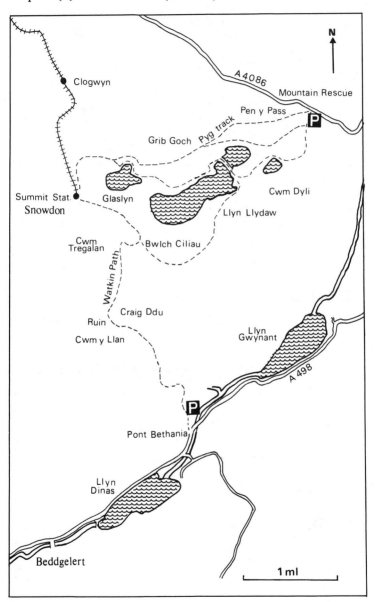

Map 14: Traeth Lavan

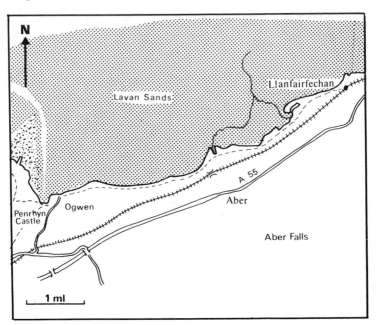

Map 15: Aberystwyth and the Rheidol Valley

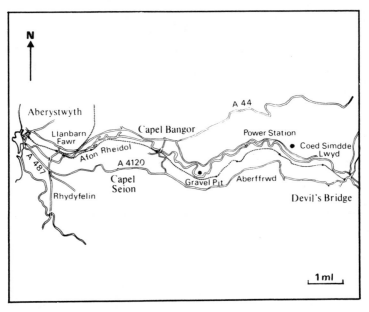

Map 16: Cors Caron

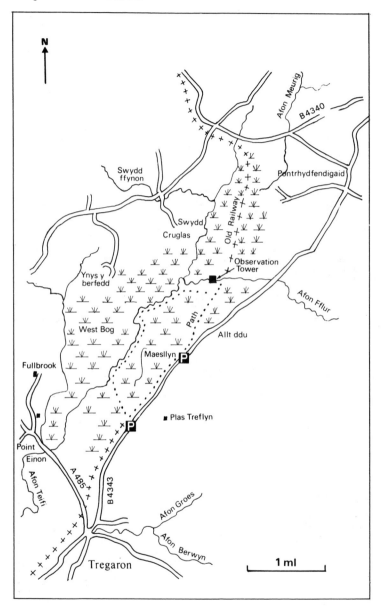

N

Afon Meurig

B4340

Swydd
ffynon

Pontrhydfendigaid

Swydd
Cruglas

Old Railway

Observation
Tower

Ynys y
berfedd

Afon Fflur

West Bog

Path

Allt ddu

Maesllyn

P

Fullbrook

P

Plas Treflyn

Point
Einon

Afon Teifi

A485

B4343

Afon Groes

Afon Berwyn

Tregaron

1 ml

Map 17: Dyfi Estuary

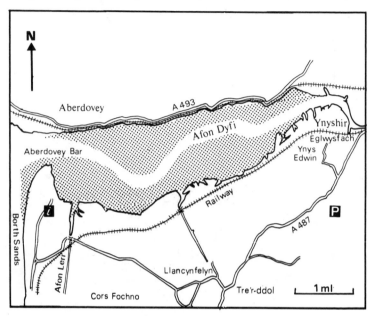

Map 18(i): South Cardiganshire Coast (New Quay)

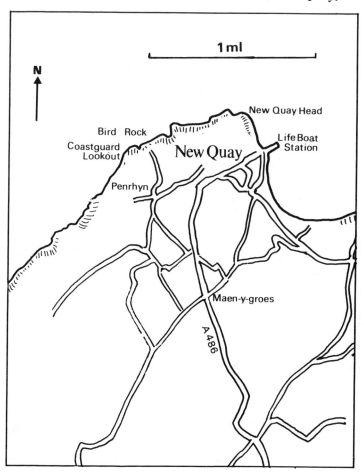

Map 18(ii): South Cardiganshire Coast (Lochtyn Peninsula)

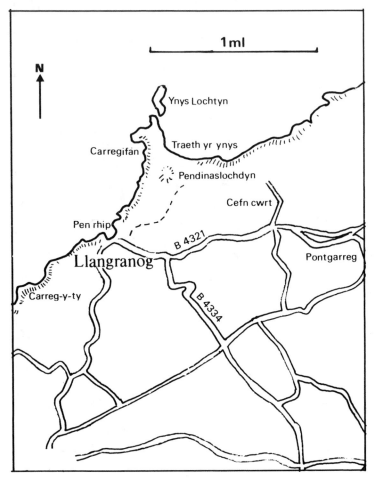

Map 18(iii): South Cardiganshire Coast (Teifi Estuary and Cardigan Island)

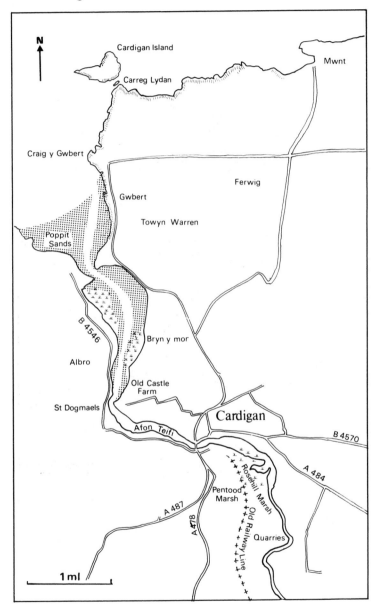

Map 19: Burry Inlet (north) and Loughor Estuary

Map 20(i): Lower Tywi Valley (east)

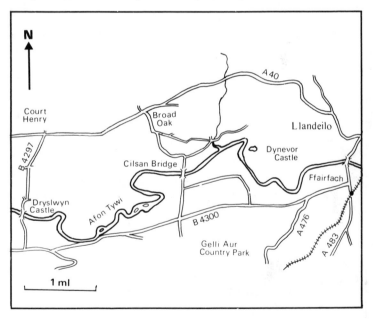

Map 20(ii): Talley Lakes

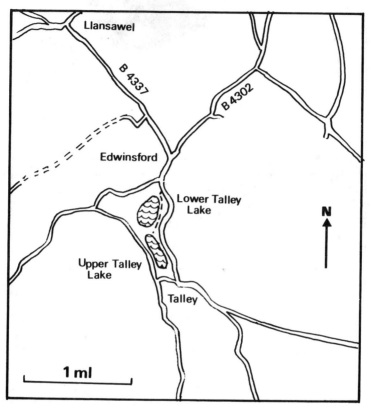

Map 21: Taf, Tywi and Gwendraeth Estuaries

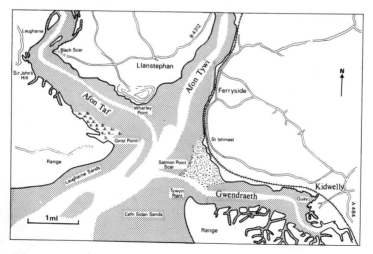

Map 22: Upper Tywi Valley

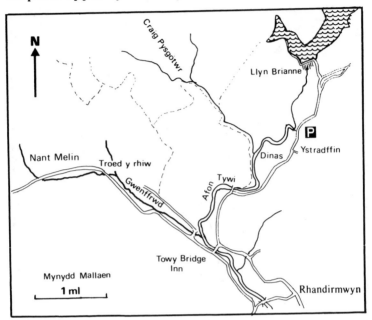

Map 23: Berwyn Range

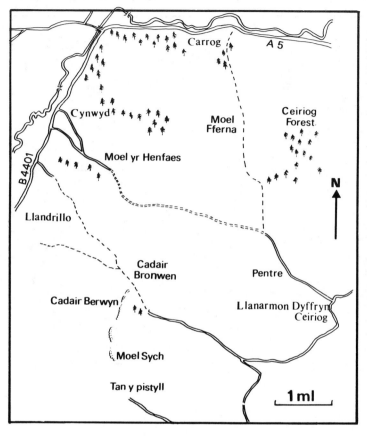

Map 24: Mynydd Hiraethog

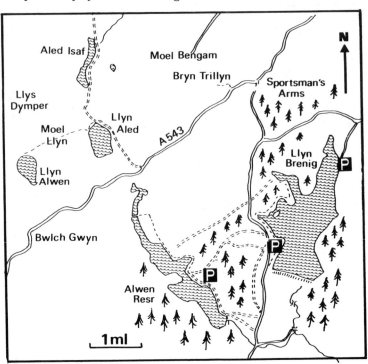

Map 25: Rhos-on-Sea

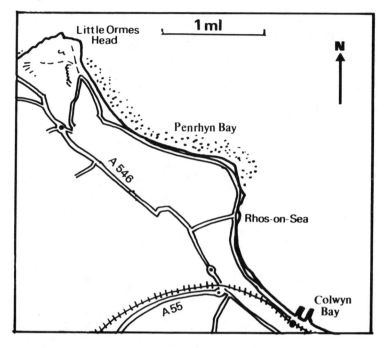

Map 26: Dee Estuary

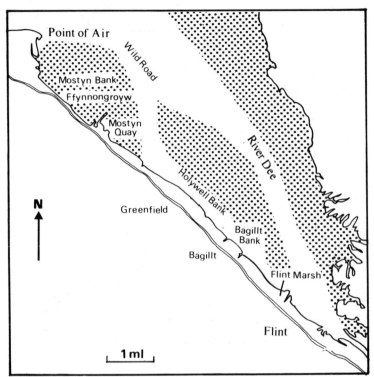

Map 27: Point of Air

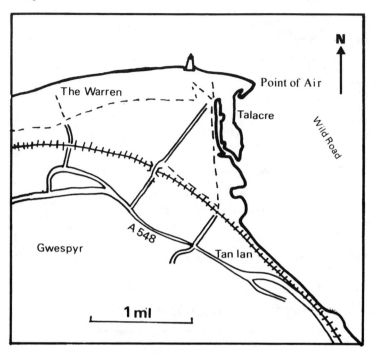

Map 28: Shotton Pools

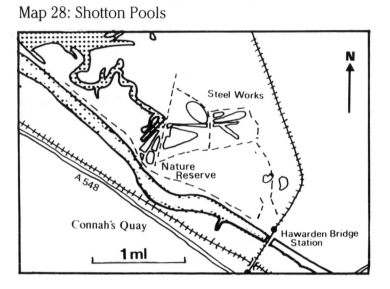

Map 29: Burry Inlet (south) and Whiteford

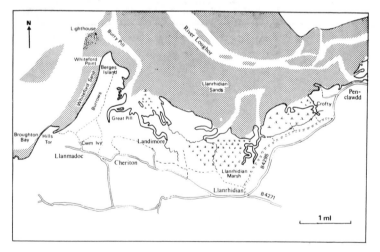

Map 30: Cwm Clydach

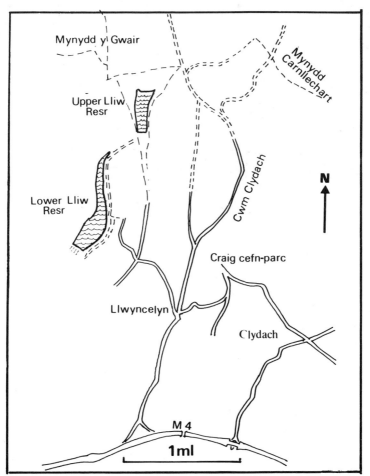

Map 31: Flat Holm

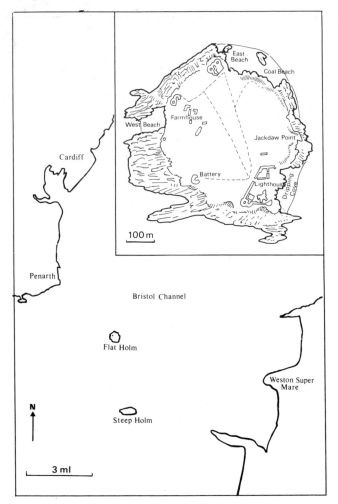

East Beach

Coal Beach

West Beach

Farmhouse

Jackdaw Point

Cardiff

Battery

Lighthouse

Dripping Cove

100 m

Penarth

Bristol Channel

Flat Holm

Weston Super Mare

N

Steep Holm

3 ml

Map 32: Kenfig Dunes and Pool

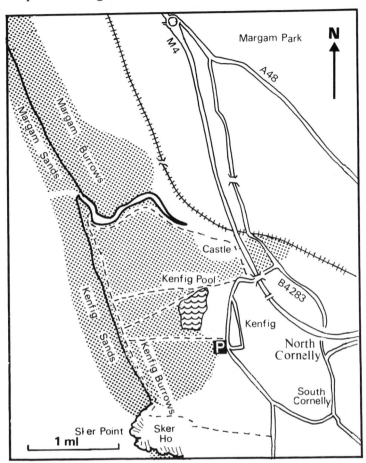

Map 33: Lavernock Point

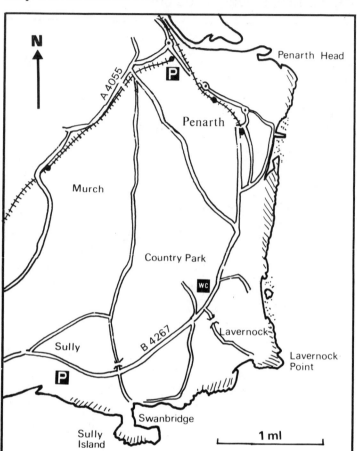

Map 34: Oxwich

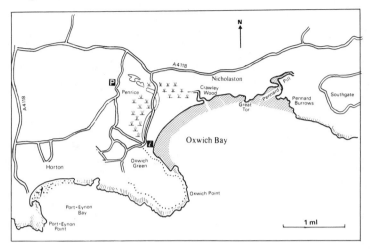

Map 35: Swansea Bay

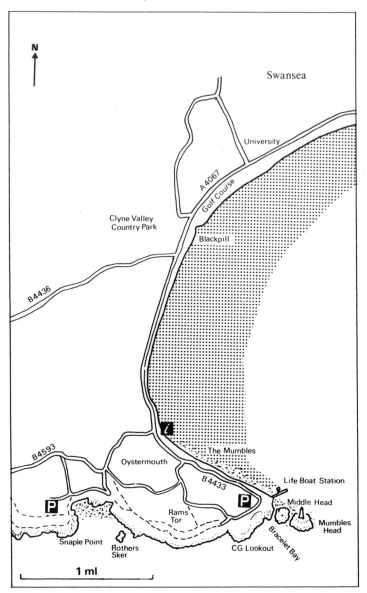

Map 36: Worms Head

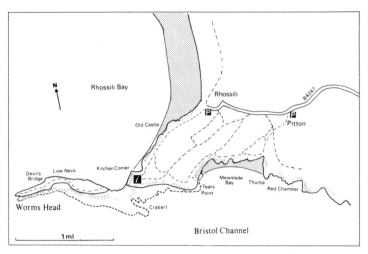

Map 37: Craig yr Aderyn

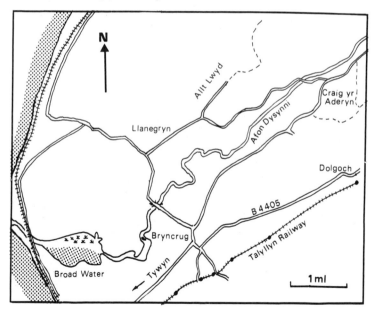

Map 38: Mawddach Estuary

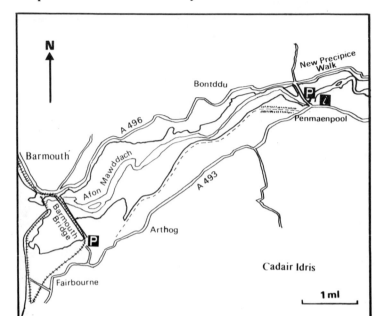

Map 39(i): Morfa Harlech

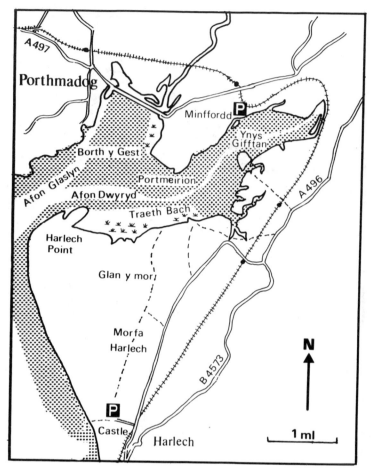

Map 39(ii): Morfa Dyffryn

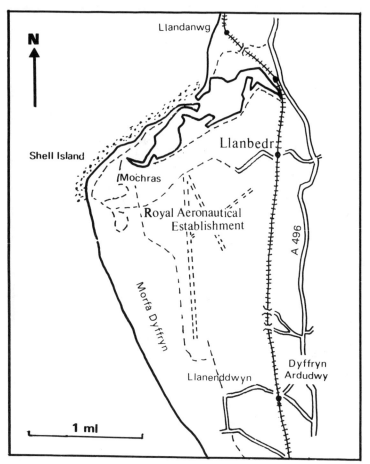

Map 40: Vale of Ffestiniog

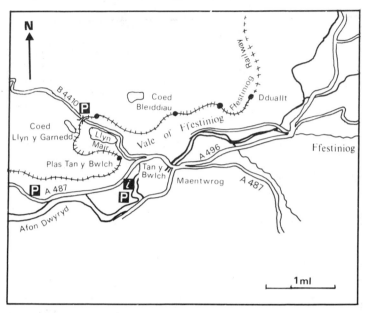

Map 41: Llandegfedd Reservoir

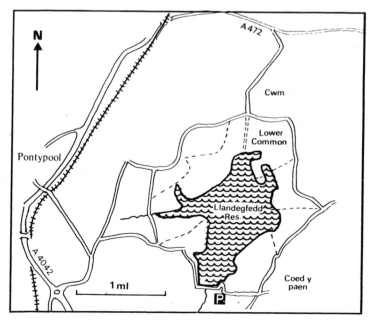

Map 42: Severn Estuary and Gwent Levels

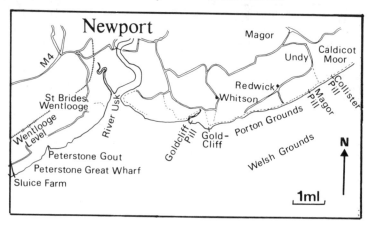

Map 43: Lake Vyrnwy

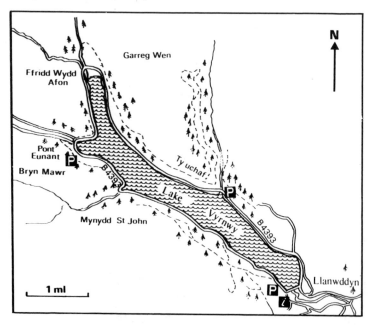

Map 44: Leighton Flats

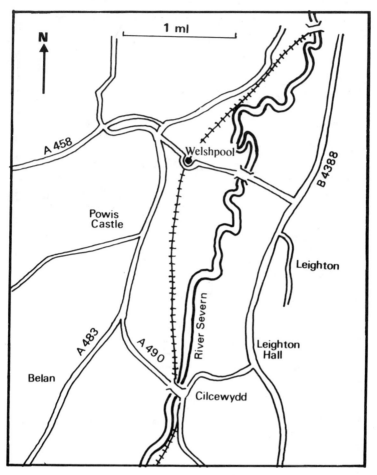

Map 45: Vyrnwy Confluence

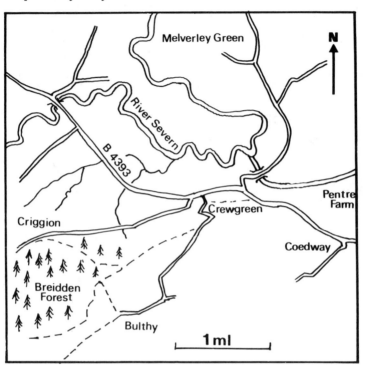

Map 46(i): Milford Haven Waterway (Cleddau Rivers)

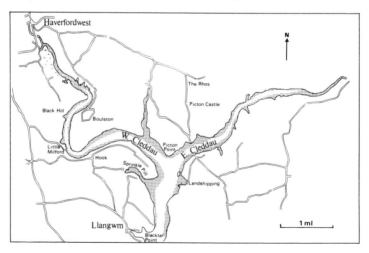

Map 46(ii): Milford Haven Waterway (Angle Bay)

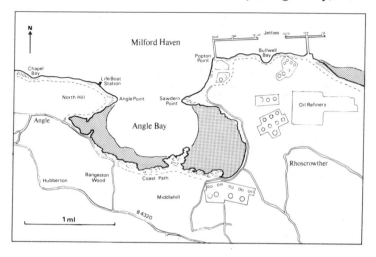

Map 46(iii): Milford Haven Waterway (Dale Roads)

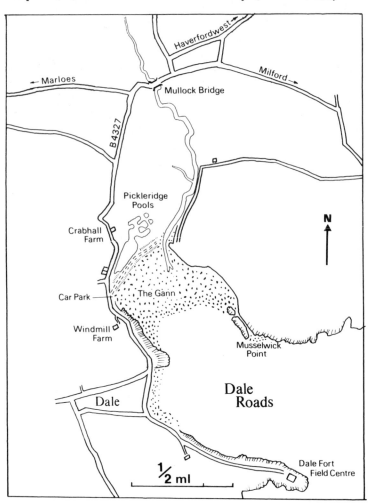

Map 47(i): Grassholm

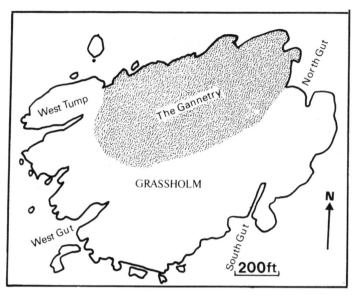

Map 47(ii): Ramsey Island

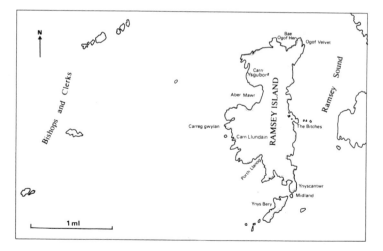

Map 47(iii): Skokholm

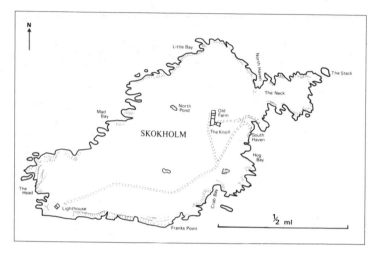

Map 47(iv): Skomer Island

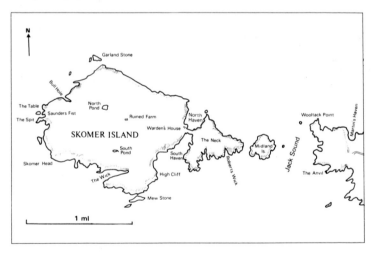

Map 48: Pengelli Forest

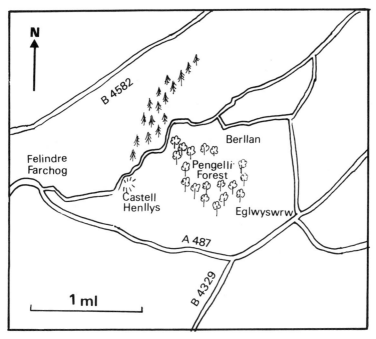

Map 49: St David's Commons

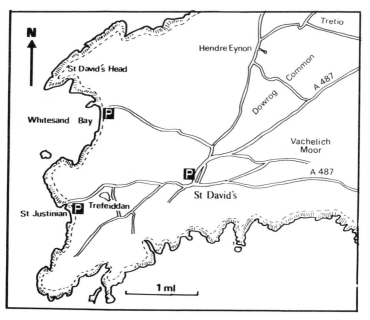

Map 50: Stackpole and Castlemartin

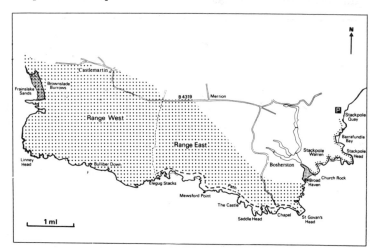

Map 51: Strumble Head

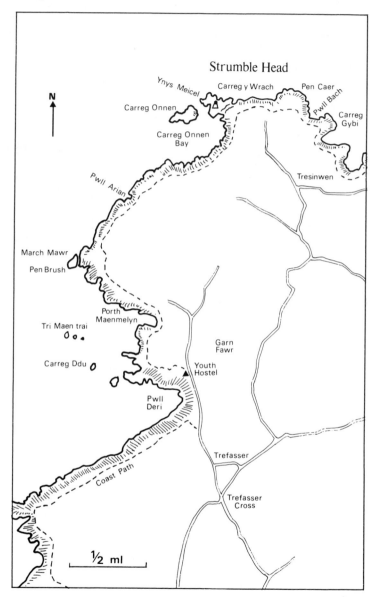

Strumble Head

Ynys Meicel
Carreg y Wrach
Pen Caer
Carreg Onnen
Pwll Bach
Carreg Gybi
Carreg Onnen Bay
Pwll Arian
Tresinwen
March Mawr
Pen Brush
Porth Maenmelyn
Tri Maen trai
Garn Fawr
Carreg Ddu
Youth Hostel
Pwll Deri
Trefasser
Coast Path
Trefasser Cross

N

½ ml

Map 52: Elan Valley Reservoirs

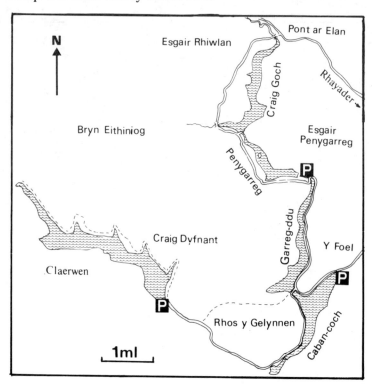

N

Esgair Rhiwlan

Pont ar Elan

Craig Goch

Rhayader

Bryn Eithiniog

Esgair
Penygarreg

Penygarreg

Craig Dyfnant

Garreg-ddu

Y Foel

Claerwen

P

Rhos y Gelynnen

Caban-coch

1ml

Map 53: Glasbury

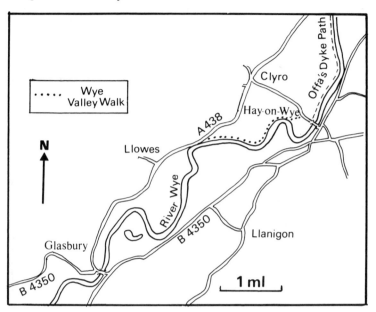

Map 54: Maelienydd

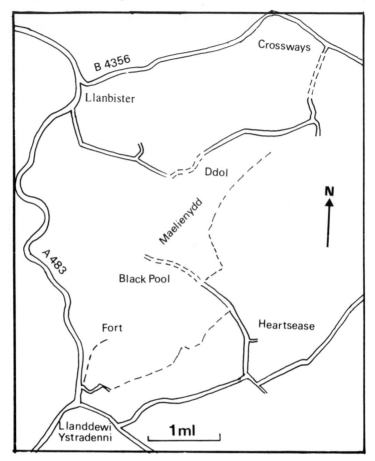

Map 55: Wye-Elan Woods

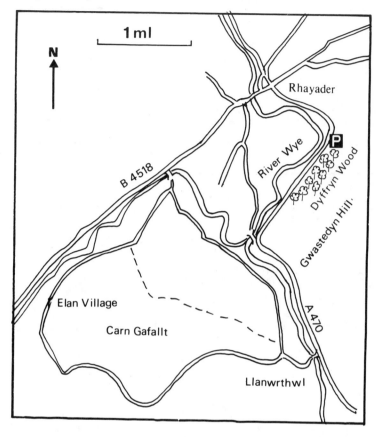

INDEX TO SPECIES

Figures denote site number; 'AS' indicates that species is mentioned in 'Additional Sites' (Appendix A).